REFLECTIONS OF CATALOOCHEE VALLEY

AND ITS VANISHED PEOPLE FROM THE GREAT SMOKY MOUNTAINS

Best Regards
Hattie C Davis

Hattie Caldwell Davis
P.O. Box 274
Maggie Valley, NC 28751

Same copy as hardback
Cataloochee book

Publisher: Hattie Caldwell Davis

Cover   Photographed and designed by the
publisher

Copyright   © 1999 Hattie C. Davis all rights
reserved

It is unlawful to use any part of this work for any type of reproduction without permission of the copyright owner, except brief quotations in accordance with the Copyright Act of the United States.

ISBN 0-9670689-1-6

Previously ISBN 1-56664-108-X

The author has made every effort to get true facts for this book; however, its accuracy is not guaranteed. Neither the author nor the printer will be liable for any damages caused by or alleged to be caused by this book.

This book can be ordered by mail. Each book ordered will be autographed by the author and shipped promptly. For each copy, send check [book: $14.95; shipping: $3.00; NC (only) sales tax: $.1.30 payable to

>Hattie C. Davis
>P.O. Box 274
>Maggie Valley, NC 28751

Also available by the same author is *Civil War Letters and Memories from the Great Smoky Mountains*, about two hundred pages, paper back. Price for each book $19.95 plus $3.00 shipping and handling and $1.20 NC state tax for a total of $24.15.

Printed in Waynesville, NC.

CONTENTS

Dedicated To His Memory 7
A Word From The Author 9
Questions 11
Judge Felix Alley 13
The Founding 15
    Cataloochee Wilderness 15
    Big Cataloochee, Little Cataloochee 16
    Caldwell Fork 16
    First Land Entry 1814 17
    The First Two Log Cabins 18
    The Second Land Entry 1828 19
    Claims, Hunting, Trapping, and Ranging 20
    Turning on the Range and Drovers 20
    Drovers—A Sight to Behold 21
    Smoky 24
    The First Permanent Settlers 24
    The First Families 1836 27
    Wild Animals 30
    The Trail of Tears 1838 31
    Other Families Move into Big Cataloochee 32
    The Hannahs and Nolands 34
    1st Settlers on Little Cataloochee 35
    Prices in 1859 36

Those Early Years 43
    Building The Log Cabins 43
    Corn Shuckin's 44
    Furniture 45
    Around the Winter Fires 46
    The First and Second Roads into Cataloochee 47
    The Dug Road 1854-1856 47
    The Corn Mill 49
    Levi's Second House 50

    First Church/School 52
    Accidents 54
    Renegades 56
    Granny Pop and the Panther 58
    Knee Length Shirt about 1868 60

The Civil War Years 63
    Patriotic, Religious Family and War 63
    The Cataloochee Turnpike — A Road of Trouble 67
    Kirk's Raiders On Big Cataloochee 68
    Raiders at the Schoolhouse Patch 1865 72
    Levi Captured 74
    Granny Pop - Civil War 75
    Cataloochee Herb Doctor and War 76
    The Reconstruction, Hard Times 78
    Scalawags and Carpetbaggers 79

The Century Turns 83
    Go To See The Train 83
    Indian Flats 84
    Funerals 85
    Guns 86
    The Bear, The Panther, and The Buck 88
    Panther Nine Feet Long 88
    Panther & Bear (Hair Raising) 89
    Hunters 90
    Bear Sign 90
    Turkey George 91
    Fayte Goes to Raleigh 91
    Tobe & Bears 93
    Bear Hunter 94
    Wolf Dog 96
    Ola Baptist Church 96
    Circuit Riding Preacher 1909 99
    Eldridge Remembers Caldwell House and Barn 104
    Hogs and Cattle and Snakes 111
    Cattle Drive to Cherokee about 1914 116
    Shear Sheep 117
    Blacksmiths 119
    Hiram's Last Bear Hunt 121
    Voting Precinct 122

Cataloochee Schools 123
    The Second Schoolhouse 125
    Little Cataloochee School 128
    County School Board Minutes 128

Little Cataloochee School 130
- Last Year Of Little Cataloochee School 132
- Beech Grove School 133
- Swimming Hole and School 1918 135
- Caldwell Fork School 137

The Twenties 139
- Second Improvement of the Cataloochee Turnpike 139
- Making Hay Early Twenties 141
- Divorce 143
- Old Age 144
- Influenza 145
- Spring Tonic and Blood Letting 145
- Horse Saves Rider in 20s 146
- Dog Saves Rider 148
- Caldwell Fork 148
- Helping Neighbors 151
- Farming 152
- Reminiscing 157
- House on Fire 1927 161
- Gold 163
- Timber and Railroads 164
- Whiskey 166
- The Model T 173
- Post Offices 173

The Depression 177
- Civilian Conservation Corps Camps 177
- Palmer's Chapel In The Early Thirties 179
- Indians Spend the Night 1930 183
- Fox Hunt 184
- Cataloochee Ranch 184

The Park 187
- Heartbroken 187
- The Sad Exodus 189
- Goodbye 195
- Much Elizabethan Speech 195
- Deceived 196
- What the Park Purchased 200
- Trade Hound Pups for Land 203
- Twins 203
- Carl Woody moves out of Little Cataloochee 204

The Park is Dedicated 207
Mr. Hiram Wilburn and The Museum Collection 207
President Roosevelt Dedicates the Park 208
Museum? 210
Corn Mills 213
Aunt Mag's Buggy 214
Locations They Moved To 217

Memories 221
Memories of Music 226
Flora Caldwell Laws 232
House Flies 237
Food and Remedies 239
Home Remedies 240
Mary Davis Palmer 242
Clay McGaha 245
Kyle Campbell 247
Ethel Palmer McCracken 251
John Cordell Noland 255
Raymond Caldwell 258
Mrs. Pearl Caldwell 259

Today 263
They Kept Their Promise 263
Speakers at the Cataloochee Reunion 264
Education, Schools in Cataloochee Township 266
Our Thanks and Appreciation 267
Reunions 268
Palmer's Chapel 269
Palmer's Chapel Restored 269
About the Pictures of Homes 272
Cataloochee Homes and Families 274
Bennetts Honor Ancestors, 1993 276
Dancing 278

Appendixes 288
Debt of Gratitude 288
Genealogical Information on Caldwells of Cataloochee to 1860 by Roy Carroll, 1984 290
Acknowledgments 297

Bibliography 297
Index 301

DEDICATED TO HIS MEMORY
Eldridge Caldwell, our kind, gentle, wonderful father.

Eldridge Caldwell, born January 8, 1898 in the log house his grandfather, Levi Belese Colwell, had built in 1858. He was a generous, kind hearted, gentle person never raising his voice, except to call his animals. He was always ready to help any of his neighbors or loan them farm equipment or tools. He would loan a horse or even a milk cow to some family whose cow had gone dry so their children would not have to do without milk. He always helped those who could not help themselves. He helped in the church and community affairs but never spoke of it.

He was a good blacksmith and had a special talent in making things of iron. He made plow points, hinges, pot hooks, wagon parts, single trees, double trees, and one time he made a triple tree to hook three horses to pull a plow, instead of the usual one or two horses. The ground was so rocky and rough, three horses were needed to pull the plow. He was ingenious at figuring how to make various tools and things he needed.

He loved animals and was especially good at training young horses to ride and work. He had a special way with training dogs to help with the cattle roundup or to drive hogs. He was sort of a veterinarian who gave his cattle shots for various reasons. He also made medicine to pour in the cattle or sheep if they got sick. Sometimes he would saddle his horse and ride to Waynesville to get medicine for them, and sometimes the old remedies worked well.

Eldridge Caldwell was about seventy years old when this picture was made. Eldridge, son of Hiram and grandson of the original settler Levi Belese Colwell. Photo courtesy of Philip Caldwell.

Daddy was a good farrier. He shod many horses of his own and neighbors. He was careful to shape and turn the horse shoes to fit near perfect. Each horse had different sized and shaped feet, and he knew their hoof prints so well he could identify who had gone up or down the road when he saw the tracks. Eldridge Caldwell was a good cattle man, drover, horseman, teamster, and farmer.

He was an excellent barber. On Sunday afternoon he cut hair for many of his relatives, neighbors and their children. He always loved children. Some cried on their first haircut, but soon he had them smiling with his kindness.

When Daddy took the wagon to town, he took a list of things to get for the neighbors. He did every good and kind deed that he could while here on earth. He died in 1973. He had always said it was so hard to go to funerals, especially where the preacher talked so long. He requested a short simple funeral, which is what we had. He wanted to spare others of as much grief as possible. We still miss him so very much.

He was good at most anything he did, but best of all he was a loving daddy. We will never forget him. He will be remembered for his many kind deeds and generous ways.

Mrs. Ethel P. McCracken, speaking about Eldridge Caldwell said, "Oh honey, he was a wonderful, wonderful person. Never harmed anyone in his life. He did good for everybody and everyone loved him. He went out of his way to help people, as long as he was able. He was a prince of a man."

A WORD FROM THE AUTHOR

The purpose of compiling this history is to pay homage and honor to our ancestors who were the pioneers of Big Cataloochee, Little Cataloochee, and Caldwell Fork. It is to chronicle the events and to tell how these people shaped their destinies. It will illustrate their courage, achievements, sacrifices, quality of life, and their faith.

This is by no means a complete history but we have enough information and true stories to show that we had ancestors worthy of any honor we may bestow upon them.

They blazed their way through the rugged wilderness and rough mountain terrain, which is now a part of the Great Smoky Mountains National Park. These brave, strong, courageous people cleared the wilderness, planted crops, built homes, raised livestock, farmed, and raised large families and called it home for one hundred years. I am of the third and last generation born there, and I went to school in the Beech Grove School, for first grade.

This book should help the descendants, especially the younger ones, to realize what a rich heritage they have. When their ancestors were forced to leave Cataloochee, they were so hurt and heartbroken to have to sacrifice their beloved homes and land they had worked one hundred years to make productive. They couldn't bear to talk about it, or to recall their disappointments, the anguish, and the awful sacrifice they had been forced to make. They just suffered in silence; therefore many stories were lost.

When our ancestors were forced out of Cataloochee, the great depression was on. Life was hard for most everyone, but it would be especially hard for the Cataloochee people to live in unfamiliar places and farm a different kind of soil.

                      Hattie Caldwell Davis
                      P.O. Box 274
                      Maggie Valley, N.C. 28751
                      704-926-1291

Palmer's Chapel, Big Cataloochee

QUESTIONS

When people visit Cataloochee Valley in the Great Smoky Mountains National Park today, they are surprised to see the few remaining nice homes, the church, school, and barns. They wonder, how did they get here? When were they built? Who lived here? What kind of people lived here? Who built these buildings? Why did they come to such an isolated place? How did they make a living? How many homes were here? Why are there no log cabins here? Where did these people come from?

When did the people leave? Why did they leave this beautiful place? How many people lived here?

All of these questions and others have been asked of this writer. All of the answers will be found in this book. It is one hundred years of history.

The first reason they came here was free range for their cattle and hogs. From early spring to late fall the cattle could range on the great grassy balds, the hogs could roam around in the mountains, finding all the food they could eat, especially chestnuts and acorns.

There were many of the grassy balds on the mountain tops surrounding Cataloochee. Many cattlemen from all around Haywood County, even from Buncombe County, would drive (on foot) their animals there for the summer, having someone stay in some type of crude camp to look after their animals.

Pioneers wondered how there could be such lush, green

Cataloochee Valley

grass growing on the balds in a wilderness. Some thought the Indians had cleared these places because they ranged their animals on some of these balds, too. These early pioneers had made friends with the Indians. Someone asked an ancient old Indian if they had cut the timber and cleared these places. Answer was, "Indian, he no got big axe for big trees." He said, "No, been like that many, many moons. Great Spirit make um."[1]

After these early drovers put their animals on the pasture, they looked around and could see the great potential of the rich, fine soil and the magnificent forest.

In the 1830s there were not many jobs, no manufacturing plants or other paying jobs in the area; so raising live stock to sell and farming was about the only way to make a living. These people had a longing for independence and freedom. They found it here in Cataloochee.

They enjoyed their freedom to live life as they saw fit. They did not mind the hard work. They were a proud people. Seeing their farms take shape gave them a sense of accomplishment. They loved the land. But above all, they loved their families and took great pride in their children. This land was to be their children's inheritance.

In 1860, the Cataloochee Turnpike was the only road through the Smokies. Those first early pioneers only had an old chopped out cattle road. Somehow they managed to travel it by horseback and pack mules for some thirty years before the Turnpike was built.

---

[1] Information from Eldridge Caldwell, about 1968.

JUDGE FELIX ALLEY
An Acknowledgment

Judge Felix Alley was born July 5, 1873, on Whiteside Mountain in Jackson County, N.C. He was very much offended by the outside writers who came here and found a few strange or unfortunate people (like there are everywhere) and they wrote about all of us mountain people, as though we were all alike.

Judge Alley did not like what they said, and he did not fear to express his opinions about those writers. He had quite a bit to say about them in his book *Random Thoughts and Musings of a Mountaineer*. He upheld all the mountain people, as I have attempted to do. As you read this book, you will find his quotes all through it. Judge Alley really described the true mountaineers. Most other writers have stereotyped us, as backward, and uncouth people.

Perhaps this book will enlighten those who have been misinformed about mountain people. You will understand the pioneers had to be very intelligent to survive in a wilderness. Their courage, kindness, honesty, generosity, hospitality, dignity, honor, and friendliness were extended to all, just as long as they were treated the same way.

*The Conquering of a Wilderness
by a Race of Heroes*

They go up by the mountains. They go down by the valleys unto the place thou has founded for them. He sendeth the springs into valleys which run along the hills. They give drink to every beast of the field. By them shall the fowls of heaven have their habitation, which sing among the branches. He watereth the hills from his chambers. He causeth the grass to grow for cattle, and herb for the service of man. He appointeth the moon for the seasons. The sun knoweth his going down. The sun riseth. They gather themselves together. Man goeth forth to his work and his labor until evening.
—*Psalms, chapter 104 parts verses 8-23 inclusive.*

Judge Felix Alley P. 256 Random Thoughts and Musings of a Mountaineer.

I

THE FOUNDING

Cataloochee Wilderness

This was part of eastern and middle ground of the once roving, warring Cherokees. They had compact settlements or villages and hunting camps widely scattered here and there throughout this mountain region. Here Indians lived and cultivated patches of ground around their villages.

Except for this it was the land of the primeval, never ending forest and save for the Indian trails here and there and those made by the wild animals, this whole mountain country was unbroken, untraveled, and almost unknown.

Imagine the time after nightfall in this vast wilderness of those days. The stars are out and except for the light overhead, all is shrouded in darkness. The calls and cries of the wild animals heard in daytime but far more plentiful at night, come from far and near. Listen! Tis the spine-creeping scream of the panther, the howl of the hungry wolf, or the cry of a catamount.

Some buffalo were to be found here in those days (the smaller, eastern breed). Bear and deer were plentiful, as were of course, all the smaller wild animals. Also there were fish in abundance, since rivers and creeks of all this mountain country ran crystal clear. These streams and this land were almost unknown one hundred and sixty years ago. But the wonderful tales of it lured our forefathers on. Many of

Cataloochee Valley

them traveled far—but they found it. They came and saw it was a goodly land, laden with all the rich potentials of virgin soil, prime forest, fine climate, abundance of fish and game, the best of water and also mineral wealth.
 —Mr. W.C. Medford *The Early History of Haywood Co.*

Big Cataloochee, Little Cataloochee, Caldwell Fork

By 1834 most of the good farm land along the eastern seaboard and the piedmont and much of the mountain land had been settled. Land was getting scarce.

Large tracts of land had been granted to privileged individuals. One was John Gray Blount, a brother of the Governor of the territory south of Ohio. The land was supposed to be homesteaded. Mr. Blount sold 150,000 acres to Col. Robert Love who had come down from Virginia and was one of the founding fathers of Waynesville N.C., in 1808. He was of Revolutionary War fame. He became a land speculator. He was required to get permanent settlers to buy the land and live on it. This large tract was in Haywood County. It included all of Big Cataloochee, Little Cataloochee, Caldwell Fork, and others.

Big Cataloochee is a big, oval-shaped valley surrounded by the Appalachian Mountains ranging from three to six thousand feet high. The mountains form a natural barrier separating the Cataloochee area from the rest of the world. Little Cataloochee is separated from Big Cataloochee by a small mountain called Noland Mountain. It is about three to four miles between these two areas if you go over Noland Mountain. But to travel by road, it is a much longer distance.

Caldwell Fork lies on the south side of Cataloochee Creek. In some places it is very steep then levels off. And there were several large farms and nice homes and log cabins, but the only road was a wagon road. When the park took over, they made a jeep road to go up there.

All of the Cataloochee areas were referred to as the "back of beyond." There were no roads, just trails made by the Indians and the buffalo that once roamed there. They always took the line of least resistance on the best grade possible. The road today follows mostly the same old trails.

There was some evidence that a few Indians have lived or camped in Cataloochee prior to the white man's arrival. The Cherokee then lived about six miles from Big Cataloochee. They mostly used that area for their hunting and fishing. The Indian trails led through Big Cataloochee, Little Cataloochee, up Mt. Sterling into Tennessee and Kentucky and other places. They had trails up Cove Creek Mountain and down into Jonathan Creek into Waynesville, through Maggie Valley, up Soco Mountain and back into Cherokee.[1]

Some of these trails had been traveled so much, they were worn down a foot or eighteen inches deep in some places.

First Land Entry 1814

In the "Land Entry Book 1809-1842" for Haywood County (p. 63) No. 131, Henry Colwell enters 100 acres of land in Haywood County on Cataloochee Creek beginning on a large maple tree on the north side of said creek running down the creek including a "punchin" camp of Thomas Coldwell for complement entered January 20, 1814.

A punchin was a thick slab of wood, which was split from a large log, roughly hewn out with a broad ax. This was a crude camp, but there for herders to stay in while they watched after the cattle they had grazing on the large grassy balds on the mountain above the valley. Since this wilderness was full of wild animals, it was a dangerous place. So naturally they would have built their camps of strong, thick planks to sleep in.[2]

The Cherokee Indians had given up Cataloochee forty-five years before any white man ever lived there permanently. There was probably much fear, due to all the killing and

---

[1] Info from Eldridge Caldwell.
[2] Dr. Carroll research: 1820 Henry still living in Buncombe Co. He was living there in 1807, and so was son James. Living near them are several Woodys and Cooks and in the same part of the Co. the Palmers – all names associated with the early settlement of Cataloochee.

Cataloochee Valley

scalping that had taken place prior to the signing of the Holston Treaty (1791).[1]

Cherokee was only six miles from Big Cataloochee by trail, and the Indians would be the only neighbors at that time of 1834.

Three generations of Caldwells spoke fluent Cherokee. They were Levi, his son Hiram, grandson Eldridge, and many cousins including Jim and Homer. This is probably the reason they were not afraid to live near the Cherokees. When the white man was friendly and able to speak the Cherokee language, they felt very much honored because in 1834, they had not learned much of the white man's language. They became steadfast friends of our family and traded and bartered all the years and long after the people had to leave Cataloochee. They came to visit and trade after we moved to Maggie Valley.

Perhaps the Caldwells were part Cherokee because they knew the language. Some pictures of the ancestors indicate that they had black hair, dark skin, and black sparkling eyes. Some relatives still have these features. Recent inquiries of three older relatives yielded "Yes, everyone always said the Caldwells were part Indian." No one knows anything more about that.

Daddy (Eldridge) always said if you ever made a friend of the Cherokee, you had a friend for life and you could absolutely depend on what they told you. They never lied, and if any white man had ever lied to them or cheated them, he had better never set foot on their territory. (This was in the 1800s and early 1900s.)

The First Two Log Cabins

January 20, 1814, Henry Colwell, father of James and grandfather of Levi, bought the first land in Cataloochee. This 100 acres lies up past the schoolhouse, the big field where the Caldwell barn

---

[1] Everyone knew the Indians had been treated very badly by the white man. The stirring up of the Cherokee against the frontier white settlements at the outbreak of the Revolutionary War was the work of British agents. The British were trying to take control and rule all the land. The British were paying the Cherokee for the scalps of the whites. Then there was the French and Indian war. The Cherokee were raiding, killing, and scalping the whites. Then the U.S. Army was sent to burn the Indian homes and crops and to kill men, women, and children and to destroy all their villages. It is no wonder they hated the white man, for they had kept them in one war or another for about one hundred years. –Mr. W.C. Medford, *The Early History of Haywood Co.*

sits on the edge of the road. This is the land Jimmy, Levi, and Young Bennett went there to homestead in 1834-1836.

They built the first two log cabins about three hundred yards above the Caldwell barn that sits on the edge of the road, several hundred feet to the right of the present road. Later there was a road there called "The Charlotte Lane." These first two cabins were back beyond where Uncle Andy later built his house. Charlie Ray Caldwell and his family lived in the house last. Then they called it Charlie Ray Lane.

The Second Land Entry 1828

The second entry for Cataloochee in the Land Entry book for 1809-1842 for Haywood County is June 24, 1828, No. 470 (page 218).[1] William Colwell enters 100 acres on Cataloochee Creek beginning on a dogwood tree marked AC up the creek for complements.

The 1830 census for North Carolina lists Haywood County, Fines Creek area (C. stands for Colwell).

William C. Sr. (45+)   Thomas C. (40-50)
William C. (40-50)   Daniel C. (50-60)
James C. (40-50)

Also in the same area of the county were Palmers, Nolands, and Hannahs who later settled in Cataloochee.

In 1830, Henry Colwell and family were still in Buncombe County. On December 12, 1832, Henry bought twenty-five acres in Spring Creek.

According to the 1840 Buncombe County census, Henry and James and their families lived in the Spring Creek area. A later adjustment of the county line moved Spring Creek to Madison County. Living nearby were listed Jonathan Woody, Silas Woody, William Woody, and two other Woodys, Jackson Andrew, James Plemmons, and Levi Hannah.

On December 12, 1842, James Colwell and his son, Levi, and James Plemmons purchased two tracts. One was 700 acres, and one was 300 acres on Davis Branch. They paid $1,000 down, and all three signed a note for the balance of $1,000 more.

---

[1] Dr. Carroll research

On May 25, 1850, Plemmons (or Clemmons) gave over his interest to the Colwells. The obligation was paid, and the deed was made out to the Colwells alone (Haywood County Deed Book G. page 104). This made 1,000 acres plus the first 100 acres Henry bought in 1814, in possession of the Colwells in Big Cataloochee.

The 1850 census for North Carolina lists: Buncombe County, Spring Creek, Henry Colwell, age 91, birthplace, Pennsylvania; Daniel, age 70, his wife Betsy, and others.

Claims, Hunting, Trapping, and Ranging

In the 1830s, especially 1832 and 1833, a whole flurry of claims were entered in the Land Entry book. Felder Davis, 1832, Ruben Moody, 1832 and 1833, John L. Smith and Edward McFalls (Ned, famous hunter), 1832, Jacob Smith, Jr. 1833, Samuel Leatherwood, Jr. 1833, Keder Boone, 1834, James Conley, 1834, Edwin Davidson, James L. Howell, David Howell, Nelson Howell, 1840, and John Messer, 1838. Most of those men were from Jonathan's Creek area of Haywood County.

They were hunting, trapping, and ranging cattle up there but did not settle and live there. Most likely they had overnight cabins or camps. Many of those claims are vague, overlapping and contradictory but indicate growing interest with the Cataloochee area. Several clains refer to the old Indian camp, and several refer to the Barnes camp as well as other well-known points of interest.

Note: A William Noland, father-in-law of Evan Hannah, did live in Cataloochee, and the mountain between Big and Little Cataloochee was named for him. It's called "Noland Mountain."

Park Historian, Ed Trout wrote, "Entering" land was a paper exercise that often did not mean "permanent occupancy." Gaining land on paper did not guarantee any headway against the forest, tree stumps, and rocks, or panthers, bears, and wolves.

Turning on the Range and Drovers

Turning on the range was taking the cattle out on the grassy balds to pasture for the summer. The stock range law was in

Wormy Chestnut tree with salt licks chopped out to hold salt for the cattle.

Photo courtesy Great Smoky Mountains National Park.

effect for about 125 years. In many sections of our county, it was voted out in favor of the "stock laws" in the early 1890s. But in certain sections like Cataloochee and Big Creek, Hurricane and White Oak, it was kept well into the present century. It was a much prized privilege because, from an economical standpoint in our county and throughout this entire region, turning on the range meant fully half the living. It was free ranging. No one had to pay for the summer pasture.

They did not use branding irons on their cattle, instead they cut V notches in the cows' ears. They each cut them in different places. Example: two V's in the top of the left or right ear, or two on bottom of the ear and one on top etc. They had to register these marks of identification with the rangemaster in the courthouse. This had to be done before the cattle were turned on the range.[1]

Drovers—A Sight to Behold

They were to start early next morning on the long drive; so the herds would be corralled in order to get an early start.

---

[1] Mr. W.C. Medford, Early History of Haywood Co. P. 85-86.

Cataloochee Valley

The call was the same kind that had echoed over the hills of Old England, Scotland, and Wales centuries ago. There has been considerable change in the English language, but the cattle and sheep calls and that for the hogs - *"pig-ee, pig-ooh!"* and for sheep it was *"cooie co co cooie"* - the calls had varied but little over the centuries.

Mr. W.C. Medford writes in the late 1880s and early 1890s: I watched the drover's herds go by. It was a sight that brought every farm family (those who lived near the old highways) to the door, where they were held in almost breathless interest until the last of the herd was out of sight.

These drovers were descendants of the English, Scots, Irish, Welsh, and Dutch—to the third and fourth generations of those who had herded and driven and given the same calls in the mother country. At first these drovers had to drive their animals all the way to Charleston, S.C., to market. As the railroads made progress, they came closer to the mountains through Spartanburg, Greenville, and finally to Asheville. But this didn't happen until after the Civil War. That shortened the distance the drovers had to go. The days of driving stock and fowl (cattle, horses, sheep, swine, and turkeys) to markets required a sort of professional knowledge and understanding, gained mostly by experience. The men who were fond of these animals, who understood their different natures, habits, and ailments, and also liked to work with them, made the best drovers. Horses, in case there was a small drove, might be haltered or tied by the neck. In that way a mounted man could handle two or three; also one or two would be tied behind the wagon. Then the better broken or trained animals could be depended upon to follow along untied.

Horses and cattle were the easiest to move or drive through. Hogs and sheep tired more easily and wanted to lie down, the hogs especially, whenever a stream or mud hole was reached. At the approach of sundown, turkeys on the drive would begin to run out of the road where there were trees, bushes, or even high stumps trying to find a roosting place.

Late summer or fall, before it got cold was the best time for driving. October was perhaps the best time of all after the cattle, sheep, and hogs had been rounded up and taken in from the mountain ranges off the mast.

On these drives, the first day out was a very important one. They wanted to drive as far as possible, while the herds were fresh and well-rested. Therefore, they were often on the road before sunup. A wagon would be taken along for hauling necessary supplies, also for picking up any animal (sheep, hog, or calf) that might become crippled or sick. Those that had little chance of survival would be left in the hands of the roadside innkeeper or other person. They would stop to see about it on the return trip.

The drovers would make from ten to twenty miles or more in a day, depending on what the herd consisted of, condition of the herd, road, weather, etc. On these long drives, trained cattle and sheepdogs were almost indispensable.

Those who have seen panting turkeys, grunting and squealing swine, pushing cattle, and woolly sheep all pressing together so closely that they seemed almost in a state of suffocation can never forget it.[1]

Eldridge Caldwell talked about being on the drives. He said, "The turkeys were the most aggravation. They would fly up in the trees to roost before dark, or even if some dark clouds came over. It took extra people to keep them on the ground and traveling because these drovers needed to make as many miles each day as possible. We had well-trained cattle dogs that could keep the other animals in line, but the turkeys could fly over their heads. We would have men on each side of the road with brushy limbs, shaking them to keep the turkeys going until we made camp or found an inn."

When these drovers went to market in the fall, they would bring back the winter's supply of salt, coffee, and sugar. They also brought a quantity of dress cloth, pieces of tableware, kitchen-ware, powder, and lead. Much of this would be done by barter.

On these drives, there would be several men and sometimes three or four covered wagons. After making about twenty miles for the day, at nightfall they pulled off the road and made camp for the night. They talked and laughed as they cooked, joked, and told of their experiences until time to lie down and pull their heavy blankets up over them. If there was no camp house, and usually there wasn't, they slept on the ground. If it rained, they got

---
[1] W.C. Medford, Early History of Haywood County P. 190

Cataloochee Valley

> ## SMOKY
>
> "SHA-CONA-GA" (SA-KA-NA-GN = Brogue)
>
> The name Smoky itself tells of the ever present veil of ethereal blue haze that hangs over the mountains, softening their rugged outlines and bringing a rare beauty of coloring. The name dates from the early days for when in 1789 North Carolina ceded its western lands to U.S. The boundary was described in part as "to the Painted Rose" of French Broad River, thence along the highest ridges of said mountain to the place where it is called Great Irons or Smoky Mountain, etc. This is the first use of the name we have found. However, the idea of the name may have been influenced by the Cherokee.
>
> –from a note of Mr. Hiram Wilburn F.3 215

in the wagons or underneath them. There were a few inns along the way where they could get a bath, a hot meal, and a bed to sleep in. These inns also had large corrals where the animals could be kept for the night. They had feed for them and a big watering trough for them to drink from.

The Tennesseans and Kentuckians used the Cataloochee Toll Road to drive their stock to market after the road was finished in 1860.[1]

The First Permanent Settlers

In 1834 and 1835 in the spring, summer, and fall, James Colwell from Sandy Mush brought his nineteen-year-old son, Levi, and another young man whose name was Young Bennett, into Big Cataloochee. Mr. Bennett was from East Fork on the Pigeon River. They spent these two summers clearing the land, that Henry Colwell purchased in 1814.

---

[1] Mr. W.C. Medford, Early History of Haywood County.

Some others may have come to help them while grazing cattle on the grassy balds. Levi's Uncle Thomas had a punchin camp there, referred to in an old deed. They probably lived in it while working there before they got their cabins built.

Coming into a wilderness like this to live took a tremendous amount of strength, courage, and above all, faith. It would take much hard work to clear and farm this ground, but it was fine virgin soil and their efforts would be rewarded.[1]

They brought their pack horses over the steep, crooked, narrow cattle road which had been chopped out, up over Cove Creek mountain, more than 4,500 feet high and down into Big Cataloochee Valley, elevation 2,620 feet. This rough old road had been chopped out in 1825 by a few Jonathan Creek citizens, Joshua Allison I, being one of the leaders (W.C. Medford, P. 81).

There was danger from the wild animals, the panther, the bear, the wolf, and the wild cat. There was also danger from the copperheads and rattlesnakes or maybe a hostile Indian or a group of them. It was a long, hard trip from Sandy Mush in Buncombe County or from East Fork, up on the Pigeon River in Haywood County.

They would need supplies and all sorts of tools—axes, mattocks, picks, wedges, plows, adz, a broad axe and others. Clearing the land to farm was a big job. Some of the trees were so large they could not chop them down. They would peel a wide strip of bark from the tree all the way around. This prevented the sap from getting to the top next spring, eventually when the tree died they would set it on fire. It would smolder and burn for a long time until it finally burned down to the stump. They probably plowed around it for a few years until the stumps rotted; then they dug the stump and roots out. This practice which gave more land to plow and farm was called grubbing. The ground was rocky, rough, and very hard to plow, but oh, such rich, fertile soil. There were other trees they could cut, but it took many, many chops with an axe. Those trees had to be cut in lengths and hauled off and those stumps and roots dug out. There were other obstacles. Huge old trees had fallen, due to the ravages of time. When these were cleared away, there were lots of rocks which had to be carried or hauled off the land.

---

[1] Mr. W.C. Medford, Early History of Haywood County.

Cataloochee Valley

A photograph of the Jim Hannah house taken on October 9, 1991 by Paul Woody.

Yes, it would be a hard job, but they could see the great potential, the rich fertile soil to farm, the grassy balds to range their cattle and hogs. Plenty of the American chestnuts would fatten their hogs. They were also a money crop. The big clear, rushing streams were so full of native trout, there was hardly room for them to swim.

What a beautiful place. There were huge trees with their branches spread out like great lofty cathedrals. Some trees had fallen and were covered with lush green mosses of different kinds. Some had lichen and fungi growing on them. There were many beautiful ferns, some waist high, and there was the wonderful fragrance of the giant hemlocks with the deep soft beds of needles underneath. It was a quiet place with natures sounds of crystal clear water singing as it tumbled down the stream and soft breezes blowing through the pines making them hum peacefully. It was a paradise of birds singing and wild flowers and rhododendrons filling the valley with fragrance.

There were plenty of good, cold springs, which were very much prized then and for the next hundred years.

Levi Colwell was proud to be one of the three founding families of the Cataloochee Valley. He had the fact engraved on his headstone.
—These stories from Eldridge Caldwell, grandson of Levi Colwell.

It took much hard work to clear the wilderness, but that was where they wanted to live. The hardy people broke into the wilderness undaunted by the mountain barriers or anything else. It was a challenge and they loved it.

The First Families 1836

Levi Colwell and Young Bennett had brought their wives to live in Big Cataloochee in 1836. Jimmy (father of Levi) had gone back to Big Sandy Mush in Buncombe County, for a spell to see about his wife and family there. We believe that Young and Allie had four children while living at East Fork. Then they became good friends of the Colwells while ranging cattle on the grassy balds on the mountains around Cataloochee. At any rate, they moved into little log cabins, with roofs made of hand-rived board shingles.

They planted corn in the new ground they had cleared, but the frost came early that year and the corn got frostbitten. They had counted on having plenty of cornmeal for their bread that winter. Now that the corn was frost bitten it would be bitter to eat. No matter, that was all they would have for bread, so they would take it to mill to be ground into cornmeal.

The long meal sacks were made of heavy material. Each one would hold a bushel of shelled corn.

They harvested their corn, dried it, shucked, and shelled it. They sacked it up the night before, so they could get an early start to the mill next morning. Each man put the sack of corn around

Cataloochee Valley

his neck, with about half a bushel of corn on each shoulder to balance the weight. They had to carry this heavy load up the mountain over Caldwell Fork, then on to the Deadend, on up over the Purchase on down Hemphill to the mill on Jonathan Creek, which was located about where the Rockhill School was. It is now a church called "The Good Samaritan."

A Mr. Howell was the miller. When he saw the corn he said, "Why you fellows can't eat this stuff, it's frostbitten and will be as bitter as gall. I will give you good cornmeal for this. I can feed it to my horses." They were happy to find this generous, good man, and they were steadfast friends ever after.

The Colwells and the Bennetts were the only people living here in this wilderness. In the fall of the next year, it was time to go to mill again. They had killed hogs and had food stored for the winter. The men shelled the corn and sacked it up and went on the long, hard trip over the mountain again to mill. The trip took all day, so they would spend the night and return the following day.

The women, Mary Ann Colwell and Allie Bennett, were left alone, each in their own cabins. The two cabins were built fairly close together. The women decided to cook a big pot of the fresh pork for their men when they returned. It would take hours to cook it in the big iron kettles hanging over the fire in the fireplace. Along about dark the women were cooking the meat, and they heard wild screams that sounded like a woman with a high-pitched voice, screaming for her life. It was a bloodcurdling sound. The sounds got closer and closer to their houses, and more joined in screaming. The women knew these were panthers, maybe half a dozen or more, coming out of the dense forest. The panthers' terrifying, shrill voices piercing the night air made the hair stand up on the ladies' heads.

Evidently the panthers smelled the fresh pork cooking and they were hungry. They jumped on top of the log cabins scratching and tearing at the shingles. They were scratching and tearing at the chimney trying to tear away enough rocks to get down into the house. Each woman stayed in her own house and kept a big roaring fire in the fireplace to keep the panthers out.

The two log houses were built just a few feet apart. Both had

A photograph of the fireplace of the Jim Hannah house taken on October 9, 1991 by Paul Woody.

a window opening with wooden shutters, so the women could holler back and forth. Through the tiny cracks they could see the panthers on each other's roof.

The panthers stayed all night, clawing, scratching, and screaming. Just before daylight, Mary Ann (my great grandmother) was so tired and sleepy she fell asleep in her chair. All of a sudden she was awakened by the sound of a rock falling into the fireplace and vigorous scratching.

Her fire had died down to just a hand full of coals, and a panther was clawing his way down the chimney! He was half way down and more rocks were falling! Lordy, that thing was getting in! She had to do something quickly.

She jumped up and grabbed a string of dried red hot peppers, threw them on the fire coals, then started fanning as fast as she could, as the dirt and rocks were falling.

Finally, the peppers flamed up. They sent hot gasses up his nostrils and into his eyes. He got himself out of there and ran back into the woods screaming louder than when he came. The others left just at daybreak. Another example of life as pioneers!

Cataloochee Valley

The men and women of Cataloochee prayed a lot and had great faith that God would watch over them. They not only had faith, they had plenty of red-blooded courage.

I first heard these stories from grandma Lizzie Howell Caldwell as they were passed from my great grandmother, Mary Ann (Granny Pop), and later I heard stories from my father, Eldridge.

These hardy, intelligent pioneers went about braving this wild territory, working at their task with determination, faith, hope, and courage.

Dr. Carroll's research reveals that Levi Colwell married Mary Ann Nailand (Nalon), who was probably his childhood sweetheart because the 1830 census shows that Patrick Nailand was a neighbor of Henry Colwell and James Colwell in Buncombe Co.

Mary Ann was born May 27, 1817. She married Levi in 1836. They had twelve children; their first was Harriett, born June 11, 1837, when Mary Ann was twenty years old.

There have been other stories of Mary Ann coming through Cataloochee and marrying at a much younger age. Evidently these were just stories, but after so many years it is easy for the information to get mixed up. On two of Mary Ann's children's death certificates Mary Ann's maiden name was listed as Doughty. Here we have the facts according to the 1830 census, marriage records, birth, and death records.

Wild Animals

In these times, 1996, we are making great effort to save every species of wild animal, bird, fish, frog, snail darter and all. But back in the early pioneering days, it was a far different story. There in that beautiful wilderness full of God's gifts, were also wild, dangerous animals. The spine-tingling screams of the panther who was so powerful that one stroke of his paw could split a bear wide open, the howl of the hungry wolf, or the cry of the catamount could put fear in the strogest heart.

Those few pioneers there in the midst of the wilderness were thousands of times outnumbered by the dangerous wild animals, not only of danger to the people but also to the livestock. It was a matter of survival. In order to survive, they had to kill dangerous predators.

It was not unusual to hear the screams, cries, and bellowing of a calf or sheep. They would run to the edge of the woods and see a wolf sitting on the animal, its innards torn out and eaten along with part of its hind quarter, while it screamed in pain.

Sometimes when they went to the pasture to check on the cattle and take salt for them, they would find several of them killed by the bears and half eaten. There was one bear they nicknamed Honest John, because he only killed one and ate what he wanted, then carried the rest of it off and put it behind a log for his next meal.

The Trail of Tears 1838

The Colwells and Bennetts had only been living in Cataloochee for two years when others started moving in. The Government started the removal of the Cherokee Indians from Cherokee to Oklahoma. They were good friends with Levi. He spoke their language, they had traded and bartered, and being their only neighbors, had much respect for each other.

When Levi heard of their being taken away, he was sad. He heard some of the Indians had escaped into the forest, but if they went back to their homes, they would be caught and put into stockades. They would have to stay hidden in the woods all winter. Their only food would be roots, nuts, and small game. They would have to live in caves and maybe freeze to death.

Levi worried. He would have gone looking for his friends, but the area was so vast, he knew he could not find them. He hoped they would come to him, and a few months went by. It was winter and the weather was bitter cold. Then one very dark night he heard a certain call of a hoot owl, but he knew it was his friends. He made a sound similar to theirs, indicating that all was clear. He went out and asked them in to warm. It was obvious they were nearly frozen and much in need of food. He fed the three of them and gave them food to take back to the others. He also gave them all the blankets he could spare. They came back at other times that awful cold winter, but only when they were desperate. Levi kept this a secret because it would probably have been a serious federal offense to help the Indians stay when the government was trying to get rid of them.

Cataloochee Valley

Other white men felt sympathy for the Indians too and helped them but kept quiet about it. Mr. Will Thomas, a white man who had grown up near the Cherokees, was so honored and trusted they elected him their chief. He bought their land in his name, so later on they could own it again. Mr. Thomas was a fine, honorable man who worked his whole life to help the Indians gain title to their land. Since he was their chief, the government did not bring any charges against him.

Other Families Move into Big Cataloochee

These first families of Colwells and Bennetts, the only white people here, were already settled and doing well. Then their friends and neighbors from Sandy Mush in Buncombe County and Spring Creek in Madison County started moving into Cataloochee.

George Palmer married Polly Surrett from Virginia. They lived in Sandy Mush farming and raising livestock. George took a bunch of hogs to market and sold them. According to his great grandson, Linton Palmer, "He fell in with the wrong crowd, got to playing cards and maybe drinking, too. He lost all of his money. He was so disgusted he told his wife to load up the wagon, they were moving." They traveled to Jonathan Creek. George told a Mr. Howell that he wanted to go where there were not too many people. He was told that Cataloochee was like that. They came on across the mountain into Cataloochee in 1838 according to Linton Palmer.

Linton said, "It was passed down to me that Fayte, Linton's grandfather was two years old when they arrived in Cataloochee." Fayte was born July 17, 1836, so that puts them there in 1838.

George built the house that now houses the little museum. The structure was made of logs, cut on the nearby property, hand-hewn by George and neighbors. It was one story with two big rooms separated by a dog trot. It was typical to have one room for cooking and eating and the other for sleeping or visiting. One or two beds in the back of the room, and in front, chairs around the fire. As the family grew, they needed more room. Linton said Fayte raised the roof and put in a sleeping loft in the mid 1870s.

Fayte married Nancy Jane Colwell (Levi's daughter). They

*Nancy Jane Colwell Palmer,
Wife of Fayte Palmer*

*Fayte Palmer,
son of George Palmer*

had twelve children. Fayte inherited the home and land from his father George. Fayte died in 1910, then Jarvis Linton inherited it from his father. Jarvis's brother Harley and sister Maria never married and lived on at the homeplace with Jarvis and his wife, Velma Childers Palmer. Aunt Maria was postmistress. The south room was used as the post office, which was called Cataloochee Post Office.

By 1858, George Palmer was well-established in Cataloochee. George held 210 acres, as homeplace and paid $200.00. His wife held 100 acres; 50 acres on Davidson Branch worth $25.00 and 50 acres on Little Davidson Branch for $100.00 with only $25.00 down. His son Jesse held 150 acres at the mouth of Indian Creek, extending to Shanty Branch for $150. His daughter Julia held 240 acres adjoining the home for $400.00.

The Palmers had 700 acres for which they paid $800 cash and $75.00 remaining.

In Dr. Carroll's research, he says that George and his brother Jessie Palmer were the best farmers or produced more farm products than any of the others according to the 1880 census.

Cataloochee Valley

Prices and Wages 1835-38

Whiskey 50¢ a gallon
50¢ lb. for gun powder
$2.50 Fur hats
12¢ lb. for bacon

Wine 25¢ a pint
$12.00   Bearskin coat
$1.00 for 6 lbs. salt

$1.84 for hauling 92 pounds from Augusta
75¢ a day for bartender–long hours
25¢ to shoe a horse

The Hannahs and Nolands

The next family we have record of moving to Cataloochee was Evan Hannah who was born in 1802, son of Alexander and Rebecca Wilkins Hannah of Wilkes County. They moved to Fines Creek in 1815. So did William Noland (of Wilkes Co.). In 1829, Evan married the Noland's daughter, Elizabeth. Before the marriage was solemnized, Evan had to make a bond in the sum of ten thousand dollars to guarantee the support of his wife and there is no record that he ever broke this matrimonial bond, which is yet on file in the office of the register of deeds of this county (1935) Annals of Haywood County, W.C. Allan page 425.

In 1829, Evan and Elizabeth moved to Ironduff in Haywood County. Then in 1839 they and her father, William Noland, moved into Big Cataloochee, down at the lower end of the valley below the iron bridge. The place later became known as the preacher Hall place, because Rev. William Hall had built a home and lived there. Lowell Hannah says his great-grandfather's house was on the southside of Cataloochee Creek.

The Hannah's closest neighbors would have been the George Palmer family. Then the Levi and Jimmy Colwell and Young Bennett families at the upper end of the valley. After the Civil War Jonathan Woody moved in permanently (1866). He had moved his family there earlier from Spring Creek in Madison County. His wife

William Palmer, High Sheriff of Haywood County for four terms—His wife Milia Caldwell (daughter of Uncle Andy) son Glenn, center. Back- Bill, baby Pauline, daughter Hattie. Son Gudger was born a few years later. Photo courtesy of Gudger Palmer.

wanted to move back there to Spring Creek, which they did. Some years later his wife died. After that he and five of his nine children moved back into Big Cataloochee. Jonathan, like others could see the endless possibilities and complete freedom they could have.

Uncle Steve could remember that he was about ten years old when they moved into Cataloochee and there were only four or five families living there in 1866.

1st Settlers on Little Cataloochee

On Little Cataloochee, a few miles across Noland Mountain, another settlement was springing up. Jack Vess, who married Elizabeth Palmer, daughter of George Palmer of Big Cataloochee, moved over to little Cataloochee and cleared a part of the place, later owned by W.G.B. Messer. This was about 1854. Vess later moved to the state of Washington, where he died.[1]

Also, in 1854, Levi Colwell's daughter, Harriett, married Daniel J. Cook. They lived on Coggins Branch in Little Cataloochee. In 1856, another of Levi's daughters, Louisa Matilda, married Creighton Bennett the son of Young Bennett and they moved to land adjoining the Cooks. (Dr. Carroll's research)

---

[1] From The Annals of Haywood County. W.C. Allan, P. 428

Cataloochee Valley

Prices in 1859

Just to give you some idea of prices, I have listed below: Account of sale of property belonging to the Estate of George Palmer, sold by G.L. Palmer administrator on 26th of April 1859.

1 log chair .... 50¢	1 loom .... 50¢
1 (auger) .... 66¢	1 wagon (2 horse) $10.00
1 shovel & hoe .... 26¢	1 gray mare & colt $33.00
1 sword cain .... 35½¢	1 saw & six pigs $1.00
2 water vessels .... 25¢	1 lot geese, ducks, chicks ... 50¢
1 clevis & pins .... 36¢	1 sow & five shoats ... $14.00
1 clack. .... 25¢	1 grind stone .... 5¢
1 pot rocks .... 25¢	1 cow $10.75
1 table .... 25¢	1 black heffer $6.00
8 chairs .... 25¢	1 bell & collar .... 90¢
1 bedstead & furniture ... 25¢	1 cow $5.00
1 bedstead & furniture .... 90¢	1 steer $8.05
1 bedstead & furniture .... 50¢	1 cow $14.00
1 shovel .... 56½¢	1 cow $20.10
1 sheet .... 12½¢	1 calf $2.87½
1 beehive $3.37½	1 cow $20.50
1 coffee mill .... 6½¢	1 bull $23.50
1 check reel .... 12½¢	1 ax .... 25¢
1 spinning wheel .... 25½¢	8 sheep $3.00
1 wash tub .... 13½¢	4 shares in Cataloochee Turnpike Co. ... $425.00 per share
1 bread tray .... 6½¢	
1 pr. sheers .... 25¢	

This list is not complete; the estate was much larger.

Harriett and Dan Cook's children include Mary (B. 1856), Sarah (B. 1858), Joseph (B. 1860,) Ragan (B. 1863), James (B. 1870), Harrison (B. 1872), Hester (B. 1875) and Rachel (B. 1876). The 1900 census states there were ten Cook children but only eight can be identified from existing records. Harriett died of pneumonia October 25, 1903, and Dan died of cancer on January 17, 1908. Both were buried in the graveyard of the Little Cataloochee Baptist Church.[1]

Milas Hannah who came from England, settled first at Crabtree,

---
[1] This info from Historic Structures Report, Little Cataloochee, N.C. by Dr. Roy Carroll.

and was a brother of Evan Hannah, or may have been his father. Evan Hannah was father of John J. Hannah who came into Cataloochee. The Muster Ground was located on Cove Creek mountain beside the old trail not far west of the old Hoglen place. It was a comparatively broad, flat area. Here soldiers were mustered, political campaigns held, big picnics enjoyed, and elections and shooting matches were held.[1]

My father and Jack Vess had a contract for grading the road from the Kerr place to Mt. Sterling. This was before the Confederate War, and before I was born in 1859. Jack Vess had a laborers camp beside Vess Branch. This camp was just below the road, a half-mile below the gap. The remains of the Vess Camp burned when I was fourteen years old. My father's house (John J. Hannah) where James A. Hannah lived for a long time, was built in the year 1880. I helped hew the logs that were put into it. A big Indian Chief had been killed and buried there. Tine Woody and William Bennett opened the grave about 1900. (Note: The Indian Chief was buried at what is known as the "rock pile" Indian grave. This location is beside the old Cataloochee trail about a mile south east of Mt. Sterling Gap. A spring is located at this point. Considerable Indian relics were found here, chips, broken arrowheads, and so forth.[2]

Neil Sutton had a camp on Little Cataloochee just below Ras Hannah's place. He was a cooper. He went to the Balsams to get spruce to make piggins and tubs. He made maple syrup and maple sugar and sold it to people in the area.[3]

About 1855, John Jackson Hannah left the homestead on Big Cataloochee and came over into Little Cataloochee territory. He cleared a farm, built his home, reared a family, and died there in 1909. John Jackson Hannah was married to Martha Simmons. Their son William J. Hannah was born in Cataloochee township. He was educated in public schools at the Waynesville academy at Wake Forest College and State University from which he graduated with a degree in law.

Other children of John Jackson and Martha Simmons Hannah were Andrew Thomas, married Sara Denton and lived on Little

---

[1] From The Annals of Haywood County, W.C. Allan.
[2] Note: We believe this was the Indian trail leading from Cataloochee into Tennessee and beyond. Legend has it that each time the Indians passed the grave they would pile another rock on the grave–probably why it was referred to as "rock pile grave."
[3] Aug. 23, 1939 – Hiram Wilburn talk with Mack Hannah.

Cataloochee Valley

Cataloochee; Mack W. who married Fannie Hoyle; Jane who moved to Tennessee; Margaret who married J.M. Black of Tennessee; Julia who married John W. Cannon of Jackson County; Judie Emaline who married Jack Moody; Mila who married John T. Messer of Tennessee; Roadman who lived in Macon County, N.C. and James A. who lived on Little Cataloochee. (Annals of Haywood Co., W.C. Allan P 426.)

One of Mack Hannah's sons, Mark, was born in Little Cataloochee. After the government took over, he applied for and got the job of Park Ranger. He and his family moved to Big Cataloochee and lived there until he retired thrity years later.

Probably all the land in Big Cataloochee was taken and these people wanted to own their land, so they started the settling of Little Cataloochee. Of course, they multiplied. Each couple had large numbers of children, same as in Big Cataloochee and Caldwell Fork, and they all worked together in house raisings, barn raisings, corn shucking, bean stringing, and quilting. They enjoyed their work and to them it was a contest or some kind of game. They laughed and talked as they worked.

They had pride in the work they did. Do it right or not do it, was their motto. Most of the people were talented and could make most anything, or his neighbor would make it for him.

These families were growing, other people moved into Little Cataloochee. Dan and Harriett Colwell Cook's daughter, Rachel, married Will Messer. He was very ambitious and could make anything of wood or iron. He was a hard worker and had good business sense. When the park came in, he owned lots of property and operated a store with a post office named Ola, after one of his daughters. He had a corn mill, a sawmill, and a canemill, and also farmed and raised cattle. He was a leader in educational and church affairs. He invented farm equipment or fixed it to work better or easier.

He started growing apples for commercial use and hauling wagon loads to Knoxville, Tennessee. He was the most prominent man in Little Cataloochee. Will and Rachel had eleven children, ten girls and one boy. Mr. Messer loaned money at interest. He established a cattle scale and a stockyard and charged five to ten cents per head to weigh cattle.

Mary Ann Rogers Palmer, born October 7, 1834, died June 11, 1914. Jessie R. Palmer, born June 28, 1833, died September 8, 1895. William Palmer, who became High Sheriff of Haywood County was one of their thirteen children. Photo courtesy of Gudger Palmer.

Mr. Messer saved the finest lumber from his sawmill to make coffins. He made them, and his wife Rachel sewed the linings. He sold them for $7.00 each but provided them without charge for any impoverished person who couldn't pay.

Mr. Messer went to Big Cataloochee to see the Hiram Caldwell house. Evidently, he was much impressed. He decided he would build one just like it, only larger, probably because he had eleven children. The house was completed in 1910. It had hot and cold water and an acetylene lighting system. Even up until the park took over, most people were still carrying water in buckets from the spring and using oil lamps. A few had acetylene lights, including Jarvis Palmer and William Palmer.

A daughter of Will and Rachel Messer, named Loretta, married Claude Valentine, from a little place called Catons Grove, between Cosby and Newport, Tennessee. They lived at Little Cataloochee and had two small daughters and were expecting another baby. Loretta told his mother, Emma Valentine, that if anything should happen to her, she wanted her to take care of her children. This was sometime in 1919. World War I was on and the influenza epidemic was killing thousands of people. Apparently it did not strike in

Cataloochee Valley

Will Messer house and family, Little Cataloochee

Cataloochee until near 1920 because Loretta and her sister both died within just a few days of each other in that year.

Loretta was seven months pregnant, when she got the flu. She went into labor and the premature baby girl was born, but poor Loretta died. The baby weighed a little over two pounds.

Emma Valentine was living in Tennessee with her two youngest children, Pearl age sixteen and Ressie age twelve. She closed her house and brought her daughters to Little Cataloochee. They lived with her son Claude and his two little girls, Ivelta and Arletha, and baby Gladys.

Emma wore the long dresses and long aprons. She put the tiny baby in her apron and pinned it up. She had warmed some sand, poured it in a sack, which she placed beside the baby. She said by this method the baby would stay warm on one side being against her belly, and the bag of sand would keep it warm on the other side. (Was this a homemade incubator?)

Emma fed the baby milk with a medicine dropper. She carried the baby all day long for two months, keeping the sand warm all along. At night she pinned the baby to a big pillow because it was so tiny, and she was afraid of turning over on it. Emma had ten children she had raised before this. She was successful with this one. She continued to live there with Claude and the children. Pearl and Ressie went to the Little Cataloochee School. When the park took over, Emma was getting too old to care for the grand children. Then the Messers were moving to Lenoir in Caldwell County. They took these three granddaughters with them.

Emma (my grandmother) went to live with some of her daughters who were all married and had homes. She would alternate her visits, staying a while with one then the other. She kept her house and farm in Tennessee for several years, renting it out, but finally sold it.

Will Messer was the richest man in Little Cataloochee. He, as all others, felt cheated having to sell to the government. He received $35,000 for his holdings and moved to Caldwell County, near Lenoir, N.C. He bought more than 1200 acres of land. When he divided his property, there were eight of his children living, but he never forgot his daughter Loretta, who died leaving three daughters, Aletha (Melton), Ivelta (Watson), and Gladys (Dillard). So he divided the land into nine parts and gave Loretta's portion to her children. He was a wise and generous man.

Dan Cook house, Little Cataloochee. This is how Levi Colwell's 2nd house looked until it was abandoned in 1903. (Cook, son-in-law of Levi built 1854-1856) Photo courtesy of GSMNP.

Cataloochee Valley

The purest Anglo Saxon blood, the strongest and most magnificent bodies, the clearest brains are found among the Carolina Mountaineers. They have furnished leaders in all vocations of life.

—Judge Felix Alley

Random Thoughts and Musings of a Mountaineer Judge Felix Alley, P 271.

2

THOSE EARLY YEARS

During serious illness in a family, rich or poor, the neighbors came in and rendered every possible service, until the patient recovered or died. If the patient died, the neighbors made the coffin, dug the grave, and buried the dead. (And wept with the family for their terrible loss.)

They lived honorable, clean, wholesome lives, and usually lived to an extremely old age. When they died, they were at peace with their neighbors and their God.

Building The Log Cabins

After the new ground was cleared and planted, they had a house raisin'. Although these occasions did not lack for color, they were rather tame affairs, and were not as popular as the corn shuckins. The individual would invite eight or ten of his neighbors (if he had that many) to help in his house raisin'. He did not need so many hands. What he needed was four good corner men (that is notchers and fitters) and about the same number of strong fellows, with hand spikes, to hoist the logs up the skid poles. Sometimes if the wall got too high to depend on hand spikes altogether, ropes and grabs would also be used. The "corner men" helped the men on the ground get the logs up. It was not only hard work, it required skill.

If the walls were to be of hewn logs, the hewing was done with a broad axe before the raising begin. The logs were elevated or

Cataloochee Valley

Dressing a log to be used in a log cabin. The log has to be flattened on both sides. Photo courtesy of GSMNP.

propped up, and then the broad axe man would make his scoring mark on the log with a dye soaked line. Then he would get upon the log and begin hewing to the line, walking back and forth as he worked.

Corn Shuckin's

Of all the community get togethers of this period, there were none more popular than the corn shuckin's. They were an annual event lasting for a month or so. With four or five a week in the communities, they drew out nearly all the people.

They were held in the fall of the year. Some farmers would send out invitations for his shuckin', then they went the rounds of the community. They lasted all day or up until nightfall and with a favorable moon, they would often run well into the night. These late shuckin's always called for a big supper and happy festivities to follow. The women folk would cook all day.

The old tune masters brought out their fiddles and banjos. All the furniture would be moved out of the big room, and they would choose partners for the old Virginia Reel.

There would be fifteen or twenty men gathered around the big pile of corn in the shuck, piled under the barn shed. Most of the men would have their little steel shuckers, attached to a leather strap around the right hand, while others would shuck with their bare hands.

Then the race would begin to see which one could be first to reach the jug, which was hidden about the center of the pile of corn. The host had put it there, knowing the "ardent spirits" would be an incentive for better work.

Sometimes the prize for the best shucker would be the privilege of a kiss from the prettiest girl present. The hands at these events were supposed to play fair. If they counted off as they shucked a hundred good ears of corn, there would be a bushel.

After the work was done, there was lots of good food, good music, lots of dancing and partying.[1]

Judge Alley wrote, there is more peace in the humblest cabin, where roses bloom around the door, and happiness and contentment reside within, than all the gilded palaces of the earth, where happiness and contentment are not.

Furniture

All of the early pioneers of Cataloochee had to make their furniture after they got there because there was no road, except the narrow chopped out cattle road, until 1860. They were good craftsmen and could make anything they needed.

Levi B. Colwell made a long table of pine boards for the top, which was put on with handmade nails. The base and legs of the table were walnut held together with wooden pegs. He made a peg leg bench, by splitting a small pine tree, using half of it with the legs pegged in at an angle. This bench has an especially, fine slick finish on it because it was sat on by so many people. It was probably hand planed at first, but we think Levi made these in the 1840s or 1850s when his family was so large.

We know the bench was used by Levi's family of twelve children, and then by Hiram's children and many many cousins

---
[1] Mr. W.C. Medford, Early History of Haywood Co., P. 72

Cataloochee Valley

and friends. Next it was used by the Eldridge Caldwell family and many cousins and many friends. We know this table and bench were used over a hundred and fifty years ago and are still as sturdy as when they were first built.

This table and bench can be seen in the kitchen at the Shelton House in Waynesville, N.C. It is now called Museum of North Carolina Handicraft.

The museum does have lots of hand crafted items, such as quilts, coverlets, dolls, pottery, woodcraft and other things, but the entire house is furnished with furniture donated or on loan, from the early settlers here in Haywood County. It is a pleasure to visit there.

Around the Winter Fires

All this hard work—growing crops sufficient to feed all the livestock through the winter, food to last all winter long for the family, plenty of wood cut, pulled down to the woodyard, sawed and split for firewood and stovewood, hogs killed and dressed, hams and bacon cured, sausage made and canned, lard rendered, soap made, meal ground, and preparation against the winter months—could be seen going on busily during and after harvest time. In this way, all thrifty families raised enough food stuffs and put away enough food to last them through the winter. Our great ancestors knew this must be done, if the proverbial wolf was to be kept from the door. We of today must remember, there were no factories, no payrolls, or pensions. They had to manage to take care of themselves. Also when the cold, frozen months of winter came on, there was little marketing that could be done. So most of the time was spent doing chores, going to mill, feeding and looking after the stock, keeping on hand plenty of firewood, and warming around the big fire. This was true especially of the men folks.

"...If Pappy had no company, the women folk might work at their knitting, sewing or spinning by the fire in the big room. But if a friend or two or three, had come in for a social chat and perhaps a little "ardent spirits," the women folks went to another room or to bed...." –Mr. W.C. Medford

The massive stone chimneys with big fireplaces often five foot wide was the rule. It took a big fireplace for the big families to get around comfortably in cold weather. Besides, the cooking was often done at the same place.

The First and Second Roads into Cataloochee

Before 1825 a rough, narrow road had been blazed and made sufficient for a stock drover's road. Then a toll road was authorized by the county court as the result of a movement by a few Jonathan Creek citizens led by Joshua Allison.

The toll road led from the right hand prong of Cove Creek, above the Davis place (where the toll gate was) to the Cataloochee Creek, and was called "Cataloochee Turnpike."[1] Allison was made keeper of the toll gate. He was to have the gate fees as his for keeping said road in good repair and etc. Here are the stated fees Allison was to collect:

> For a man and a horse 18-3/4 cents
> For an extra pack horse 6-1/2 cents
> For each head of hogs, 1 cent each
> For cattle, 2 cents per head.

No fees for vehicles were mentioned whatsoever, because we suppose it was entirely impassible for such, except possibly a half sled.

The people who came into Cataloochee before 1860 had to travel by way of the old, rough, cutout cattle road for thirty-five years before the Cataloochee Turnpike was built.

The Dug Road 1854-1856

It was called "Cook Lane," and it started below Palmer's Chapel along the branch behind the church. When it left flat land it went to the right of the Dillard Caldwell house, then on up that branch on the left side.

---

[1] Note: We must not get this first old cattle road into Cataloochee confused with the much later and remarkable turnpike road which was finished in 1860. –Mr. W.C. Medford, Early History of Haywood Co. P. 81

Cataloochee Valley

Wagons were common, but sleds were more common. They were easy to build with two bent sourwood runners. There seemed to be one for every purpose: tobacco, hay, logging, and general hauling. Sleds were cheap and went where wagons couldn't go. Photo courtesy of GSMNP.

It turned off to the right. That section went on by the Jack Woody place, then across the mountain to Ball Gap, then on down to Little Cataloochee. That was the mail route between Little Cataloochee and Big Cataloochee years later. (Interview with Gudger Palmer, Sept. 4, 1995.)

While visiting with Mark Hannah, in April, 1990, and inquiring about the Dug Road, he seem surprised that we had ever heard of it. He said, "Them first two couples to live on Little Cataloochee in 1854, they made it forty-eight inches wide so they could get a narrow sled through there from Big Cataloochee. They had to have some way to get supplies over there. Some places there wasn't much digging to do, but other places they would have to dig through three and four feet of dirt and rock. This was the shortest distance between the Big and Little Cataloochee."

What a hard backbreaking job that was with mattocks, pick and shovel. Eventually, there was a road built into Little

Cataloochee going toward Mount Sterling, then turned off to the left. That is a much longer distance than going across Noland Mountain.

But for many years the only way to travel from Little Cataloochee to Big Cataloochee was this "dug road."

The Corn Mill

A corn mill was built by Jessie Palmer about 1850 or earlier. The water was transported from the mill pond by a raceway (or trough) four feet wide and three and one-half feet deep into a fobay or tank constructed of logs and boards. This trough was a quarter mile or longer. The fobay was eight feet wide, twelve feet long, and twelve feet deep. The frame was made of logs, mortised together (notched to fit) then heavy one inch boards nailed inside the frame to hold water.

Water was transferred from the bottom of the tank, down a chute at about a thirty degree angle, and hit a wooden wheel made of oak about three feet in diameter. Cups were chopped out in the wheel for the water to hit and turn the wheel, a square yellow heart pine shaft fit in the center of the wheel, and the

The Jessie Palmer Mill on Indian Creek (now Palmer Creek.) Painted by Mrs. Hilda Palmer.

shaft went up about ten feet through the stationary mill stone. On the top of this shaft was a piece of plate steel tapered out to a sphere, extending through the stationary mill stone. There was a heavy steel piece that fit over the sphere to carry and balance to the top mill stone as it turned counter clockwise. There was a mechanism to lower and raise the top mill stone. This was to adjust the wheel so as to grind the corn fine or coarse. The corn was poured into a hopper and fell down through an opening between the two mill stones. These stones weight 1,000 pounds each.

Occasionally, these stones wore smooth and had to be turned up on the edge and sharpened. That was done with a metal pick. We sat there and pecked, pecked, pecked until it was uniformly roughed up; then it was lowered back into place.

The park destroyed the old handmade mill about 1940. It was on Indian Creek (now called Palmer Creek) near the horse camp. Jessie Palmer passed the mill on to his son, Thomas Palmer. Jarvis Caldwell bought the Palmer place and operated it until 1938 when the park took over. The miller took one half gallon of the corn meal for each bushel of corn ground in payment. There were several mills in the Cataloochee area. All of this information came from Raymond Caldwell on May 27, 1994.

Levi's Second House

In 1858 Levi Colwell built a larger log house of hand hewn poplar logs fitted together with dovetail corners. It was two stories high. It had the kitchen built out back with a dogtrot between the two buildings. There was a porch all the way across the front. One end of it was enclosed for an extra bedroom. This was the first house in Cataloochee to have a closet in it. He was very proud of his house, especially the closet, which was enclosed space under the stair steps.

Later Hiram Caldwell, lived in the house, and he showed the closet to visitors. Mark Hannah was one of the visitors and related this to us. Usually the clothes were hung on the walls on wooden pegs. Levi made a clothespress for their clothes, too. That was a large cabinet with three shelves.

This second house was built about three hundred yards above

Levi's corn crib and buggy shed. Behind it is the house Levi Colwell built in 1858. Eldridge's barn can be seen in the distance. Photo courtesy of GSMNP.

the Caldwell barn on the same side of the road. You can still see some old apple trees out near the woods. Those were back of the second homestead.

Near the house he also built a corn crib with space on one side to keep the buggy and the other side, harness etc. He also built a barn of logs.

In 1923 Eldridge Caldwell (grandson of Levi) got Jim Caldwell and some more of his cousins to help move the barn. They numbered the logs so they could reconstruct it exactly as it had been. Now the barn sits close to the road, directly across the creek from the Hiram Caldwell house. The log stalls are the same as they were in 1858 or 59. The loft and other parts were added.

Levi also built a small log house for his sheep. Levi built all of his buildings of hand-hewn logs. He made shingles for the roof out of oak, riving (split) them with a froe and a maul. The little sheep house was moved down behind where the barn is now. After Eldridge got these buildings moved, he built a large red cattle barn of rough sawed lumber, with a shed on the end for his mowing machine, hay rake, plows, and tools. Now only the big barn stands.

Cataloochee Valley

Levi did not get to enjoy his second house very long, due to the Civil War. He was captured in 1863 and died in 1864. He only got to live in it five years. This is the house Jonathan Woody and his children moved into with Levi's widow, Mary Ann and her children. After her husband died and his wife died, they got married and raised the fourteen children there.

Hiram Caldwell, one of Levi's sons worked as a teamster to Greenville, S.C. for ten cents a day, saved his money, and bought the home and some of the land from the other heirs. Hiram married Mary Elizabeth Howell, daughter of Albert Howell and Eleanor Ferguson Howell from Cove Creek. They lived in the house Levi built. All of their children were born there. William, Harriet (Hattie), Dillard, Reuben Eldridge, and an infant named Connie who died early.

First Church/School

The first school in Cataloochee was built on land donated by Julia Ann Palmer ("...for the love I have for the promotion of religion and education.") to trustees, George Palmer, Young Bennett, Levi Colwell, and Newton Bennett, for a meeting house and a school house for the Methodist Episcopal Church South in December, 1858. It was on the north side of Cataloochee Creek, on one acre of land, between the present ranger station and campground. The families themselves donated time, labor, and materials to provide a place of learning for their children. It was called "The Schoolhouse Patch."

The first school met in the log church. It was likely a subscription school, financed primarily or totally from local contributions, and was surely primary grade level only. No information is available as to the length of school term or teacher's salaries, but in the state of N.C. as a whole in 1858 the average salary for teachers was $28.00 for an average term of four months.

There was a decline during the great difficulties of the Civil War. Counties were released from the obligation to levy and collect school taxes, and at the end of the war the public school system virtually collapsed in North Carolina. The period 1865 through 1867 was an especially bad time. A state law of 1866 allowed the justice of the county courts to levy and collect taxes at their discretion for common school support and also gave them discretionary powers to grant aid to subscription schools and to allow such to be operated in the district. The new constitution in 1868 provided the general assembly should provide by taxation or otherwise for a general uniform system of public schools, wherein tuition shall be free of charge to all children of the State between the ages of six and twenty-one years. Counties were divided into districts, with at least one public school for at least four months a year. County Commissioners who failed to comply were "liable to indictment."[1]

For several generations, the children of the pioneers had little education from books because there were no public schools and few subscription schools. But it must be understood that they were not without knowledge. The open book of nature was before them. They knew the ways of the wilderness, they understood the storms, the floods, the trees, the forest, the wild animals, the Indians, and many other things that most people did not know.[2]

The first public school law was passed in 1838. At the time education was only available to children of the upper and middle classes who could afford to pay for it. We have no record of who attended or who the teacher was at "The Schoolhouse Patch." Dr. Carroll says we should note that the 1839 law required counties to provide school but not necessarily a schoolhouse.

Judge Felix Alley, wrote that the first school law ever enacted for North Carolina was in 1838, but much earlier than that, lots of families throughout the mountains hired private teachers for the education of their children, each family paying part of the teacher's salary. This was called subscription school.

Mrs. Ethel Palmer McCracken was interviewed on September 24, 1994. She was born in 1894 on Cataloochee and remembers the first Church/School at "The Schoolhouse Patch." She said her sister Lura and brother Jarvis Palmer went

---
[1]Dr. Roy Carroll, Historic Structures Report
[2]Random Thoughts and Musings of a Mountaineer. Judge Felix Alley, P. 269

Cataloochee Valley

to school there, and she told names of four of the teachers. They were Andy Hall, Doctor Caldwell, Charlie Carpenter, and Mr. McElhaney. She said it was always called "The Schoolhouse Patch." She could also remember later teachers at Big Cataloochee.

They were: Verlin Campbell, John Queen, Mattie Hayes, Mary Henry, Rass Owens, Josie Owens, Lillie Ferguson, Glenn Palmer, Jarvis Allison, Juanita Medford, Gussie Martin, Eula Noland, Lee McElluth, Jane Brown, Frank Rogers, Falsom Davis, Hugh Rogers, Maggie Chambers, and Mary Davis.

We don't know who wrote the next list but all of these taught school in Cataloochee.

Eleanor Palmer (one school before she married,
   two schools after marriage.)

Frank Rogers	Clara Leatherwood
Burnice McMahan	Levada Palmer
Maggie Allen	Flora Palmer
Eula Green	Della Palmer
Miss Simmons	Cromer Chambers
Ruth Smathers	Magola Caldwell
Roger Ferguson	Eula Noland
Will Howell	Letha Noland
Lillian Bryson	Hazel Settlemire
Mamie Leatherwood	Mayme Leatherwood
Ora Ferguson	Thelma Sutton

Accidents

Two of Levi's sons lost their lives at an early age on Big Cataloochee. David Marion, born in 1847, was a young married man. He was out plowing in a field where some of the large trees had been deadened. By removing a wide band of bark, so the sap could not rise, the tree died. After it dried out some, maybe a year or two, it would be set on fire. It would burn and smolder for weeks on end.

This tree had been burning for sometime. Marion was plowing and he did not realize the tree was about to fall. He went on plowing and suddenly the tree fell, killing him. This happened in early 1883, when he was only thirty-six years old.

In 1866 or 1867, Marion married Eliza Cagle. She had apparently been married before because in the 1880 census, Marion had a stepdaughter named Elizabeth, age seventeen. For more information on this family see appendix, The Second Generation of Caldwells in Cataloochee, by Dr. Roy Carroll.

In the 1880s people needed doctors very much, but they were few and far between. In those early census, there were twenty men named Doctor in Haywood County. We do not know why. Almost all communities had herb doctors who were successful in helping many people.

Another of Levi's sons, Doctor L., was born in October, 1856. He married Sarah Palmer, February 4, 1885, daughter of Jessie and Mary Ann or "Polly" Rogers Palmer.

Doctor was driving a group of hogs when a large hog ran into him and gored his leg deeply. It became infected, blood poisoning set in, and red streaks ran all the way up his leg. They doctored him with every known remedy and sent for a doctor, but he was dead in a short time at age forty-five.

In those days with no antibiotics, patients with blood poisoning often died. Lots of times the old-fashioned remedies like Epson salts and warm water were used to bathe the injury. Then they would apply some salve, or sometimes fat meat was sliced thin and placed on an infected area to draw out the infection, but this time nothing helped. He died.

Doctor was a school teacher and a farmer. He and Sara Jane had seven children, but she died when the last child was born. He managed to keep the family together for three years, but he died in 1901. There were six boys, and then a girl was born in April, 1892, who they named Minnie. She was raised by Uncle Hiram and Aunt Lizzie Caldwell. Uncle Harrison and Aunt Susie took a child named Hardy to raise. Then there was a child named Thomas raised by Thomas Palmer and Aunt Lou. William Palmer took Herbert, who died at age fifteen. Frank Palmer took Jessie. George and Mag took Eston.

Though Doctor did not become a physician nor did his son, Eston, he married Maggie Cope Caldwell, and they had several children, and the oldest, E.R., became a physician, specializing in

Cataloochee Valley

Left: Doctor L. Caldwell Born October 12, 1855 Died November 19, 1901 Son of Levi & Mary Ann Colwell. Right: Sarah M. Palmer Caldwell Wife of Doctor L. Caldwell Born March 20, 1867 Died June 30, 1899. Photo courtesy of Frank Davis.

internal medicine. He married Yvonne Phelps of Winston-Salem, N.C. Their accomplishment was remarkable. They had five children, three boys and two girls, all professionals in the medical field. Dr. David Caldwell specializes in rheumatology at Duke. Dr. Bob specializes in pediatrics in Winchester, Virginia. Dr. Steve is a specialist in gastroenterology in Charlottesville, Virginia. Both daughters became registered nurses. Susan Caldwell Madison of Statesville and Lynn Caldwell Vessel of Midlothian, Virgina, both worked in the operating rooms and emergency rooms.

Renegades

There was an incident that was not known by many people. This was told to me by (Daddy) Eldridge Caldwell just a few years before he passed away. This happened in the early years of Cataloochee.

There was one summer they had a drought that lasted all summer. It was so hot and dry most of the crops failed. The branches almost dried up. The creeks were very low. By fall of the year it was clear to Levi Colwell there would be a food shortage that winter, and he set out to hunt some wild game.

As he walked through the woods, the dry leaves under his feet made crackling sounds, which would alert any animal. He would have to travel to a spot where he expected some wildlife to pass and wait quietly.

He waited for hours at several different places. No game came by. Finally, in late afternoon he got lucky and shot a deer.

He put the deer across his shoulders to carry it home. He had taken the time to reload his gun, which he carried under his right arm with the barrel in his left hand. He had walked for about a half mile, when suddenly he heard a limb snap! He jerked his head back just in time to see a tomahawk fly in front of his face and stick in a tree! It barely missed his head. He whirled around to see an Indian coming at him. He wanted that deer. Levi had his gun positioned to where he could get his finger on the trigger and fired point blank from his waist. There was no time to lay the deer down, to sight his gun. He shot and killed that Indian. Levi was badly shaken because he was almost killed, then had to kill someone in self defense. He threw the deer down and ran over to see who he was. It was not one of his beloved Cherokees, but a renegade passing through Cataloochee. Back in those days, occasionally there would be a roving band of renegade Indians passing through the county stealing from whites and the Cherokee too. The group would split up and travel alone, steal what they could, then meet up and travel on together.

Levi didn't know if the others would be coming along soon or not. He buried that Indian fast. It worried him and he didn't talk about it for a long time and then only to a trusted few.

Mr. Hiram Wilburn interviewed people about the time the park was taking over. Uncle Steve Woody knew about it. He told Mr. Wilburn, "Levi Colwell was hunting at the ford of Indian Creek, leading to the ledge. An Indian threw a tomahawk at Levi's head, and he dodged behind the tree, the tomahawk sticking in the tree. Levi shot at the Indian. It was not reported whether he was killed or not." The tomahawk was kept in the Caldwell family for many years. Uncle Steve, George H. Caldwell, and others

Cataloochee Valley

reported seeing this tomahawk many times. It was a square bladed axe with a short wooden handle.

Mr. Wilburn records that Turkey George told him, "Indians stole cornmeal from Jesse Palmer's mill and some meat from Creek George. They were tracked some distance to their camp. This was the Mull mill. This was before the Civil War. There was a large Indian camp along beside the creek back of my barn. I was going to see my place one time early and two Indians scared me very badly. They had been sanging (digging ginseng, a root which was sold for a very high price) and were laying out, wrapped in two white blankets. I talked with them. They were friendly. This was forty years ago, when I had but three acres cleared at the time." This is Indian Bottom and Indian Creek.[1] (The same creek that the park named Palmer Creek.)

The Mull mill was 100 feet past the present mill. Then my father built a mill and sawmill at the present place. Old Saser's son sawed lumber for my house. It ran a little while after that time. That saw could cut 1000 ft. to 1200 ft. per day if it ran well.[2]

Granny Pop and the Panther

Mary Ann Colwell got a nickname. She became known as "Granny Pop." No one knows why she was called that, but during the Civil War she had to be both Mom and Pop, then after the war when she was raising fourteen children, maybe if they did not obey her, she gave them a big pop on the rear end. When you look at her picture, you see she was very stern. In those days, children were disciplined, and they loved and respected their parents. They respected themselves and were taught to respect others, all according to the Bible. The children were taught all the manners and did not call older people by their first names. They were taught to call them Uncle and Aunt when they actually were not, but it was just a way of showing respect. Someone said it was an old English custom. Sometimes they referred to older people as Mr. or Mrs.

---

[1]Hiram Wilburn notes [116] 291
[2]Hiram Wilburn note #28

Mary Ann Nailand Colwell, also know as "Granny Pop."

Older folks used to tell about Granny Pop going over to Little Cataloochee to visit her married daughters. On her way back home along the trail, she saw a panther perched in a tree ready to pounce on her. She left the road and continued on her way circling through the woods. She was thinking she had left the panther behind, but when she had circled around through the woods a long distance then came back into the trail, he was coming along some distance behind her. She wondered what to do. He was getting closer. She knew she could not out run him so, she took off her apron, dropped it in the trail, and walked on as fast as she could. Glancing back, she saw the panther was curious, smelling and examining the apron. She kept walking briskly, but when she looked back, he had left the apron and was following her. As he got close again, she dropped another piece of her clothing, and he stopped to examine it again while she gained a good distance. Then the panther was following her again. This happened over and over as she traveled the three or four miles. She finally got home, but she was practically naked. After hearing her story, the men folks went hunting him, found his tracks, set a trap, and caught him.[1]

Uncle Steve Woody talked about moving out of Spring Creek when he was just a boy about ten years old. His father

---

[1] This story was told to us in June 1975 by Floyd Woody. We had heard the story before, but he had all the details.

Cataloochee Valley

had decided to move back into Cataloochee. He loaded up five of his children in the old wagon with quilts and what clothes they had and some food and stuff to camp along the road. He said, "The rough old road was not much more than a trail and in places it was washed out. It was an awful hard trip. They camped and cooked along the way and slept in the wagon at night."

Uncle Steve said, "There in Cataloochee were only a few families living. There were not many fields cleared then, mostly just woods." He talked about the herds of deer, and lots of bears and wolves. The sheep had to be put up every night or wolves and bears would kill them. He said the big herds of deer, just up and left. Nobody knows why, but there were all kinds of animals, plenty to eat, turkey, pheasant, coon, bear, and more fish than we could eat, and lots of mink and other fur to sell.

"We could always make a good living; never had to borrow any money. Back in them days people in Cataloochee kept their money at home. They felt like it was safer than way off yonder in a bank."[1]

In the last few years of Eldridge's life, he could finally talk more about Cataloochee. As much as he had been hurt by the government taking his home and land, he never had bad things to say about it; but when he was old and not able to keep his pastures mowed, they grew up in weeds and briars. He said, "If the government wanted a 'dad blamed' wilderness, they ought to have taken this place." (Meaning Campbell Creek in Maggie Valley where he lived thirty-nine years until his death in 1973.)

Knee Length Shirt about 1868

At the time and before Granny Pop and Jonathan Woody were raising that large family, she grew flax and wove it into material. Flax is pure linen after it is processed. It is noted for its strength, coolness, and wearability. She made knee length shirts for the boys. These shirts were so durable, they probably never wore out and got passed down to the next child when the first ones out grew them. At this same time the young Indian

---

[1] As told to Eldridge Caldwell by Uncle Steve

Levi's log cabin.

men wore the knee length deer skin shirts.

We know about the flax shirts because there was a funny story about Hiram told by his son Eldridge.

When Hiram was sixteen or seventeen years old, about 1868, he had a sweetheart. One day several of the family (Woodys and Caldwells) were out hoeing corn when Hiram happened to look down the road and saw a group of girls coming up the road, and his girl friend was in the group. He did not want to be seen in that long shirt; so he ran to the house and up the stairs to change into some pants. He jerked off the long shirt in such a hurry he was totally naked and forgot that some planks in the floor had not been nailed down. He happened to step on the end of a loose plank, flipping it up and dropping him naked as a picked bird right down in front of the door, just as the girls were entering. Oh! He was so embarrassed he ran back up the stairs and would not come back down until the girls left.

All the family had so much fun laughing and teasing him, every summer as they hoed corn. It became a family joke and was passed down to me.

Cataloochee Valley

The Ravages of War

In the Civil War, the loss of our men was great. There was much sorrow and grief. This county made slow progress since it became a county in 1809, it was originally part of Buncombe County. The Civil War set it back, mostly the agriculture, because their economy was built around farming and livestock. Since all the young men and even up to middle age, was drafted into the ranks of the Confederacy.

So it was that the farmland grew up (much of it) into briers, weeds and bushes, it was often improperly cultivated by the womenfolk and children left at home. Also fences and buildings went down for lack of repairs. It had been a period of four years of war, for it to go to waste.

Business fell off woefully because of the depreciation and lack of purchasing power of the Confederate currency, especially toward the last of the war. Stores and supplies became limited, and the bare necessities often could not be obtained. It was a period of want, stint and often suffering here and elsewhere.

—Mr. W.C. Medford, *Early History of Haywood Co.*, P. 164

3

THE CIVIL WAR YEARS

Patriotic, Religious Family and War

Aunt Lizzie Caldwell was one of five children born to Albert Howell and Eleanor Ferguson Howell on Cove Creek. When Grandma Lizzie was just a young child, her father was killed. He went to South Carolina, probably on a cattle drive and met his death, but the details were never known.

At any rate that left her mother with five little children. There was no way a woman could support her children and herself in those days. There was an orphanage in Haywood County, but only the poorest or unfortunate were sent there.

The family members usually took one or two of the children to raise. In this case, little Mary Elizabeth was taken in by two of her mother's brothers, Garland and Burder Ferguson before the war. They were both in the terrible Civil War.

Lt. Burder, C.O.E., gave valiant service in the East Tennessee campaign and at Vicksburg, Rome, Kenesaw Mtn. and the big battle in Atlanta, Ga. After the war, he taught school and later practiced law with his brother, Garland. They also enjoyed farming.

We still have copies of the letters he wrote to his parents. He signed it, "I remain with due consideration, your obedient son," Burder, 25th NC Regt. He writes from Tennessee: "While the enemy had possession of this country, they destroyed nearly all the property of Southern men, took horses, hogs, cattle, and

Cataloochee Valley

Negroes, hay, wheat, even the last peck of grain. Wrecked all the household furniture and arrested both men and women. You have but little idea of destruction and harrow of war." He always inquired about the family and crops. He mentions that beef was ten cents a pound in 1863 and worries in every letter about his brothers. Several were in service.

This is a copy of a letter (in part) from Burder Ferguson to his younger brother Andrew.

Louden, Tenn.
Feb. 17th, 1862

Mr. A.M. Ferguson
Dear Sir:
In haste I write you. Late last night we received our marching orders to Morristown, Tenn. There have been very heavy battles in the last few days. A heavy fight of the last five days ended on the Sabbath at Fort Donaldson. More heavy battles. Passengers on the train say this place will soon be in the possession of Lincoln forces. Now is the time to try men's souls. Let every son of the South that can shoulder a musket, resolve to do or die. Awaken you sons of our sires. Come to the rescue, our country, our all is at stake. May God give us the victory and then express himself. If die we must in bloody gore, may God help us to die like Christian heroes, fighting for country, freedom and all that is dear and sacred to generous spirits and noble hearts. Be not panic stricken, for he who cannot brook defeat never survives.

Yours truly
W.B. Ferguson

In a letter Burder Ferguson's brother Garland writes:

"Once I had a dear and affectionate brother with me, Nathan is gone, Ebed is gone, never will I have them to give me advice again. No more, shall I have their much loved company for the narrow grave contains it. Dear parents, I can hardly give up dear Nathan, but we must be resigned to the will of the All Mighty. Mother, if you have a chance a pair of socks would be very acceptable. Give Elenor and Annie and children my best love and tender them the heartfelt sympathy of a brother. My love and deepest sympathy are with you all.

>I am ever your affectionate son,
>Garland."

Lt. Garland S. Ferguson, was wounded three times, the last time at Petersburg, Va. Those wounds caused him to be crippled the rest of his life. He was hospitalized five months and held as prisoner of war. He was wounded in his left thigh in 1865 and bones worked out for the next thirteen years. After the war, he became a lawyer, a politician serving in the NC Senate, and later a judge.

A letter from Burder in which he says he is forty-seven miles from Cumberland Gap.

> "We marched last night and came up, tired and feet blistered, many of our boys are still barefooted. Several days the only water is a pond so stagnant it had a very unpleasant smell. Some sickness in our group. We have had quite a severe time. We have two days food cooked in our haver sacks.
>
>>I remain your obedient son
>>WB Ferguson"

Burder writes:

"Nothing is impossible with God. God can shield us with the hollow of his hand and preserve our lives. If this should not be his will, we have within our grasp to lay hold of the blessed promises, given to us in the new testament. We had cornbread and beef for breakfast. Several days stinging, biting cold. No warm room or comfortable bed. I got a glass of buttermilk for only thirty-seven cents. It usually cost $1.00."

In another letter he is mourning and praying for Robert, his

Cataloochee Valley

brother, in a prison camp in Douglas, Ill.

A letter dated Apr. 12, 1884, states that Robert P. Ferguson died in Camp Douglas Prison and was buried in the Confederate graveyard, near Chicago, Ill. (This is just a small portion of those old letters)

These fine men, Burder and Garland, and their wives had several children each, but they were a kind and loving family, so they took in their sister's child Mary Elizabeth, raised her and educated her. She never forgot them or the religion they taught her. She later taught subscription school in Waynesville at their home. They lived in a red brick house on the lot where the library is now.

Some years after the Fergusons died, some of the heirs gave the house and lot to Haywood County for a library. The house was remodeled to house the library and was used for some years, then torn down and the new one built. Before the Fergusons gave it to the county, the library was on Main Street, the rock building beside Smith's Drug Store.

Back in the days when Hiram was courting Lizzie at the Ferguson house, he became well-acquainted with them. After they were married and lived at Cataloochee, when he went to Waynesville on business, he would always visit, sometimes spending the night with them. Lizzie would drive her buggy and go to see her Mother, still living at Cove Creek and then go to Waynesville to visit her Uncles.

When her uncles came home, they talked of the war. It made a profound impression on her. When she married Hiram Caldwell on Jan. 22, 1880 and moved to Big Cataloochee, they lived with his mother (Granny Pop) Mary Ann Nailand Caldwell, in the log house Levi had built.

Granny Pop had told some of these war stories to Aunt Lizzie, her daughter-in-law. Many years later, when this writer was born, (Grandpa) Hiram and (Grandma) Lizzie had built the large white house. Hiram had died. Their youngest son Eldridge had married Pearl Valentine, and they were living there with Aunt Lizzie. She still liked her old log home and she took me there quite often as a child. She told these stories to me and described how they lived. She knew times were changing and wanted me to know about the early years of Cataloochee. She died when I was ten years old. Many times after that, I talked with Eldridge about the same stories. That is how the stories were passed down to me, from my great grandmother, to my grandmother, to my father and to me.

The Cataloochee Turnpike — A Road of Trouble

The Cataloochee Turnpike had been finished just before the Civil War. Just in time to be used by Teague's Scouts.

Captain Albert Teague of the Home Guards and his Scouts had been active in raids on the Union sympathizers, especially in the Big Bend section (Haywood Co.) where it was mostly prounion in sentiment in at least ten or twelve families. Several of these were known as outliers (same as draft dodgers). They had been hiding out, and Teague was having trouble rounding them up.

Finally Teague and a few of his scouts succeeded in capturing three of the outliers by watching their homes. When their wives would leave the home to carry food to their husbands, these scouts would follow and find the men. Sometimes they would whip the women to make them tell where their husbands were hiding.

The three captured were George and Anderson Grooms and a Caldwell man. They were tied and marched on foot up to the top of Mt. Sterling and down about seven or eight miles on the Cataloochee side. There at a certain turn in the road, they stopped and required one of the Grooms to play his fiddle. Grooms complied with his favorite "Bonaparte's Retreat" which for many years throughout this mountain region, was known as "Grooms Tune." It is a sad one running much to the minor key, musicians say. Dogs often begin to howl whenever it is being played.

"Fare you well, farewell" the treble notes seem to cry out. But evidently it did not soften the hearts of the war hardened scouts, for there in the shadows of Mt. Sterling, Grooms held his cherished fiddle to his breast for the last time. Its sweet plaintive strains were scarcely hushed in the deep wooded silence when the lives of Grooms and his companions were hushed. No doubt the old fiddler poured out his heart, its penitence, sorrows, and hope in that one last tune.

Cataloochee Valley

All three bodies were left lying by the roadside. Hours later Eliza Grooms and others came with an ox hitched to a sled. On this they laid the bodies and hauled them back across the mountain to their home for burial in the little community graveyard on the water of Big Creek.[1]

Years later an old woman said that her grandmother would drink coffee in the morning, then look at the coffee grounds in the cup, by this she could determine where her husband would be hiding. He would have to change his place of hiding often. It's a mystery, but she declared her grandmother could read the grounds and find him. Her grandfather was never caught, but he nearly froze to death.

Mr. Hiram Wilburn recorded this in his notes. "Mrs. Ira McGee born 1853 on Caldwell Fork.

Kirk's Raiders On Big Cataloochee

The Civil War was an awful scary time for the women to be left home with little children and to know this notorious raider Kirk and six hundred men would be coming into the valley, plundering, burning, capturing, killing, and stealing. They would take all the food a family had and just leave them to starve.

These were terrible times in the mountains. All of the able-bodied men were gone off to war. Just women and children and a few old men were left at home. In order to feed their family, the women had to take on the men's work of plowing and planting the crops, chopping the wood, feeding the livestock, milking, harvesting the crops, and preserving the food for winter.

We often speak of the bravery shown and the hardships endured by our soldier boys in war times. We seemingly forget the privations, sacrifices, and brave carrying on all along the home front by the mothers and other womenfolk, children, and a few old men, as it was in the time of the Civil War here.

The women not only took the place of their husbands and sons in the fields but also had to continue to cook, clean, sew, make clothes and patch for all the family. They packed loads over long mountain trails; they doctored in case of sickness and nursed their loved ones through.

---

[1] Mr. W.C. Medford, Middle History of Haywood County

The cruel Kirk, was George Kirk from Tennessee who was first a confederate, but turned renegade and joined the union. He was given the rank of Colonel. His regiment was mostly made up of deserters and bushwhackers and criminals. They were supposed to find deserters and make them fight, but instead they killed and stole. This group and Captain Albert Teague and his confederate scouts were most feared. Both groups were looking for outliers. Since Cataloochee was in the vast wilderness, there were outliers from other areas or states that came there to hide out. They didn't want to fight for either side because communication was so poor, they hardly knew what the war was about. They did not care or did not realize what it meant if the states were united. Everything in their world was good "without war." They did not see any reason to fight.

When these outliers hid out in the wilderness of Cataloochee, they lived in the woods, in caves or hollow logs. Sometimes after dark they would slip into a barn loft and sleep under some hay, leaving early in the morning before the family caught them. They stole eggs and sometimes milked a cow before leaving. Sometimes they would beg from the settlers if they thought it was safe. If not they lived on wild game and berries and chestnuts.

Throughout the war, both armies searched the Cataloochee area for outliers. They were shot and killed if found.

The very last days of the Civil War, about the last of March or April, the notorious Federal raider, Col. George Kirk marched into Haywood, coming from Tennessee across Mt. Sterling on down into Big Cataloochee.

Captain Robert Howell, with a little company of homeguards was trying to hold the Turnpike against Kirk. The Homeguard was mostly old men and boys. The cruel Kirk and his raiders broke through about Sterling Gap.

Kirk and over 600 men, of which 400 were on horseback, 200 on foot, encountered some sniper fire from Captain Howell and his little group of the homeguard. They were so outnumbered about all they could do was bushwhack and harass, fall back and retreat, which slowed Kirk's men somewhat.[1]

In an interview dated September 9, 1994, Mrs. McCracken said, " Howell sent one of the young boys to warn the women and

---
[1] From Mr. W. Clark Medford's book "The Early History of Haywood County."

Cataloochee Valley

children to hide their food and livestock. The first house the young man came to was that of Young Bennett, and he told them 'The enemy is on the way, lots and lots of them! Hurry, Hurry! Hide everything of value, your hams, all your food, and your horses. They will take everything and leave us here to starve.'

"Mrs. Bennett helped hide some of their things and told the family where to hide the rest, while she got on her horse and galloped down to the valley to warn others."

While Mrs. Bennett was gone warning neighbors and family that the raiders were coming, is probably when they set fire to her house. Allan wrote they set the fire because Mr. Bennett was such an uncompromising confederate.

Dr. Carroll also said the Bennetts had a daughter named Sophronia, sixteen years old and she whipped one of Kirk's men. He said, "I don't know if it was before or after they burned the house." Sophronia also managed to hide a trunk of valuable possessions.

The following story was first told to me by Grandma Lizzie. She would take me up to her old log cabin where she had lived and tell me lots of stories. Later, the same story was told by Eldridge (my father).

Mary Ann Colwell was warned, we think by Mrs. Bennett. Very quickly Mary Ann carried the hams and dried apples and other food out in the cornfield and hid them under the corn shocks. Then Mary Ann quickly gathered her horses, and she rode one, with the others on a lead behind. She rode at full speed up the road, then into the creek for a distance on up past where the Woody house is now, on into the woods and up the mountain to a large cave. The same cave the Indians stayed in that cold winter of 1838. She took the horses in and tied them up, then broke off a large laurel limb. She used it to brush out all the tracks, so the raiders could not track the horses and take them.

Mary Ann heard that Kirk and his raiders were camping down at the Kerr place. She would have to be very careful when she went to feed the horses, but she managed to slip back and feed them every few days. She was successful at keeping everything hid and when the raiders came, she stood up to them with a "steel cold stare" and told them nothing.

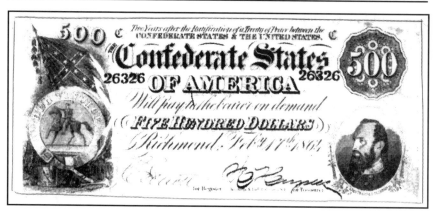

Levi and Mary Ann Nailand had saved quite a bit of the Confederate money and kept it in a trunk. After the War when it became worthless, some of it was used to paper the walls.

Mary Ann and Levi had been living there raising cattle and hogs nearly thirty years. He had taken several animals to market every year. They had accumulated lots of money because they were so self-sufficient and they made most of what they needed. They had all the good homegrown food they could eat. Their home built of logs and cost nothing except hard work. Their clothes were made from the flax they grew, also wool from the sheep they raised. They even tanned animal hides and made their own shoes, so there was very little to buy, just coffee, salt and sugar, and probably some bars of iron to make plow points, hinges, nails, horseshoes, and other farm implements.

When Levi came from the market, he brought the necessary items and always had a good-sized roll of money after paying for his purchases. He brought home the rest of the money, which they kept in a trunk. He would probably have bought more land, but the Civil War came along and the confederate money became worthless. It was finally used to paper the walls. Paper of any kind was very scarce at that time.

Gudger Palmer remembered his family talking about Kirk's raiders being camped out down at the Kerr place when his father was just a small boy out playing with some other small boys in the field below the house. They heard horses running, looked up, and saw men on horses coming after them. The little boys ran fast as they could and just barely missed being run down and trampled to death. Of course that was deliberate. The cruel raiders intended to cause all the heartbreak and sorrow they could and they didn't want the children to warn their family.

The raiders did not know the families had already been warned. They must have been disappointed to find so little to steal. Gudger remembered the family talking of hiding their beautiful handwoven woolen coverlets out in the woods in hollow logs.

Raiders at the Schoolhouse Patch 1865

Interview with Gudger Palmer April 28, 1993.

Some of the Confederate soldiers who had been wounded were sent home if they were able to travel at all. The train did not come any closer than Morristown or Knoxville, Tennessee, or to Morganton, NC, so they had to walk most of the way.

Soldiers who were wounded came dragging themselves home to Big Cataloochee and Waynesville. They were ragged, dirty, war worn, half starved, and sick. The distance was long and some died on the way home. The poor, crippled soldiers could only hobble along, some trying to help the others who had lost a foot or a leg. Some had no shoes, their feet blistered and bleeding. They had no food except what little people along the way could spare.

These had been strong, healthy, fine young men before that awful war. Now they came home crippled, thin, and suffering. It was heartbreaking to see their pitiful condition.

The Cataloochee women were already overworked and they needed to get the crops planted. Yet these sick men must be taken care of. The women decided to set up sort of a hospital in the first little log church/school at the Schoolhouse Patch. Then they could take turns caring for the men, while the others tried to farm. They bathed the soldiers, dressed their wounds, and gave them food, nursing and caring for them best as they could.

Unfortunately Kirk and his outlaws were still camping at the Kerr Place and found out about the wounded soldiers in the church/school. They came there, stood in the door and shot the poor, sick, helpless men. Shot and killed were nine men, three got away, six others were shot but not killed. Some of those soldiers were from Waynesville and other areas. They had been fighting in Tennessee and other places just trying to get home by way of the Cataloochee Turnpike, the only road through the Smokies at that time.

WC Medford: When Kirk and his raiders left Cataloochee they went up across Cove Creek Mountain, down into Jonathan Creek, killing a Carver man and another man along the way. They were plundering and stealing from many homes.

They went into Waynesville where they broke into the jail and freed the prisoners; then they burned the jail. Some of the criminals they freed from jail rode with Kirk and his men. His whole group was made up of criminals, except those they had captured.

After they burned the jail, they went to Col. Love's Mansion where they plundered and stole everything they wanted, then burned his huge house down. After that they went on back to Tennessee, by way of Maggie Valley and Soco Gap.

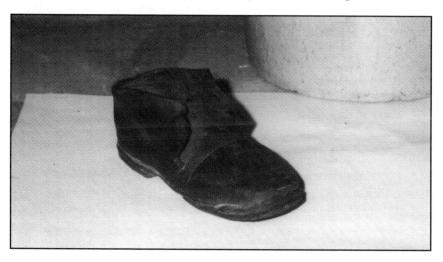

This little homemade shoe was plowed up on Big Cataloochee, more than 65 years ago. It was given to Dr. Liner, a dentist from Waynesville, NC who was there pulling teeth. He kept it many years, then gave it to his daughter-in-law, Mrs. Louise Liner who is a dear friend of mine. Now that I am writing this book, she gave it to me in January 1995. We figure the shoe is about 100 years old. It was coated with bear grease to soften the home-cured leather, which also preserved it while it was underground.

Cataloochee Valley

In a Sepember 28, 1995 interview John Carver of Hemphill said, "Yes, the Carver man that Kirk's raiders killed was my grandfather. His name was Alps Carver." John said, "My grandfather and a Mr. Rice were riding along the road just past Dellwood (now the intersection of US 276 and US 19) when they saw the raiders coming. The ran their horses off the road, back up in a cove to hide, but the raiders rode up there and shot both of them." John's grandmother was a daughter of Jessie Palmer. Her name was Burdine.[1]

Levi Captured

This is the story that has been passed down through the family. Levi B. Colwell, age forty-eight, and his son Hiram, age thirteen, were captured up on Cove Creek Mountain, where they were helping Captain Howell defend Cataloochee, by the raiders. They were tied and marched down to the Young Bennett's second house, which was located near the intersection of the road (Hwy. 184) to Cosby, Tennessee and the Cataloochee Turnpike. There they tied Levi and Hiram to a porch post of Bennett's house. Somewhere along the way, the raiders had found some whiskey. They went inside the house and started drinking and playing cards. While they were occupied, Hiram managed to chew the rope off Levi's hands, and then Levi untied Hiram's hands. When the raiders came outside, they had set the house on fire, intending to burn Levi and his son. Hiram and Levi started running, and the raiders jumped on their horses and ran after them. Levi and Hiram knew the country well. They ran down the mountain on foot off into the roughest places for a horse to get through, but the raiders managed to keep close on them. Finally somewhere around the Hall place they ran into the thick laurel. Hiram being young and strong, managed to escape but Levi being older just couldn't run anymore. The raiders dragged him to their camp. The next day they made him walk and run in front of the horses, then put him in a stockade and held him prisoner. He almost starved to death, and the severe cold was agony.

Somehow he managed to escape somewhere in Tennessee. He started on his long journey home. The trip was very hard for

[1]W.C. Medford, Early History of Haywood Co. p. 138

These are the beautiful grave markers for Levi and Mary Ann Colwell. They are located on the hill behind Palmer's chapel.

him in such a weakened condition; food was scarce everywhere. The women and children were not strong enough to do much farming and barely able to feed themselves, but somehow these kind people managed to provide a little food for this pitiful man.

Levi had to be very careful not to run into any Union sympathizers. He was gone almost a year before he got back home. He was so sick and in such pain with every breath, Mary Ann tried her best to nurse him back to health, but he lived only about a month before he died from the effects of abuse and hardships he had experienced. The family thought he had a collapsed lung from having to run so hard when the raiders chased him on horseback. He was buried in the cemetery on the steep hill behind Palmer's chapel. There is a beautiful marker at the grave for Levi and Mary Ann who was also buried there beside him in 1891, even though she had married Jonathan Woody after Levi's death.

Granny Pop - Civil War

Poor Mary Ann Colwell was left home with nine children. Her son Harrison was in the Confederate Army. After several

Cataloochee Valley

hard-fought battles, he was wounded, captured, and held prisoner in Illinois. Her husband, Levi, had been captured and taken away. Her father-in-law, Jimmy Colwell, had been of some help to her, but he was an old man and he got sick and died. Then her baby, Mary, died before she was five years old.

After Kirk's men came into the valley, they grabbed up Mary Ann's teenage son, Andy, and made him go with them to tend to their horses. Her son Hiram was with his father when they were captured. Hiram managed to get away and come back home to tell of their experience and how they had narrowly escaped being burned to death. Levi was still gone, and they didn't know if they would ever see him again.

The war had caused a shortage of everything and their Confederate money was worthless. The one thing people were hungry for, was salt. They had used all they had on hand and could not get any more. It had been very expensive, one dollar per pound, but now none was to be had.

Grandma Lizzie told me how Granny Pop had reclaimed some of the salt they had used before the war. She said Granny Pop would go out where they had always poured the dishwater, and dig up the dirt, put it in a pot, fill it with water, and boil it for awhile. This caused the salt to dissolve in the water. She let it set until the dirt all settled to the bottom of the pot, then slowly poured off the salty water into another pot. She boiled it until all the water had evaporated, thus leaving a little salt in the bottom of the pot. She said before the war was over that some people got so hungry for salt, that they would go out where they had urinated, dig up the dirt and process it the same way.

There was no soda, but these women knew how to leach a certain woodash and make it into soda. Since coffee could not be purchased either, they parched rye to use for coffee, and also made spicewood tea and sassafras tea and sweetened it with honey or molasses.

Cataloochee Herb Doctor and War

Young Bennett was an herb doctor and held in high esteem by his neighbors. They referred to him as Doc Bennett and as Mr.

Bennett. For a few generations, his first name had been forgotten, but Dr. Carroll's research revealed his first name was Young.

In 1858 Young Bennett, Newton Bennett, George Palmer, and Levi Colwell were the Trustees for the Methodist Church in Big Cataloochee. These men seemed to have been the leaders of the community at the time. Their names are listed several times as committeemen for the school and trustees of the church. Young served several years as Justice of the Peace, and at one time was postmaster, the post office being in his house.

Six of Young Bennett's sons fought for the Confederate cause. Three did not return. Sylvanus fought for two years and was killed at Chicamauga, and Archibald died from wounds he received at Murfreesboro, leaving behind a wife and two children. Wash was captured at both of those battles and imprisoned at Camp Douglas, Illinois. Amanuel was captured toward the end of the war. Newton served with his brother, Creighton, in the 62nd Infantry Regiment, and was captured at Cumberland Gap and sent to Camp Douglas, where forty percent of the 522 prisoners from the 62nd died, sixty-nine of them from Haywood County, including Creighton.

In 1858 before the horrible war started, Levi had built his second house which was probably about the time that Young built his second house. He built it near the intersection of the road to Mt. Sterling (Hwy #284) and the Cataloochee Turnpike. He was one of the stockholders of the Cataloochee Turnpike. It was most unfortunate that the road was built just before the Civil War. General Kirk's first stop was at Young Bennett's house. They burned it to the ground. After that, Young had to declare bankruptcy in 1870. Young's son, Newton, also had to declare bankruptcy, due to poor health and injuries suffered in the war.

In 1869, Newton was granted 100 acres of land for $12.50. The land had been obtained by treaty from the Cherokee Indians. Newton, his wife Jalie Gillett Bennett, and family were living in Fines Creek township from 1870 through 1890. Jalie died in 1907 and Newton, 1909. They are buried in Greenhill Cemetery in Waynesville, NC. Their children were well-educated. Two were attorneys, one a physician, two ministers (a Baptist and a Methodist) in New York, and one was a professor.[1]

Creighton Bennett fought in the Civil War, 62nd Regiment, and was captured at Cumberland Gap and sent to Camp Douglas, Ill., where he died and was buried in the Confederate cemetery near Chicago. According to the genealogy records of Robert Medford in Canton, N.C.. Matilda, Creighton's wife, then a widow married the second time to J. Valentine "Tyne" Woody in Oct. 1880, when she was forty-two years old. She died at age fifty-eight and was buried in the cemetery at the Baptist Church in Little Cataloochee. There were some of the Bennetts living in Little Cataloochee when the park took over. Bartlett, George, and Eldridge and their families moved to Franklin, NC, in the Iotla community. Tyne Bennett moved to Sylva, NC, and George Bennett to North Georgia.

The Reconstruction, Hard Times

In late spring and summer of 1865, when our soldiers were ragged, dirty, weary, war worn, half starved, and some battle scarred they came struggling home. There was no time to be lost for those who were able to work after they had rested up a spell. Returning in the late spring and early summer, it was too late to plant more crops, but they could help with the crops that had already been planted.

There was urgent need for repairs to be made to the dwellings and barns, also to the roads, fences, hedges, and ditches. Chores such as getting in provisions, came first. Skimpy times would have to continue for a while, certainly for another year, but it was much better now.

The so-called "Reconstruction" was soon to cast its dark shadow, beginning in 1867. Vice President Andrew Jackson, who became president after Lincoln's death, believed that there was no need for Congress to pass a Reconstruction Act to put the South back into the Union, since these states had not succeeded in leaving the Union.

But the northern Republicans, led by Butler and Deward,

---

[1]This information is from Mrs. Carolyn Bennett Mahaffey of Atlanta, GA.

Then followed for the South about three years of misrule and political corruption, the like of which, perhaps, has never been known here, before or since.

Scalawags and Carpetbaggers

The Carpetbag and Scalawag regime was so called because the northern office seekers and exploiters flocked in here, carrying little more than a change of clothing in a carpet bag.

Here the southern scalawags and others joined them, and under the protection and backing of the Federal Army stationed here, they altogether ruled the South for about three years.

It was indeed a bitter experience for a proud people to face. But it was tolerated until the administration of President Hayes, when the last of the Federal Troops were withdrawn and home rule was restored in Haywood as well. This county did not have it as bad, however, as many of the eastern counties with much larger populations of scalawags.

Our citizens were required to take the Amnesty Oath—a bitter pill for them—but for a brief time, they were mistreated and misruled. Time can be the instrument of cruel fate, or it can be a ministering angel to soothe and heal. Gradually the healing began.[1]

Following our State Constitution Convention in 1868 and shortly thereafter, 1870-72, most of the Northern Scalawags, militia regiments, and corrupt politicians had left the state or been run out. This was first under Governor Zeb Vance and then under Governor Todd Caldwell.

After the State Convention and the new Constitution took effect, the worst crisis in our history as a country and state had passed. We entered upon a new era as a defeated people militarily, much poorer, broken and disheartened, but not in will and pride and determination to carry on.

The Woody Family

The 1860 census for Madison County, NC (created from Buncombe and Yancey counties in 1851) lists Jonathan H. Woody, age forty-one, and his wife Malinda Plemmons, age

---
[1]Mr. Clark Medford, Early History of Haywood County, P. 167

Cataloochee Valley

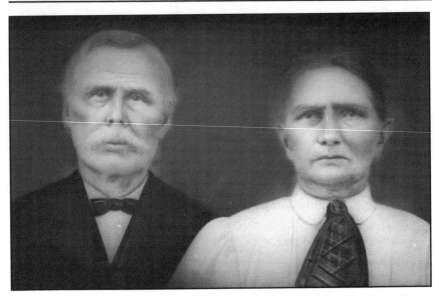

Harrison Caldwell and his wife, Susie Woody Caldwell. Aunt Susie delivered many babies at Cataloochee. Photo courtesy of Claude Caldwell.

forty-one, and their nine children: William M., born 1843; Martha Jane, born 1844; James Valentine (called Tyne), born 1846; Susannah A., born 1848; Nancy, born 1850; Lucinda E., born 1852; Stephen L., born 1853; Robert Jackson, born 1856; and Rebecca E., born 1860.

Jonathan's wife died about 1861. He and five children, Susan, Nancy, Stephen, Robert, and Rebecca came from Spring Creek to Big Cataloochee about 1866. He and his family had known the Caldwells many years. They had been neighbors. (Dr. Roy Carroll, Second Generation of Caldwells in Cataloochee)

Mary Ann Colwell's nine children were Andrew, born May 19, 1845; Harrison, born Feb. 9, 1844; Marion, born 1847; Reuben A., born 1849; John W., born 1854; Hiram, born June 3, 1851; George H., born 1857; Mary; born 1864, and Doctor L., born Oct. 1856.

With Mary Ann and Jonathan's families combined, there were fourteen children. But there were no children from their marriage. Jonathan and his children moved in with Mary Ann and her children after the marriage. They lived in the new house Levi had built in 1858.

Now that there were sixteen of them, they needed more room. The first smaller log cabin Levi had built was still

Hiram Caldwell and his wife Mary Elizabeth Howell Caldwell.

standing and in good condition. They decided it could be moved down near the newer house.

Mary Ann's sons and her husband and his sons worked together. They cut long poles, slid them under the small log cabin, with enough length stuck out to hitch several teams of horses. They placed round poles across in front of it, all the way down the hill to the other house. They slowly pulled it like a big sled. These round poles made it possible to pull. It was a successful move.

All fourteen children grew up together, but they were no relation to each other. Jonathan's daughter, Susan, married Mary Ann's son Harrison on April 27, 1870. She became known as Aunt Susie and was a much loved and respected lady. She was a midwife and delivered many of the babies on Big Cataloochee, this writer included. She was a large woman, always ready to deliver a baby whenever needed. She got on her horse and went, no matter how dark, cold, or wet the weather. She lit a lantern and traveled with her satchel and delivered the baby. She had ten children of her own. She died Jan. 6, 1929.

Jonathan was buried in the Little Cataloochee Cemetery, Nov. 30, 1894. He was born Mar. 9, 1812.

In Mr. Hiram Wilburn's notebook he records that Uncle Steve Woody told him, "I built my house in 1880." (The one that

Cataloochee Valley

The Steve Woody House

still stands.) It was originally a log structure then covered over and added on to as the sawmills came in.

In 1880, Mary Ann's son Hiram married Mary Elizabeth Howell, and they lived with his mother until he gained enough money to buy property. Later in 1898 he started building the large white house, completed in 1903.

Jonathan probably went to live with his son Valentine Woody (called Tyne) on Little Cataloochee in his later years, or at any rate that is where he was buried.

George Lafayette Palmer with his wife Nancy Jane Colwell Palmer, builder of Palmer House. Both are buried on the hill above the Palmer Barn.

4

THE CENTURY TURNS

Go To See The Train

Before the Civil War, the railroad was built almost to Morganton, N.C., but due to the Civil War, the work was stopped. Then sometime after 1865 the work started on the railroad again. By 1873, it reached to Old Fort, NC and finally on to Asheville by 1880. This was built by 500-600 men with pick and shovel, mules and drag pans. Most of the people in Cataloochee had never seen a train, didn't have any idea of what it looked like, except pictures they had seen in the toy section of Sears, Roebuck Catalogue. They had heard about trains that could haul big loads.

Sometime after 1873, Steve Woody and Hiram Caldwell, both young men with good riding horses, decided to ride off down to Old Fort to have a look at the train. They were gone for a week or more. Everyone at Cataloochee knew where they had gone and were anxiously waiting to hear what Steve and Hiram had to say about it.

When they arrived back in Cataloochee, it was reported that they were much impressed that the train could haul such large loads and said it was "very exciting to see all that smoke pouring out if it, and that they had never heard such a loud noise and rumbling." When the train started pulling off, Hiram and Steve raced along to see if it could run as fast as their horses. As soon as the train got its steam up, it left them. Their horses couldn't keep up with it. One of them said, "Boys, that thing could run! No

Cataloochee Valley

Hiram Caldwell in his hay field in Big Cataloochee. Son of Levi and Mary Ann Colwell (also grandfather of this writer).

telling how fast it can go. It outran our horses." That surprised everyone because they knew these were two of the fastest horses on Cataloochee. One man spoke up and said, "That ain't so! God never made anything that could outrun a horse!"

Indian Flats

This site is known by local people as "Indian Flats." The location is just above the late Turkey George Palmer's home, and at the mouth of Pretty Hollow Creek. Mr. Palmer stated to me that when he and his father, sometime before 1875, came upon this site with an idea of purchasing it, there was much evidence of Indian activity. This evidence consisted of a small field that had been cleared, but at the time was growing in briars, brush, and small trees. There were "fire places," broken stones, and pottery. There was some evidence of recent camping activities.[1]

When the white people moved into Cataloochee, the Indians were still traveling through there on foot, carrying bundles of baskets on their back. Sometimes they carried their babies (papooses) in a sheet on their backs, too. These trails went into Tennessee, Kentucky, and other places. They had been traveling these trails so many years that it was said the trails were worn down twelve to eighteen inches deep.

---

[1] Mr. Hiram Wilburn Title Abstracts, Book 8, p. 787

Funerals

We discussed funerals with Flora Burgess Caldwell, since Cataloochee did not have a funeral home or any way to embalm a body. When a person died, some of the family or friends would bathe the body and lay it out on a cooling board and lay coins on the eyes to keep them closed. Then the body would be dressed and put in the coffin.

In Big Cataloochee, the coffins were made by Jim Caldwell and Jarvis Caldwell and maybe others. They saved all of the finest lumber to make them. They used cherry, walnut, poplar, and pine and were usually lined by the wife of the man who made them. Jim's wife was Avie and Jarvis's wife was Bonnie. They always used some nice material for this. They probably kept a few of the caskets on hand in different sizes, for man, woman, or child because it took time and skill to make them.

When a body was dressed and placed in the coffin ready for viewing, it was left in the home, and neighbors all came and brought food and made coffee. They sat up all night with the corpse, and the family gathered around, talking and remembering all the good things and good deeds the person had done. Sometimes they sang religious songs.

The next day the funeral service would be held at the gravesite or in the home. Gudger Palmer remembers Hiram Caldwell's service was held in his home. After the service the casket would be loaded on a sled and hauled to the cemetery for burial.

Then the graves were looked after, kept clean, and flowers placed on the graves. When flowers were not in bloom they made flowers from crepe paper to decorate the graves and to decorate the home.

Elizabeth Howell Caldwell, wife of Hiram, was always known as Aunt Lizzie. She was a very religious person. She was eighty years old when we had to move out of Cataloochee and she was very much saddened, having to sacrifice her life long work, her home and all. She had her headstone put in the cemetery there in Cataloochee between Hiram and her child, Connie who had died young. She knew she would soon be coming back there to be buried. She died in 1937 only three years after we moved to

Maggie Valley. Having to leave their home was a harder adjustment for the older ones. She prayed daily about it.

A short time after we moved, Grandma Lizzie got a Mr. Roten at Dellwood to make her coffin of walnut wood. It was hauled to Maggie Valley on a wagon. She lined it with white cloth, satin or taffeta, then it was stored until it was needed. She made her burial clothes of white cloth. No one had ever seen her wear white before. She had always worn navy or black. Her hair was still black, only a few gray hairs under the ball of hair she wore on the back of her head. When she died, her body was taken back to Cataloochee for burial as she had planned and buried in the family cemetery, upon the hill back of the barn.

Flora Burgess Caldwell (Laws) told of some man that died, who for years had rheumatism or lumbago as they called it, and he was drawn over very badly. When he died, they really had a hard time getting him straight enough to fit in the coffin. But after a lot of work, they finally got him straightened out enough to put in the casket.

Then, as customary, everyone had gathered at his house, talking and eating. And suddenly the corpse sat up in the casket, and nearly scared them to death. They all ran out of the room hollering, and screaming, "Lord, have mercy! How could such a thing happen?"

Evidently his muscles contracted back to the way he had been drawn over, thus setting him up. She could not remember who the man was.

Guns

A flintlock was a long-barreled rifle used by the pioneers. They had to be good marksmen. If they missed a shot, they would have to wipe out the rifle, recharge with powder from the powder horn they carried, take a bullet from a shot pouch, ramrod it down the rifle barrel, and finally prime the flintlock with powder. All this took so long the animal would be gone.

The pioneers looked to the limbs. Into the woods they went and out of the woods they came at noon or eveningtime loaded with game. They told of the merits of the beloved old flintlocks or

Brown Bess and bragged about the way their hunting dogs could unerringly scent and keep the trail. "I can hit a squirrel, pine blank (bragging) in the head on the highest limb with this here gun, yes sir-ee! She seldom misses." Think back one hundred-fifty years ago of the conditions in our new, struggling county.[1]

Pioneers of all this mountain country in those days were good marksmen. This training was necessity. They had to make every ounce of powder count because both powder and lead were expensive and our ancestors had little to buy with. Trading was nearly altogether by barter. All seasons were hunting season back then. There were no such things as "open and closed" seasons and limits. A hunter's limit was his ability to bag the game—and often times his bag was all he could carry home. Game was plentiful—squirrels, fox, coon, groundhog, deer, bear, opossum, wildcat, wolves, wild turkey, pheasant, quail, etc. And since it was profitable to take the hides of most of these animals, the pioneers, profited in two ways. One day's hunting might furnish the table for a week or more, but that was not the only benefit. The good hides of the day's hunt must be taken, dressed, and cured, and that was no easy task. Hides were better taken in the fall and winter when the fur was vigorous, full, and glossy. It was then that the pioneer looked forward to a good store of hides and the coming of the fur trader.

The hides, after being skinned off the carcass carefully and trimmed, were drawn inside out tightly over a board (which had been shaped for that purpose) and tacked in places to the board. This was how they dried and cured the hides. They had to be kept straight and smooth. The hides were then hung against the walls on the sunny side of the house, smoke house, or barn and left to dry.

When properly cured, the hides would be taken off the boards, inspected and stored away where there was plenty of ventilation. Then the owner would await the fur trader or take his hides to his favorite "general merchandise" dealer. There he would trade for powder and bar lead (for making bullets), salt, coffee, indigo, or whatever was needed.

It was the days of hunting and most everybody did so. For not only was it a cheap and rather enjoyable way of furnishing meat

---

[1] Mr. W.C. Medford, Middle History of Haywood County

for the table, it was necessary that many of the wild animals such as the wolves, panther, bear, wildcat, and groundhog be thinned out and kept down for better protection of crops and domestic animals, as well as for personal security of the settlers.[1]

The Bear, The Panther, and The Buck

Mr. Crate Bennett was in the low gap of Fork Ridge, between Cataloochee and Caldwell Fork. He came there every morning. Often there was a light snow on the ground. He came to watch for a buck deer. A large log lay across the gap. As he approached, he heard a considerable commotion in the brush and presently a panther and a bear appeared from opposite ends of the log and clinched in a fight. The bear gave an awful roar and ran off through the brush. Mr. Bennett shot the panther from the log, and approaching the scene, he found a large bear lying there that had been killed by the panther. The bear had been savagely cut by this attacking panther, and on inspection it was found that his belly had been literally ripped open by a stroke from the panther's paw. Evidently the panther had killed the buck, and the bear coming upon the scene to share in the catch was immediately attacked by the panther. Here were three dead animals—buck killed by panther, bear killed by panther, and panther killed by Bennett.[2]

Panther Nine Feet Long

Uncle Turkey George Palmer, eighty on January 24, 1938, says that when the first white people came to Big Cataloochee, three or four panthers were thought to be in the Cataloochee area. My father and Levi Caldwell caught one on Maple Stand Ridge in a pen. This one was nine feet from tip of nose to tip of tail and said to be the longest ever caught in this area. (Was it the one that stalked Granny Pop?)

Panthers were the most feared. Bears killed more livestock. There were organized bear hunts every fall, and anytime a bear killed someone's cattle, all the men took their dogs and got on the

---

[1]Mr. W.C. Medford. The Early History of Haywood County.
[2]Mr. W.C. Medford, Early History of Haywood County, p. 34, p. 35

trail. Most of the time they killed him, if not he would return and kill over and over until they got him.–source W.H. Wilburn

Gudger Palmer talked about his grandfather, Andy Caldwell, who was coming home one dark, cloudy night with a wagon and a team of horses.

The horses started to rear and pitch. They were very excited, and he could hardly control them. Evidently the horses could see or sense something. He knew there was danger nearby, but it was too dark for him to see what it was. He knew that his horses would not act that way without reason. Finally, he got to his barn and put his horses up and fed them. Then he went to the house. After they had gone to bed, they could hear scratching on the roof. Next morning he found some of the shingles torn loose. A panther had been stalking him and the horses.–source Gudger Palmer

Panther & Bear (Hair Raising)

J.C. Hopkins says that Jonah Phillips was father of Jo Phillips who was in turn father of Jonah Phillips. Old Jonah Phillips was generally known as "Tobe" Phillips. He set a gun trap for a bear at a big log on Big Creek. There he had quite an experience with a panther. It was probably in the 1880s. A large bear had been crossing Big Creek into Mouse Creek country regularly and had been waylaid several times by Tobe Phillips at a crossing over a big log that lay several feet off the ground and above the water. The gun trap was set so as to shoot the bear as he crossed over the log. Phillips got under the log and waited. While he was waiting, a panther came upon the log, and spent some time squalling in answer to another panther some distance in the woods. Tobe related how his hat was pushed off his head by hair raising on end, and other extreme expressions of fright.

However, he lay still and the panther lay still. Later the bear came along and the gun trap got him. The bear fell over dead in the brush, and Tobe, there in the dark, cut him open, removed the entrails, and went home for the night. He came next day with help to carry it home.–source W.H. Wilburn

Cataloochee Valley

Hunters

Old hunters used to have a camp at what was the Hub Caldwell place (now the Ranger station.) They would all leave camp in daytime, to hunt and while they were gone, panthers would come into camp and carry away their collection of deer skins. The hunters would find them buried on Rough Ridge. The place they crossed the creek to recover the skins they named "Lucky Button."

In an interview on July 21, 1937, Mr. Mitch Sutton talked to Hiram Wilburn about panthers. Mr Sutton lived near Mt. Sterling and was about sixty years old at the time. Mitch knew about the panther caught by John J. Hannah and others about 1884 or 1885. "I had a personal experience with a panther myself," he said. "I had been fishing by the Big Bend Area and was walking home with a string of fish about 1905. It followed me about five miles. At the time I was working for Haddock-France Lumber Co. In following me, the panther kept mostly behind and out of sight, but would run up on the steep bank above me and look down and growl. I saw its tracks next day and knew it had to be a panther."

Bear Sign

Someone in Cataloochee had found bear signs, and all the men were excited and planning a bear hunt. They had gotten together for that purpose. Then a female tourist heard them talking of bear sign and couldn't wait to find out what it was. She felt their excitement. She walked up to Old Man Woody (we do not know which one) and interrupting asked, "What is bear sign? What are they talking about?"

"They said bear sign right over there."

"What does it mean?" she quizzed.

"They saw bear sign over on Jim Ridge," he replied.

"What is bear sign?" She fired all those questions so fast the old man got irritated because he wanted to hear all the details of the coming hunt. The hunt took careful planning and he needed to know how he was going to participate, so he became annoyed at her rudeness and decided to get rid of her quickly.

She demanded again, "What is bear sign?"

Woody replied, "Sh-t and tracks, Ma'am, sh-t and tracks."

She was stunned, but if she had been more patient and asked later, she probably would have been taken to the place to see.

Turkey George

There were three men named George on Big Cataloochee. People there put a nickname on each one, so they knew which one they were speaking of. "Creek" George was a brother of Jessie Palmer. "Turkey" George was the son of Jessie and then there was "Big" George Caldwell, son of Levi.

Turkey George's house was built in 1890 just after his marriage in February of that year. (He married the daughter of Uncle Andy and Aunt Charlotte Caldwell–Alice Cumi Caldwell. The barn was built a year or two later. All the lumber for the house and barn was sawed on a sash mill near the Jesse Palmer place.

Turkey George got his nickname because he had built a pen, then dug a hole under the side of it. He shelled corn and made a trail of it going into the pen. He had studied the habits of turkeys and knew they would not come out through the hole he had dug, but they would try to escape by flying up. He had closed in the top. He went on home for the night. Next morning he returned to find eight or ten big, wild turkeys in his pen. He decided he would crawl in and grab one. He got it all right, but when he grabbed one, all of the others fought him, beat him with their wings, and stomped on him as he made his escape back through the hole. But no matter. He got his bird. Everyone laughed about it as he told the story, including him. He was always called Turkey George after that. He was a great hunter who killed 105 bears.

Fayte Goes to Raleigh

Eldridge Caldwell talked of the stories he had heard from the older generation about the early settlers. They told about how the wolves were killing all the hogs, sheep, and little calves. Wolves

Cataloochee Valley

would make a raid on them and kill a whole slew of them at one time.

George LaFayette Palmer (called Fayte) thought it would be great if they could get the governor to put a bounty on the wolf. He just got up early one morning, saddled his horse, and rode off. He would go see if he could talk the governor into paying a bounty. It would be a very long trip to Raleigh, but it would be worth it if he was successful.

Upon arrival, he soon got to see the governor and explained how the people in Cataloochee may as well move out if they didn't get help and they needed it right then. He said, "The packs of wolves are raiding and killing all our animals, making it awful hard on us. I have an idea how we can get rid of them, but only if you help us."

"Well," said the governor, "how can I help?"

Fayte replied, "If you would put a $10.00 bounty on every wolf, then all the people there will trap and hunt until they are gone."

Governor Worth said, "I'll do it. I will give you an official order that you can take back to Cataloochee. Tell those folks for every wolf scalp they mail down here, they will receive a check for $10.00."

Fayte thanked the governor and hurried back home to tell the folks the good news. It took three weeks for the trip on horseback. Everyone was happy because $10.00 was a lot of money back then.

As soon as the men received the good news, they went hunting and trapping.

Steve Woody knew there were wolves above his house on the mountain. He had heard the mother wolf whipping her whelps (pups) because she was weaning them. That meant they were getting big and strong. It would not be long before the whole pack of wolves would raid and kill the livestock.

The good news came just in time. Early next morning he took his dog and put her on the trail. Soon she had found the den. There were eight whelps. Altogether he sent nine scalps to Raleigh and soon received a check for $90.00.

He took the check to the Loves in Waynesville, who were

owners of the land at that time. He told them he wanted to buy land in Big Cataloochee. They inquired how much money he had, and which land he wanted to buy. He told them he wanted certain boundaries including part of Spruce Mountain, Woody Creek, and some on Sugar Creek, about one hundred seventy acres. Most of the valley had been settled. He bought at the very upper end. They sold it to him for fifty cents an acre. When the park bought it, they surveyed it and made an offer.

Uncle Steve did not like their offer. He and a few others sued to get a better price, and did receive a little better than had been offered. On July 18, 1931, Uncle Steve received $11,655.00 for 151 and a half acres. It cost him $1,000.00 for lawyers and court cost. Most of the people would not sue. They had a saying: "If you go to court, the only winners are the lawyers."[1]

Tobe & Bears

George Phillips said his grandfather, Tobe Phillips, was a great bear hunter and trapper. He used a flintlock rifle. He would watch where a bear crossed Big Creek. He used white turnip hull on the front sight of his gun. When bear darkened this white spot, he would fire at the bear. He also killed many panthers. He killed panther mainly to keep them from destroying game and livestock. He would not shoot panthers if he saw one while watching for a bear.

"I," said George Phillips, "never saw a panther but heard them often. A panther ran Bill Campbell off Mt. Sterling Creek. He had a string of fish, and the panther followed him. He dropped the fish and ran. My father went and saw the tracks and other sign and said it was a panther. This was when I was sixteen years old (now fifty-three)." It was generally believed that there were several panther in the Big Creek area at that time.

Grandfather (Tobe Phillips) would try to find a crevice or a place between big rocks near a bear trail. Then he would build a fire to heat the rocks and have a bed of live coals so he could warm his hands and be able to shoot when the bear came.

He "still-hunted" mostly. Tobe would dig a pit in the ground, in the winter time during the day and build a big fire

---
[1]Information from Eldridge Caldwell

in it to warm it up, and then stand in it to shoot the bear when they would come by in the dark. He killed several bears with his knife. In order to accomplish this, he would wait until the dogs had the bear bayed against a log or a bank, then rush in and make the fatal stab.

These and many more stories happened in 1900 and earlier. Eldridge Caldwell talked about the wild animals in an interview in June of 1969. "The old timers before 1900 had a hard time trying to guard their animals and crops, chickens and ducks. They had greater losses than we did, but I had so many losses at High Top I had to sell it to the park."

Bear Hunter

Turkey George Palmer had killed 105 bears in his time, but never hunted but one with dogs. This was on Hells Half Acre Branch near Robert Palmer's. "It climbed up a tree and I shot him with a pistol through the leg, and he fell out and the dogs got him. I continued to shoot the pistol eight times before I killed him. He sullied and rolled up like a cat. Then he flounced and scattered the dogs. He came very near catching me. I kicked him under the chin; then he ran up the tree. Again I shot straight up at him and down he come again. The dogs got after him, he run down the hill and sullied again. I finally followed him to the branch, put the pistol against his head and fired. It numbed my hand so bad, I had to loosen my fingers one at a time. I hit him several times but seemed not to do much good, until I put the pistol against him and finally got him." Turkey George told Mr. Wilburn that he got so much bear meat that he started canning it and selling it for one dollar a jar.

This same story was told by Turkey George's grandson, Judson Palmer, as he fondly remembered spending some time with him at Big Cataloochee during the summers. Jud, age six, could ride the horse named "Old Saint." He rode bareback and if he fell off, the old horse would stop until he got back on. Jud did not put a bridle on the horse. He would get on him in the pasture, and the old horse would go to the barn with him. If he got on at the barn the horse would take him out in the pasture.

Jud remembered Turkey George carried orange slice candy and always gave him some. Jud's father was Charlie. They lived near Waynesville. When Turkey George went to town, he would always spend the night with them. He always wore a double breasted suit to town. At home he wore overalls and wide brimmed black hat.

Judson said, "Turkey George died when I was in the second grade." He did not move out of Cataloochee, but he had bought a place in Clyde, N.C. so his family would have a place to live when the park put them out. The family stayed in Cataloochee until Turkey George died.

Turkey George and Alice's last child was born when Alice was past fifty. The child was healthy as were several other Cataloochee babies born late in the mother's life. They called them change-of-life babies. My father, Eldridge Caldwell, was one of those.

Judson remembered when his grandaddy killed a bear, he would hollar a loud rebel yell from the mountain tops. This was to let the family know he had killed one and for them to build a fire under a big washpot and have barrels of water boiling. He would have gutted the bear soon after killing it, then when he got the bear home it would be skinned clean and dressed (cut up into hams, shoulders, ribs etc.) It was wonderful, delicious meat, much like beef.

Judson was in the Air Force in World War II. He and his wife, Hilda Dotson Palmer lived in Washington, DC. He was stationed at the Pentagon, and Hilda worked with intelligence.

They traveled to Germany and were there a long time before coming back to Washington. They were also sent to Tokyo, Japan. Finally Judson retired from the Pentagon. He said on election day when the votes started coming in, he would go outside to watch the marquee. He knew Cataloochee would have their votes in first, because there were very few people left there at that time. He said, "It gave me a thrill to see the name 'Cataloochee' up there." They had a saying "As Cataloochee goes, so goes the nation."[1]

---

[1] Interview with Judson and Hilda 4-24-95

Cataloochee Valley

Wolf Dog

Eldridge Caldwell said, "My father had some good bear dogs. He had a favorite one that was torn up awful bad by a bear while a bunch of dogs had the bear hemmed up and were fighting it. He decided he needed a tougher breed of dog. If he could breed his bitch dog to a wolf, that would be worth a try.

When the bitch was in heat, he took her up to the mountain where he could hear the wolves howl and bark at night. He figured she would attract some male wolf. Well he was right because sometime later she produced a litter of puppies half dog and half wolf."

The next story happened when Eldridge was a baby (born January 8, 1898), just old enough to sit alone. He said one of the puppies seemed to like him. It was real gentle with him. When his mother went out to hoe in the garden, she put him on a quilt nearby. The puppy stood guard and would not let anyone near him. If a bug crawled on the quilt, he barked until his mother came to take the bug off.

Eldridge always loved dogs and had an extremely gentle way with them. He trained many shephard or collie dogs for cattle and sheep dogs. One dog he had trained knew when it was 4 P.M. Without anyone saying anything, the dog went to the pasture and brought in the milk cows only. After they were milked, he went back for the beef cattle and made them go in the correct stall for feeding. He would even bring fresh eggs from the barn loft, one at a time in his mouth and lay them on the back porch. Everybody cried when he died of old age.

Ola Baptist Church

Ola Baptist Church is located in Little Cataloochee was built about 1880 or 1881. "Doc" Hall oversaw construction which was performed by the local people. The church stands on land sold by J.V. Woody to D.J. Cook and T. H. Hannah deacons of the Missionary Baptist Church, Cataloochee Township in 1892. In 1907 Woody reserved one-half acre of his property for the adjacent graveyard.

Very early on, the building doubled as a schoolhouse in which Robert M. Hannah was one of the teachers. In 1914 the church was "constituted," meaning it was officially recognized by sister churches in the Haywood Baptist Association. The fact that it existed for twenty-four years before being "constituted" turns out to be completely normal, especially in an isolated, post pioneer situation. The Rev. William Cope of First Baptist in Pigeon Forge, Tennessee explained that broader relationships with other churches were common.

Preachers did come from Waynesville and closer communities. Services were held on the second weekend of each month. Revivals were held in late summer or early fall, and singing school (Old Harp/Shaped Notes) brought things to life in the springtime. Some remember Rev. T. Frank Arrington of Waynesville, as "the loudest preacher they ever heard." The Rev. D.C. Davis was another preacher of record. Most of them earned about $7.50 per trip from collections.

Will Messer designed and built the belfry in the early teens, and William J. Hannah donated a bell that weighed 400 pounds. When national park land acquisition began, the church was sold to the Park Commission. It was conveyed by J.W. Burgess, W.G.B. Messer, George Bennett, and Jonah Brown, Trustee of the Ola Baptist Church on December 26, 1929 (Haywood County Deed Book 81 P. 80) The Rev. Pat Davis of Hartford, Tennessee, was the last preacher (1930-32).

Ola Baptist is twenty-four by twenty feet with a ten foot ceiling height. The stud-framed walls stand on a continuous mortared river rock foundation, a trussed gabled roof system with stamped galvanized shingles. The interior of the building is devoid of ornamental trim. However, the roof system is trimmed with scalloped bargeboards at the gable ends. The people of Little Cataloochee plowed funds received from the National Park in 1929 back into "improvements" such as the continuous foundation, laid by Mack Hannah and others.

The people and their descendants of Little Cataloochee go back every year in June for their annual reunion, to pray, to sing and worship, to remember their ancestors, to decorate the graves and renew acquaintances along with eating and sharing

Cataloochee Valley

Ola Baptist Church, Little Cataloochee, inside and out. Photos by Paul Woody, September, 1981

the lunch they brought. Some call it decoration day.

The only people who can be buried in Cataloochee are the people who were born there, or a descendant of the original pioneers or someone who married a descendant. Such was the case of a young pilot from Georgia, who had married Lois Hannah, daughter of Mark and Verdie Hannah. His name was Kenneth Gardner. He loved Cataloochee so much, he told them that was where he wanted to be buried when he died. They had only been married a few years when he was killed in a plane crash. As he had requested, he was buried in the Cemetery in Little Cataloochee beside the Ola Baptist Church.

Some people from Big Cataloochee go to the reunion at Little Cataloochee and people from Little Cataloochee come to the reunion in Big Cataloochee. They are all good friends and happy to see each other.

There were no artificial flowers when we lived at Cataloochee, or if there were we did not know it. Paul Woody talked about his mother Lou White Woody, making roses from crepe paper. She worked for days making enough to go on all the graves of the family, and she also made wreaths with roses.

This writer helped her family make crepe paper flowers for the cemetery as Paul had helped his Mother.

Circuit Riding Preacher 1909

Mr. T.A. Groce was one of the last of a hardy breed of preachers. Now that era is long past, but the indelible mark of those rugged ministers of the gospel left on this mountain region has not been dimmed by time.

On horseback, by buggy, and behind the wheel of a Model T Ford, hardy men of God rode where they could, and they walked the rest of the way to tend the spiritual needs of their scattered flocks.

Preacher Groce was born September 22, 1878, in Greenville County, SC. He and his wife and four sons came to live in Western North Carolina in 1909. He had been transferred here by the South Carolina conference to be a member of the North Carolina conference. Thus began one of the most fruitful ministries in Methodism. His first appointment in the western North Carolina conference was Jonathan Creek in the Waynesville district. He said his parsonage there consisted of a house, a few sticks of furniture, and a 1200 pound horse. Big Cataloochee was on his circuit, so were Maggie Valley, Shady Grove, Hemphill, and Cove Creek.

His kind and gentle voice and a pleasant smile, always made others feel good in his presence. He never lost these valuable qualities, even in his later years. He had such a deep love for others, and was able to show it in such a wonderful way, that no one ever felt left out in his presence, nor was it possible for anyone to forget him who had once known him. His marvelous memory enabled him to never forget a name or face.

Rev. Groce first preached in Greenville, SC, for two years. Due to illness, the doctor said he should move to the mountains. He had been to Haywood County one time to a funeral and became acquainted with the presiding Elder. When he was sent to Jonathan Creek (1909) he did not know where it was. Rev. Groce and his family got on a train to Asheville and from Asheville to Waynesville. At Jonathan Creek, they spent the

Cataloochee Valley

The Reverend T.A. Groce. Photo and article courtesy of Fred Groce, the son of Rev. Groce.

night with a good friend, brother Rufus Howell, who was the Sunday School Superintendent.

Mr Groce's first retirement was in 1953. He made a speech, recalling some of his experiences.

> We caught a train to Waynesville, got off the train, me, my wife, and four boys. A man walked up, Dave Boyd, there are two, Big Dave Boyd and Little Dave Boyd. He said, "You must be that Methodist Preacher for Jonathan Creek and all them other churches."
>
> I said, "Yes, I am."
>
> Big Dave said, "I will tell you one thing; you will find some fine people out there. Old folks have the pocketbook, and the young folks have the get away." It was just that way too. "I'll tell you right now, Preacher. If you want to get these folks on your circuit to heaven, don't you go telling them about the pearly gates and golden streets and how beautiful it is. Tell them that timothy and clover hay grows waist high up there, and you will get every man in the valley."

We spent the night with Uncle Rufus Howell, and they had ham, fried chicken, and all sorts of things. We really ate. I guess me and my boys were always hungry.

The parsonage furnished a horse and buggy. The buggy cost $100.00 less ten percent, the harness cost less. At the parsonage, Dave Boyd drove up with a whole load of corn. Another man brought hay, then a cow, then hay for her. Salary on Jonathan Creek was $500.00 the first year. With pounding (gifts) and other things we got along better and enjoyed life. Maple Grove, Maggie, Dellwood, Cove Creek, Hemphill, and Cataloochee, fifteen miles over the mountain to Palmer's Chapel in Cataloochee. We went the first Saturday in November. I took my seven-year-old son, Junior.

Uncle Rufus Howell said, "You better light a candle and put it at your feet in that buggy, along with that buffalo lap robe. You are going to need it. It's blowing blue snow."

It took a little over four hours to go over that mountain in the buggy. The rough road, rocky, rocky, rocky all the way. Mr. Howell said, "Don't you stop until you get to Uncle Hiram Caldwell's. You will have to go spend the night with him first, if you don't he won't come to church the whole time you are there."

We traveled on and on up the road by the creek, and all of a sudden here come something out of the woods. A group of hogs run out across the road with ribbons tied around their necks and tied on their tails. Junior asked, "What was that!"

I said "Hogs, razor back mountain hogs."

"What is the ribbon for?" The ribbon had some kind of grease or medicine on them to keep the lice off them.

Well, when we got up to Uncle Hiram Caldwell's, he was at the barn. I drove up to the big white house with blue trim across the creek, barn on side of road. I said, "Are you Uncle Hiram?

He said, "Yes, are you that Methodist Preacher?"

I said, "yes." He looked down at the ground then looked at my boy.

Cataloochee Valley

Palmer's Chapel 1914 with a rail fence. The field in foreground was a cornfield, now used for parking at Cataloochee Reunion. In 1914 the road ran along the creek and in front of the church. The church did not have a bell tower until 1929. A wood stove was used for heat. Picture and information courtesy of Gudger Palmer.

He said, "Well, go on over to the house, Lizzie will fix you some supper. I'll be over there soon as I finish feeding here." Well we went on to the house. They had a big roaring fire in the fireplace. Aunt Lizzie welcomed us then went off to cook supper.

We were starved, hoped to eat soon. Uncle Hiram came in from the barn, and we got good and warm. We talked and talked, all the time hoping to eat. Well, along about nine o'clock we were called to come eat. I tell you, Aunt Lizzie had really fixed a fine meal, all kinds of fine food. Me and Junior ate and ate. I was so hungry I just kept eating. Finally Uncle Hiram looked over at me and said, "Preacher, you don't need to bother about hurting yourself. We plan to have more food here in the morning."

I said, "I may not be here in the morning, I aim to

satisfy myself tonight." Well, Uncle Hiram had quite a sense of humor.

Next morning when we were leaving, Uncle Hiram walked out a ways with us. He said, "Now Preacher you can come back and stay with us any time, the latch string is always out (meaning you're always welcome). That's an awful good boy you have. In fact, I don't know but what I like him better than you (with a grin on his face). Other people bring kids here and they are into this and that and down in the spring house, into the butter, messing and spilling things. Your boy is really good."

We had many more happy visits with Uncle Hiram and Aunt Lizzie. Hiram was always joking and laughing.

We always went over on Saturday. We had to rest up to preach and visit, spend Sunday night, then go back to Jonathan Creek. We went to visit and spend the night with just about everybody. We went to Cataloochee one weekend each month. Later on I got my first T-model Ford, and it got about like an old horse.

The Rev. T.A. Groce retired, but he never stopped working. He had preached on many circuits all over North Carolina. Sometimes he had to preach three times a day at 11 AM, 3PM and 8PM to cover all the charges. The much beloved minister observed his seventy-fifth birthday, looking forward to his newest pastorate—the Groce Methodist Church, Beverly Hills, Asheville, N.C.

In 1917 he entered the army chaplain corps and returned to the Waynesville district in 1919. He helped to build and organize many churches. Mr. Groce helped to organize the Groce Funeral Home. To the Groce Methodist Church he contributed an organ. His sons later gave a set of chimes as a memorial to their mother and Martha Groce, the late wife of Alvin Groce. His life was unusually full and complete with seven sons, one of whom continued his work in the active ministry, a host of devoted friends, the establishment of new churches, thousands of people helped by his ministry. Many who were led to Christ testify to the effectiveness of his devoted life.

Cataloochee Valley

All of this information and picture was from Fred Groce, son of Rev. T.A. Groce. He was at the Cataloochee reunion Aug. 1991, found out this book was being written, and sent me this information and picture to do with as I pleased.

Eldridge Remembers Caldwell House and Barn

Hiram, Mary Elizabeth, and their four children, Hattie, William, Dillard, and Eldridge lived in the Levi Belese Colwell house until 1903 when they moved into their new frame house.

After Levi died, his son Andy, who was the executor divided the land with his sisters and brothers. Hiram worked as a teamster, driving a wagon and horses to Greenville, South Carolina for ten cents a day. He bought his tract of 154 acres and log house for twenty-five cents an acre from his sisters and brothers. He built a prosperous farm and started building the nine-room, two-story white house in 1898. It was finished in 1903.

First, trees had to be cut, trimmed, and sawed into lengths, pulled by horses to the sawmills. The lumber had to be sawed and stacked to air dry. They selected only the finest number one lumber (no knot holes). These builders weren't only carpenters; they were fine craftsmen. Every plank had to fit perfectly. You can see how they fitted the beaded ceiling and walls, the different designs made by installing it at various angles. They joked about the beaded ceiling of pine being imported from Waynesville.

It still stands. Eldridge Caldwell remembered moving into the new house when he was five years old. He was born January 8, 1898. It took five years to complete the house because there were no power tools. It is definitely handmade. The men who built it came over there and stayed to work on it, in between going back to their homes to make crops.

These fine carpenters were Charlie and Taylor Medford and Vaughn Massie. They built a water-powered sawmill on "Cataloochee Creek" in front of the house. If you will check on the very oldest deeds, you will see the name of the creek was "CATALOOCHEE." It was NEVER called Ugly Creek as the park calls

Creek George Palmer and Family. Photo Courtesy of Ethel Palmer McCracken.

it, somehow they came up with that name. Must have been someone's weird idea of a joke because it is a perfectly beautiful crystal clear creek. It should be changed back to the original name. Some distance above the Caldwell house, the creek is called Woody Creek.

After the lumber was sawed and stacked to air dry, they were ready to start building. The beaded ceiling and bricks for fireplace, chimney, and kitchen flue were brought from Waynesville in a wagon. It took one whole day to travel to Waynesville with an empty wagon. When it was loaded they had to travel up Cove Creek Mountain, which was very steep and crooked.

It took four horses to pull the wagon when loaded with brick or other heavy material. The road had many deep ruts cut in it from the heavy loads pulled over it, by the narrow steel-rimmed wagon wheels, especially in rainy weather.

It would take another day when the wagon was loaded for them to travel up to Cove Creek Gap. There they would spend the night, sleeping on the ground. Starting out early next day

Cataloochee Valley

The frame house that Hiram Caldwell completed in 1903.

down the steep crooked rutted out road, finally down into the valley and about five miles up Cataloochee Creek to the Hiram Caldwell place. We wonder how many trips it took to bring in all the materials with all the trips taking three days each. These dirt roads became so cut up and rough, sometimes they had to plow them up, then drag heavy boards to level and flatten them out.

The walls and ceilings upstairs are made of hand-planed yellow poplar, which with age has a beautiful golden patina. The poplar lumber was cut on the property. It took many days of painstaking work to hand plane the rough sawn boards. But Oh! The ugly graffiti that some of the park visitors have cut and marked on the fine old wood. It's a shame! They don't care about all the hard work, but if they read this maybe they will respect it more.

During the many years we lived there and with the large numbers of friends, relatives, teachers, fishermen, preachers, and even an opera singer from New York who were guest in this house, there was never a mark on the beautiful old wood. They all respected what had been earned from hard work, and they respected other people's property.

Interior hall of the Hiram Caldwell house built 1903. See the perfect fit of the narrow pine panelling. After the park service took it from us and no one was living in it, much damage was done.

The large room upstairs had several beds in it. It was also used for weaving, spinning, and quilting. The quilting frames were suspended from the ceiling and could be raised with cords when the room was needed for other uses. The quilt could be lowered to about lap level, and several women could sit around it in chairs, quilting when they had time.

This big room also had a wooden rack suspended from the ceiling by four heavy wires. This rack was used to store extra supplies, several fifty pound bags of flour, one hundred pound bags of sugar, and salt. They always bought it in one hundred pound sacks because the cattle had to be salted often. There would also be dried beans and coffee and other supplies stored there.

When the cattle and hogs were taken to market in the fall, the men would come home with a wagon load of supplies for the winter because it was nearly impossible to travel the wet, muddy, rocky road in the winter time except by horse back.

All these supplies were kept on the rack, so that if mice got in

Cataloochee Valley

Mack and Fannie Hannah lived on Little Cataloochee. Hannah was one of the granny women who delivered so many babies. She was called "Doctor Woman" by some. Photo Courtesy of Lowell Hannah.

the house, they could not get into the supplies and destroy them. The little room at the end of the big room was for canned food (maybe five hundred jars). This can room had shelves all the way around. Located directly over the kitchen, the flue went up through this room and kept the food from freezing. Also the window faced due west, and it got all the afternoon sun; so none of the food froze.

When winter was coming on, all the food was either dried, canned, or root crops buried and the smoke house was filled with fine smoked and sugar cured hams and bacon. Now the women had time to quilt, weave, sew, knit, and crochet. The men folks would have time to repair or make harnesses and bridles, to repair farm equipment, sharpen their hoes, mattocks, and other things. There were always a few good bear hunts and several dances or something to do.

They created a social life that would be the envy of many today. They had high morals and principles. They truly lived by the golden rule. For the most part they were hard working, ambitious, and religious people. Moonshining was about the only time they violated the law, but only a few of them did, not the majority as has been written.

Hiram and Lizzie sent their children off to finish school when they completed seventh grade at Beech Grove. Dillard attended Mars Hill college. We think William may have, too. We don't know where Hattie went to school, but she was teaching school when her baby brother, Eldridge, was born. After Eldridge finished the seventh grade, he was sent out to Jonathan Creek to school but never got to finish. His father had worsening heart trouble, and they had to send for Eldridge to come back home to take care of all the livestock and his parents and some farm work. They had some tenant farmers, too.

Hiram and Lizzie decided to give Eldridge the home place and 154 acres to take care of them. They had already given the other children land, money, and livestock.

They made a deed to Eldridge, but it stipulated and agreed that "the said R.E. Caldwell is to keep and maintain H.J. Caldwell and Lizzie Caldwell the rest of their lives and preform all duties toward them that a boy should to them as his father and mother. If R.E. dies without performing his duties under this deed, then title reverts to them. If while living he fails to perform, then the title reverts to them, if either of them should desire. (Deed Book 51, P. 362.)"

Hiram died May 19, 1922. Eldridge married Pearl Valentine, March 23, 1923. They lived there with his mother (Aunt Lizzie) until March, 1934. They had four children: Nell, who died at age five in 1929, and Hattie, Helen, and Ken. Hattie went to school one year at the Beech Grove School; then they moved to Maggie Valley.[1]

When the house was vacated, Uncle Will and Aunt Eleanor Palmer who had been living on the mountain above the Jarvis Palmer house, decided to move into the Hiram and Lizzie Caldwell house. The dining room just had one window looking onto a wrap around porch which caused the dining room to be dark. Since the Palmers wanted more light, they took two windows from their house and installed one on each side of the single window in the dining room. That is the reason for the different

---
[1]Historic Structures Report–Dr. Roy Carroll

Cataloochee Valley

This is the barn Eldridge built in 1923 using logs from Levi's barn to build the stalls. He added more stalls and a hay loft.

sizes, those two being shorter, but more light came in.

The beautiful wisteria vine grew all the way around the front of the porch, and it hung down and gave afternoon shade. Pearl, May Miller, and Aunt Eleanor planted flowers. Sometime later the Palmers moved out of Cataloochee.

Next, the house was occupied by Lush and Maggie Caldwell and their children. Lush was a maintenance man for the park. They lived in the house until about 1968, and then they moved to Maggie Valley.

At one time the park got the big idea of tearing down the fine old house and using the lumber to make a maintenance shed. Enough people opposed it, that they left it standing. Later a small group of people lived in the house, probably Peace Corps workers. We saw their cots and an old cook stove.

In 1969, I took Eldridge Caldwell back to see the house, and everything was gone including the flooring on the front and side porch, probably burned for firewood. Then the banisters around the porch disappeared, and other damage was done to the house. Boards were torn from the back of the barn.

The man had worked to build it in his young days, and now

in his old days, he goes back and sees that his work is being destroyed. It hurts him so bad, the pain is so great, that a flood of tears pours out of his eyes and his poor body shakes all over. He was trying to hold back the crying sound, but he could not. Eldridge was sobbing and shaking so hard that he had to be helped back to the car. Perhaps he knew it was the last time he would ever be there, or perhaps it was pent up hurt and resentment he had carried all those years which he could no longer contain.

We feel sure the Caldwell House would have tumbled down and been gone by now, if the Park Historian, Mr. Ed Trout, had not been so dedicated to his job. He helped preserve all the historic structures and rebuild the spring house. He did all that he could get funds for. He had a true sense of history and its meaning. Nothing much had been done by the park to restore anything in Cataloochee, until Mr. Trout became the historian. It was a hard task to get the funds to restore the buildings that should have been kept in good condition like they were when the park took over.

Mr. Trout and his preservation crew put a new roof of hand-rived shingles on Caldwell barn and a lot of work told in other chapters of this book.

Hogs and Cattle and Snakes

Most people in Cataloochee raised cattle and hogs to sell. They could make quite a bit of money because they had free range. Hiram Caldwell had lots of hogs out on the range. He had one old sow that no matter where he put her, she would always take her brood and go into the mountains a long way from Cataloochee to Chiltose. He would have to go there late October or early November to bring her and the young ones back. He named her Ol' Chiltose.

He had hogs scattered all over. Some were in Bushy Mountain, Early Creek, Little Ford Ridge, Piney Butt Mountain, Cataloochee Balsam, and at the Orr Place down on the other side of Mount Sterling.

He would bring these hogs in and feed them corn to harden the flesh because they would be wobbling fat on chestnuts and acorns. When they were in fine shape, he would take some to

Cataloochee Valley

market, keep some for his own use, and keep some for breeding.

One fall when he brought them in, the hog lot was full and little pigs were running all over the barnyard. Some man from another community came over there and saw all those pigs. He must have thought, "Ol' Hiram has so many pigs, he'll never miss a couple of them." So he managed to steal two of them. Soon after that Hiram missed the pigs and knew someone stole them.

He went around inquiring of the neighbors, but no one seemed to know anything about them. One day he asked someone else who has been traveling over the mountain? because he knew his neighbors would not steal.

As soon as he asked, the man said, "Well, I seed a certain feller (naming him) go through here the other day with a tow sack on his back. It had something in it that wiggled. Could have been your pigs, but now I can't say fer shore 'cause I didn't seed em." Hiram grinned because he knew the man who stole his pigs. He thought he would teach that fellow a lesson. He waited about two months until he knew they would have gained several pounds. Then he rode out over the mountain and a considerable distance into another community to see the man. He admitted stealing them, and he couldn't deny it because there was Hiram's mark in the ears. Hiram told him to carry them back the next day or he would take him to court. The man sure didn't want to go to court because he was already in trouble with the law.

The next day, here he came, huffin' and a puffin' with a much heavier load than two months earlier when he stole them. If he had come to Hiram and offered to work a day or two, he could have traded his work for the pigs. He sure never stole from Hiram again.

Since Hiram had so many hogs out on mountains in all directions, it took lots of time and traveling to go check on them. If a sow had a litter of pigs, he had to crop (notch) their ears with identification marks. If he didn't someone who was dishonest could pass through and get the pigs. Hiram and his sons were kept busy with the farm work and going to check on the cattle and hogs. They rode their horses until they came upon tracks leading off into the brush. There they tied the horse to a tree, then trampled through the laurel patches and brush until they found them.

A fall hog killing in Cataloochee.

Those men were wise in the ways of tracking. They could tell what kind of animals had passed through, sometimes they climbed mountains calling the hogs and listening for their bell for two or three days before finding them. Usually they would stay in a camp a few days. They took some rations with them. They hoped to find hog tracks instead of bear tracks. If any bear sign was found, they might have also found a sow half eaten and no pigs because the bear ate them first. That would call for a bear hunt in that area. Everyone wanted in on the hunt because it was exciting and dangerous, but if they didn't kill the bear, it would kill again.

They knew every neighbor's animals by the notches and splits in the ears, and they would report to the neighbors where and when they saw them.

Some of the hogs wore a bell on a leather strap around the neck, especially the ones that had a tendency to stray to far off places. The bell helped the owners find them, but there was a problem when the chestnuts and acorns fell and covered the ground in the fall. The hogs gained weight fast and got fat, and the leather strap holding the bell had to be loosened, which meant trips more often to let the strap out until they were brought in.

Some hogs would not be driven out or tolled by eating shelled

Cataloochee Valley

corn dropped along the trail; so the men had to put a rope on one of the hog's leg to lead them out of the mountains. The hogs would be so fat that a rope would slide off over their head, requiring the men to know how to get a rope on one of the hog's leg.

There were many dangers for the men in the woods while hunting and tending the cattle and hogs. Sometimes a wild boar got after them, forcing them to climb a tree. If there was not a tree with limbs low enough for them to climb, they found way to trick the hog. Eldridge said he would stand still, the old hog aiming for him, snapping its teeth, and then he jump aside just before it hit him. Those hogs were not wild to start with, but after being in the mountains for long periods of time, they became aggressive. (Now there are Wild Russian Boar in the park. They have long tushes (teeth) and are very dangerous, much more so than the others).

Levi, Hiram, and Eldridge Caldwell, at one time or another during the one hundred years they live in Cataloochee, took their cattle to open range on several different mountains, along with other cattlemen. Those grassy balds were located on or near Pin Oak Gap, Heintooga, The Bald, The Swag, Balsam Corner, The Ledge, The Purchase, The Ledge Divide, and Cherry Cove.

They would go to salt the cattle at regular intervals and check on their cattle as well as other people's cattle. Raymond Caldwell remembers what a treat it was to get to go to The Ledge with his father Jarvis, Uncle Jarvis Palmer, Harley Palmer, and others when he was about ten years old. Before they took the cattle out to pasture in the spring, they had to vaccinate all the cattle for black leg and pink eye. Jarvis would go to town and get the medicine, and he had a big syringe and needles to give the shots. They took plenty of rations along. They took fish hooks, line, and leader and cut a pole wherever they decided to fish. They could soon catch all the speckled trout they could eat. They carried corn meal, eggs, bacon (side meat, streak of lean), salt, coffee, and a big dodger or two or corn bread. They cleaned the fish, fried the bacon, rolled the fish in cornmeal and fried them. Raymond could not remember what else, but said they had plenty to eat, and the fish was delicious. Big groups of men and boys stayed two or three days, sleeping in two logging camps, hunting, fishing, and salting the cattle.

Where there was a log lying on the ground, the men chopped out square notches to put the salt in for the cattle. They called it a salt lick. If there was no salt lick, they spread the salt on big flat rocks for the cattle to lick.

Raymond said his daddy, Jarvis, was out in the mountains at a place called Snakeroot because there were so many rattlesnakes in there. Jarvis had a shotgun. When he climbed up on top of a big boulder he looked down, and there was a big pile of rattle snakes all coiled up together below him on a flat rock. It must have made him excited because he was about to fall on the snakes but was able to gain enough balance to jump over them with his gun in hand. As soon as he could, he climbed back up, and fired that shotgun into the pile of snakes killing fourteen of them.

The snakes had dens between the rocks. There were so many of them, the cattlemen decided they had to kill them. They really could not get to them, between the rocks, but as with many of their problems, they devised an ingenious plan. They must have used all the cook vessels they had, filled them with water, and set them on the fire. When the water was hot and got to a full rolling boil, they dumped it in the rocks where they thought the snakes were. They said the place stank so bad later that they could not stand the stench of the dead snakes.

The danger of Cataloochee was not just predators, but the poisonous snakes, wasps, yellow jackets, and other things. When Eldridge was about seventeen years old he went up on a mountain a long way above Uncle Steve Woody's to bring in some hogs. Some other boys went along to help. They found the hogs and got ropes on them. It was way past lunch time, and they were all hungry. Eldridge told them to head on back, that he would go on to find one that was missing.

There were two dogs with him. He had to have them to hem her up so he could get a rope on her. He got the rope on her, but all of a sudden, he was getting stung by yellow jackets. It was a hot day in October. He had taken off his hat and unbuttoned his shirt. All the commotion of the dogs and hog had stirred up a large nest of the yellow jackets. They were all over him.

Although he was getting stung, he did not let go of the rope. This old sow would not walk in front of him, but he found she

Cataloochee Valley

would follow. He had gotten up at four o'clock that morning and ate a big breakfast, but now it was getting late, and he was starved. The bee stings were on fire and he started getting really sick. He tied the hog to a tree and walked on down to Uncle Steve's and told him he was sick and needed a horse to ride home.

Eldridge lay down on the porch, and in a short time Uncle Steve was there with the horse and helped him on.

He rode home, right up to the porch, and they helped him to bed because he was so weak and dizzy he couldn't walk. His father sent someone to get Dr. Bob Medford who lived across the mountain, at Cove Creek. The trip there and back was about twenty-five to thirty miles on horseback. Dr. Bob Medford came, but during the time they were waiting for the doctor, Eldridge vomited and vomited. Dr. Medford said that was all that saved his life. He had gotten rid of most of the poison, but he was sick long after that.

Cattle Drive to Cherokee about 1914

The Cherokee did not live in teepees. They lived in houses and cultivated the land. They made gardens, planted corn, beans, squash, and potatoes. They hunted wild game and fished for their meat. They lived in peace and friendship with their Cataloochee neighbors.

The Cherokee made very strong baskets of oak strips, and sometimes they used small, smooth wild honeysuckle vines. Their workmanship was always the very best. These baskets used to carry vegetables and apples etc. and lasted many years.

The Indians and the early settlers of Cataloochee often bartered and traded in baskets and livestock and other things. One time a couple of Indian men came to Big Cataloochee and made a trade with Hiram Caldwell for cattle. A certain date was decided on that Hiram and Eldridge would drive the cattle over there to Big Cove where the Indians lived in the Indian Nation. (It was always referred to as the Indian Nation.)

When that day came, Hiram was very sick. He woke Eldridge up at four in the morning and told him that he was awful sick and he would have to drive those cattle by himself. We can't disappoint the Indians because if you break a promise to them, they will say our word is not good; and they won't ever trust us again.

Eldridge got up, ate his breakfast, saddled his horse, and went to round up the cattle, then drove them up Cataloochee Creek and up Woody Creek. One old cow was causing trouble, running out of the trail into the bushes, and by the time he got her back to the trail, some others had scattered all over into the woods. This went on all day long. It was a very hard day for a boy sixteen years old.

It was nearly dark when Eldridge finally arrived with the cattle at the place agreed upon. He had not expected so much trouble and had not carried any lunch, so he was starving.

The Cherokee considered a man honorable when he kept his promise. They were pleased to see he had arrived with all the cattle they had traded for. That was an occasion to celebrate; so the Indians, some with beansacks around their ankles, danced around a big fire to honor him and show their appreciation.

They continued dancing and celebrating while Eldridge was starving; he had never been so hungry in his life. The women finally started cooking a big feast. He saw they were grating some kind of roots for making bread, but he didn't care about a feast. Just a piece of cornbread would have been fine.

About ten o'clock that night they served the meal. The vegetables were seasoned with unfamiliar herbs. Eldridge did not like the bread, but he noticed the others really did. He did enjoy the fried fish but pretended to like everything, though he ate very little.

They made Eldridge a bed, and totally exhausted he quickly went to sleep appreciating their respect for him. He got up early the next morning and hurried home to eat the kind of food he liked. That was in 1914, and they always remained good friends with the Indians.

Shear Sheep

We had lots of sheep, and in the summertime when the weather got hot, all the sheep would be put in a pen in the barn.

That was the time to shear the wool off each one. It was a very hard job because they had to hold the sheep and

Cataloochee Valley

Ethel Palmer feeding sheep. Photo Courtesy of Ethel Palmer McCracken.

use handshears. It usually took one man to hold the sheep and one to clip the wool. It might have taken a whole day to shear one man's sheep, next day they all move to the next man's sheep. The wool would be stuffed into tow sacks and later washed, picked clean, and laid out to dry.

After it was dry it would be packed into tow sacks with a tag wired to it with the shipping address, Chatham Mills, Kannapolis, N.C. A list was included giving the weight of wool, the number of blankets, and the color and number of yards of fine woven wool cloth to send in return. The wool was hauled to Waynesville in the wagon, then shipped by train. Sometimes they shipped the wool and received a check for it if they did not need anything made from it.

I remember the blankets were gray with red, green, or blue stripes across each end of the blanket. We had several of each.

Pearl Caldwell (mother) was a good seamstress, and she made nice coats for my sister (Helen) and me out of the wool material from the Chatham Company. Our coats were blue with a lighter blue lining.

By the 1920s almost every woman had a sewing machine and made the women's and girls' clothes and sometimes

Major Woody in the Little Cataloochee Blacksmith shop. Photo Courtesy of Paul Woody.

shirts for the boys and men. Some would order their Sunday clothes and blankets from Sears Roebuck & Company. Every family received a catalogue which we called the wish book. We stared getting modern. Think how long it took to get a new dress before the manufactured things were available.

The men could buy overalls at the Nellie post office and store. Some of the men wore their best overalls to church. Several had suits and wore hats, shirts and ties. The women wore hats and dressed in style.

Blacksmiths

We know there were several blacksmith shops in Big Cataloochee including Jarvis Palmer and Jim Caldwell, Eldridge Caldwell, and Levi Caldwell (grandson of the first Levi). The only two that we know of in Little Cataloochee was Will Messer and Major Woody, but there were probably several more. They could buy horse, mule, and oxen shoes, and nails at the Nellie Post Office and store, or at Messer's store at the Ola Post Office in Little Cataloochee.

Cataloochee Valley

The blacksmith shops had a forge where a fire was built and bellows to blow air into the fire to make it hotter. The right size horse shoe was chosen and held over the fire with tongs until it was red hot and then white hot. At that stage the shoe would be removed from the fire then put on the anvil and tapped with a ball peen hammer into the exact size and shape.

Horses, like people, have various sizes and shapes of feet. Sometimes the shoe had to be reheated and hammered and shaped to make it fit. Then it was dipped in a bucket of cold water. When it was cool, they picked up the horses foot to be sure it would fit and to see how much to turn down on each end to make a cork to keep the horse from slipping and sliding on hills and mountains while pulling heavy loads. The shoe would be heated again, the corks turned down, cooled, and finally nailed on. They had to be very careful in nailing the shoe on, or they would cripple the horse by the nail hitting the flesh. That was a hard, exacting job because the horse's hoof would be picked up and bent back and held on the blacksmith's knee while he drove the nails in.

Some people used oxen to plow and pull sleds and logs. Each of their feet was divided, taking two small plate like pieces of metal on them, with cleats or corks welded on them. They made wooden yokes for the oxen. All of this work was an art form of exact sizing, hammering, and fitting.

They could buy the iron by the pound and forge out a set of hinges or plow points, iron pieces to fit on single trees or wagon parts or anything they needed. They did not have instructions on how to make these things; they knew what was needed and were intelligent at figuring how to make it.

We inquired of Thad Sutton about blacksmiths on Caldwell Fork. His father, called Big Jim and his grandfather, Sol Sutton, were blacksmiths there. He said he could remember eleven families living there and Carson Messer ran the corn mill. A blacksmith and a cornmill were very important in each community.

Hiram's Last Bear Hunt

Bear hunting was fun for the men of Cataloochee, and it may have been more fun to tell about it because it would be the talk for weeks. It was fun, a sport, meat for the table, and protection for their cows, calves, sheep, and hogs. Bears usually slaughtered five, six, or more animals at one time. When they killed a cow, the first part of her he ate was the udder and sometimes that was all he ate.

When Hiram Caldwell was getting old and had heart trouble, he had to give up bear hunting and most of the farm work. He kept an eye out for any activity indicating a bear hunt, such as a group of men and their dogs going by, but usually someone would come to tell him. He liked to sit on the porch and listen to the dogs run and tree the bear.

The bear hunts were usually organized after someone had found his livestock killed. The men may have stayed in the woods as much as twenty-four hours if the dogs could still run. The women would fix up some food for the men in a poke.

When the men went into the mountains, they would split up and take their stand in the gaps, knowing the bear would run the easiest way to get over the mountain. Not knowing exactly where the bear would go, each man stood in a different gap with his gun ready, hoping the bear would come his way when the dogs were turned loose. Some might have shot and missed the bear; but when someone killed him, they fired three rapid shots, indicating the hunt was over, and everyone came to help carry the bear out.

One day when Hiram was no longer able to go hunting but while listening to this hunt, he heard the three shots. He knew the mountains so well, he could tell exactly where they were. He went to the barn, put the gear on the horse, hooked him to the sled, put the saddle on the horse, and rode up the road he knew they would be coming down. There he met them carrying that big bear. They had tied his front feet together and his hind legs together, and had taken a long pole, put it through the legs, one man in front and one man in back carrying the big load. They sure were happy to see Hiram, and they let the

Cataloochee Valley

horse pull the bear to a place where it could be skinned and divided between all the men. Hiram was delighted that he could even have a small part in the hunt. He knew it was his last hunt. He died a short time later on May 19, 1922 and was buried high on the hill behind the barn.[1]

Voting Precinct

The Cataloochee settlements were large enough to organize as a township in the 1850s and to establish a voting precinct. The population was 140. In 1860 there were 161. In 1870 there were 198 inhabitants in the township and ten years later there were 391. By 1900 the population had grown to 764 people occupying 136 dwellings. A majority of the inhabitants were native North Carolinians, but 116 were immigrants from Tennessee, with single representatives from Indiana, Colorado, and Canada. Farming and farm laborers were the occupations most frequently listed for Cataloochee householders, but the area also included two dressmakers, one midwife, one grocer, one teamster, and one minister. About one-half of the householders were renters, reflecting a significant amount of farming. In 1910, population was listed as 1,250 people living in Cataloochee.[2]

This large increase may be due to the logging companies. They had large camps built on the mountains and had lots of men working there including a large number of Italians. People used to talk about selling produce—honey, eggs, meat, butter, and milk to the logging camp. Then on Saturday night these Italians would hire some local musicians (string band) to make music for them to dance. Cataloocheeans thought it was strange to see men dancing together, but they reckoned that must be how they danced in Italy. The dance was something like a polka or a folk dance, where they hooked arms and danced around and around.

---

[1] Story from Eldridge Caldwell.
[2] Dr. Ray Carroll, Historic Structures Report, Little Cataloochee

5

CATALOOCHEE SCHOOLS

An address by Dr. Roy Carroll, at the Cataloochee Reunion August 11, 1991.

For almost two hundred and fifty years, the county school was the backbone of American education. All across this land the church and the school were community centers, housing the activities that joined people together in the community.

In many rural areas today, the old church and the old schoolhouse are virtually the last physical proof of communities and settlements that have withered and died because the families have moved on.

So it is with Cataloochee. Palmer's Chapel and Beech Grove School, also Little Cataloochee Baptist Church, are powerful symbols of a shared community life.

I want to talk a little this morning about education and schools in Cataloochee and perhaps shed some light on public education and its significance not just in this valley but also in North Carolina.

The first public school law in North Carolina was passed in 1838. At that time, formal education was available almost exclusively to children of the upper and middle classes whose family could afford to pay for it. Trying to make it available to everyone's children was an exciting but radical idea. We should note, too, that the

Cataloochee Valley

This is the little Beech Grove Schoolhouse that burned. Center back row is John Queen, teacher there. Mrs. Ethel Palmer McCracken said, "I was as afraid of him as I was of a bear."

1839 law required the counties to provide school, but not necessarily a schoolhouse.

From 1836 to 1850 there is no evidence of a school in actual operation in Cataloochee, at least of formal schooling. In the 1850 census, some two dozen in nine or ten households were identified as having some schooling that year. But we should remember that in Cataloochee, as elsewhere in America, formal schools were only a small part of the total educational process, at least for the first generation of settlers, and then a kind of appendage to other, far more important and far more comprehensive agencies–the church, the community at large, and above all, the families.

For most children, the major kinds of learning occurred at home. It was where they learned the basic skills, like how to handle utensils, tools and weapons for planting, fence building and mending, cooking, sewing, spinning and weaving. It was there they learned verses from the Bible, vocal and instrumental music, and sometimes the three R's.

There in the context of the total household environment, values, manners, literacy, and vocation were all transmitted from one generation to the next. The process was perhaps only part conscious and deliberate, but it was nevertheless real.

The new construction in 1868 provided that the General Assembly, "provided by taxation or otherwise for general and uniform system of public schools, wherein tuition shall be free of charge to all the children of the state between the ages of six and twenty-one years."

Hence in November, 1868, the County Commissioners of Haywood County ordered that the townships be the municipal school districts and ordered that Lafayette Palmer, Young Bennett, and Parker Hopkins be appointed as the school committee for the Cataloochee district.

The first Haywood County Board of Education was organized July 6, 1885. At the same meeting, the board condemned the "seats, desks, and convenients as inhuman, unhealthy, and not in keeping with this progressive age" and that the school committeemen of each school district be earnestly requested to supply their houses with convenient seats and desks at their earliest convenience.

The Second Schoolhouse

Sometime before 1905 there was another schoolhouse that sat on the creek bank, across the road from the present Beech Grove School.

The people had been living in Big Cataloochee about seventy years. By now they had so many children their school was very over-crowded. The committeemen had petitioned for a new schoolhouse as far back as 1893 but did not get it.

A group of the parents got together and decided some of them should go to Waynesville to talk with the County Commissioners

Cataloochee Valley

New Beech Grove School - Cataloochee 1908
1st row: Fannie Sutton, Grace Sutton, Glenn Caldwell, Linton Palmer, Elmer Palmer, Charlie Caldwell, Willie Sutton, Verlin Palmer, Chauncy Palmer, Brown Caldwell, Bob Sutton, Roy Palmer, Guy Caldwell, ——, Dave Caldwell, Lush Caldwell, Arthur Sutton, Lenn Caldwell. 2nd row: Eldridge Caldwell, Bill Palmer, Leona Canup, Hattie Caldwell, Magolia Caldwell, Addie Caldwell, Addie Grooms, Lonnie Palmer, Myrtle Palmer, Elizabeth Palmer, Inez Grooms, Fay Caldwell, Hattie Palmer, Ida Palmer, Hazel Palmer, Charlie Palmer. 3rd row: Gene Sutton, Flora Palmer, Della Palmer, Jim Palmer, Ethel Palmer, Ethel Woody, Charles Woody, Nellie Palmer, Jonathan Woody, Lura Palmer, Lillie Ferguson - Teacher, Dave Palmer, Hiram Palmer.

again and explain that their school was so overcrowded, and request a larger school.

It was decided that three of the men would go–they were Uncle Steve Woody, Grandpa Hiram Caldwell, and his brother Uncle George Caldwell. They dressed in their Sunday best, mounted their horses, and rode that long trip across the mountain into Waynesville.

They presented their case in a gentlemanly manner. The commissioners replied, "Ah, you fellows over there don't pay enough tax. We can't build you another school. You will just have to make out best you can."

These men certainly were disappointed. They were proud of

their children and wanted them educated. What to do?

They went across the street and bought a bottle of whiskey. They were mad, but as they rode all that long distance back across the mountain they debated what to tell the folks back home. They sure hated to tell them that there would not be a new school.

As they rode toward Cataloochee talking about what to do, they kept taking sips of whiskey.

They said, now it's the "law" these children must go to school and just what if that little ol' schoolhouse happened to burn down, then the county would have to build one. Yeah, By Golly! That's it. That was what they agreed to do.

When they got to the school, they went in and removed all the desks, books, and other things. They carried them out in the woods and hid them, putting the blackboard over everything so the rain would not ruin them. They would just burn down that little ol' crowded schoolhouse. They wondered what would happen if they didn't get a new schoolhouse for a while. They couldn't let their children miss school.

"Well, that's no problem," said Hiram who had just finished building a new house. He and Lizzie had moved out of the log house a short time before. "We'll have school in my old log house till they build us one."

Those three men made a pact between them. They would never tell who did it, until there was only one left alive. At that they shook hands. They set the school house on fire, and when it got started burning real well, they got on their horses and rode on up the road, noticing how it lit up the whole valley.

The new Beech Grove School was built in 1907 and mysteriously, the blackboard, books, and desks and other things reappeared. Uncle Steve Woody lived longer than Uncle Hiram or Uncle George. He told about it in his later years. He laughed and admitted they burnt it down.

The schools in Cataloochee had only seven grades. When the children finished there, many were sent to board somewhere to complete their education in other schools.

In the 1880 census of Cataloochee township, eighty-five children were attending school. It is no wonder that those three men burned that crowded little school down. Glenn Palmer

Cataloochee Valley

Beech Grove School - Cataloochee 1918
1st row seated: Fred Rogers, Wilma Caldwell, Odell Lockman, Nettie Caldwell, Boone Lockman, Julia Burress, Pauline Palmer, Arvil Caldwell, Mattie Caldwell, Reuben Palmer, Fannie Lockman. 2nd row standing: Carl Palmer, Maggie Caldwell, Arlo Palmer, Wayne Lockman, Gudger Palmer, Paul Lockman, Blye Caldwell, Boone Caldwell, Kimsey Palmer, Maggie Palmer. 3rd row standing: Nellie Rogers, Goldy Rogers, Laura Noland, Vernon Palmer, Lavada Palmer - Teacher, Flora Palmer - Teacher, Eulala Palmer, Jessie Lockman, Callie Burress, Rachel Ewart. Back Row - by window: Guy Caldwell, Robert Palmer.

taught school there, and he had fifty-eight students all at the same time in the one room school.

After Uncle Steve Woody revealed their secret, the story was often told by descendants of these three men, especially when they got together at the Cataloochee reunion.

Little Cataloochee School — County School Board Minutes

- January 1907–county school board approved a bill for sawing lumber and a lot surveyed for a new schoolhouse

in Little Cataloochee. July 1907–A deed from John Hannah and others for a new school site, and agreed to sell old school lot to Americus Hall for $5.00. In October that year $10.00 was allotted for a rural library.
- 1909–the county commissioners made a contract with Andy Bennett to furnish lumber for the building. The new schoolhouse was forty feet long, twenty-four feet wide and twelve feet from floor to ceiling. The contract called for four windows on each side and one door, weatherboards to be poplar, the framing of spruce pine, ceiling of chestnut, flooring of maple. The lumber was to be common or better grade. School board to pay $13.00 per one hundred running board feet, for framing and sheeting, $16.00 per one hundred running board feet for siding, flooring, and ceiling.
- February 1910–board agreed to pay Andy Bennett $2.00 on lumber bill, and to accept a site from W.B.G. Messer, between his house and the Little Cataloochee Church. The deed stated that all the apples from one tree on that lot continued to belong to Messer. The lot bought from John Hannah in July was not used but bought back by William Hannah in 1927 for $1.00.
- July 1910–R.M. Hannah paid $42.50 to the board as half payment for five #2 desks, ten #3 and ten #4 desks to be ordered from Sears Roebuck in Chicago. The school board to pay the other half. Minutes of the board August, 1911, record the final settlement between the board and Little Cataloochee School committeemen. It shows the following from the Board of Education to:

A.C. Bennett for lumber	$226.00
J.K. Boone & Co. for windows	39.33
H.M. Caldwell nails etc. bought for Will Messer	11.97
Mr. Parks for surveying	3.50
John Burgess for lumber	9.00
John Burgess for shingles	4.00
George Bennett for shingles	9.00

Cataloochee Valley

Charlie Ray for brick for flue	3.65
A.C. Bennett–hauling brick	1.55

From Local Committee and Citizens:

J.C. Kerley-carpenter	180.00
W.G.B. Messer-site	40.00
Work on site	22.00
hauling lumber	10.00
drying lumber	5.00
shingles	32.00
stove	7.75
painting the house	10.00

Local school districts were free to provide additional months of school at their own expense and supplement teachers' salaries if they wished. The 1925-26 school committee for Little Cataloochee chose to supplement Fred Hannah's salary by $25.00 for the first six months and to pay an additional seventh month. His salary for six months was $130.00 with $105.00 from the county and $25.00 from the local district and was the highest monthly salary ever paid a teacher in Cataloochee.[1]

LITTLE CATALOOCHEE SCHOOL

Helen Hannah Trantham, daughter of Mark and Verdie Messer Hannah, was born on Little Cataloochee and went to school there in the first grade.

Helen remembered her second grade was taught on Mt. Sterling at the school there due to the park closing Little Cataloochee School. The children had to be transported there by the teacher, Roger Ferguson, in his pickup truck. He boarded with the Hannahs. When the winter weather got too bad, the school was discontinued. It was too cold for some of the children to ride in the back of the truck. But everyone got promoted anyway.

Helen said it did not affect her grades in any way. In her third year all of the school children from Little Cataloochee were hauled over to Beech Grove School in Big Cataloochee by

[1] Historic Structures Report-Dr. roy Carroll

First schoolhouse in Little Cataloochee. The top story was used for a men's club. Photo Courtesy of Paul Woody.

Kimsey Palmer who had a station wagon. Her teacher was Gussie Martin (later married Robert Palmer).

Helen remembered other teachers. They were Martin Palmer, Tom Frazier, and Ronnie Allen. Two of Helen's uncles taught school but did not happen to be amoung her teachers. They were Fred and Mont Hannah. Helen finished the seventh grade at Beech Grove, then went to Waynesville, NC where she boarded with the Jarvis Palmer family. She went on to high school there and finished with excellent grades. Soon after high school, she went to Washington, D.C. where she worked with the FBI for some years during World War II.

We inquired of Helen if she missed all the people who had lived at Cataloochee. Her father, Mark, being the ranger kept on living there and very few other people remained. Her reply was "No, not too much. We were too busy." From the time they were big enough to carry a hoe, they were taught how to hoe in the garden, hoe corn, and plenty of other jobs. People over there usually lived miles apart or at least out of sight. Her favorite thing to do was kick off her shoes and sit in the swing and play her guitar. She said the job she hated most was carrying water to the field for the work hands.

Cataloochee Valley

Second Little Cataloochee Schoolhouse: On each side of the front door there was space for coats and lunch. The back side was mostly all windows. Courtesy Paul Woody.

Last Year Of Little Cataloochee School

The second Little Cataloochee schoolhouse was built in 1909. It closed after the school term was over in 1932. Gordon Cagle of Hemphill was the teacher that year. He only had ten or twelve students. What once had been a large, thriving community, now only had a few families left due to the park restriction.

After more than sixty years, Gordon could remember his class was made up of some of the children of Carl Woody, Jonah Brown, Mark Hannah, and Ervin Messer who lived up on Mt. Sterling. Mr. Cagle taught all grades from one to seven, whatever level the child was in, as did other teachers in one room schools.

He said, "They had a big long wood heater. We loaded her up with beechwood or maple wood. It kept us warm." The wood was cut and hauled there by different men in the community, Mercius Hall, Carl Woody, Jonah Brown, and maybe others.

There was a nearby spring where we got water, and we kept a big bucket sitting on a bench in the school. There was a privy outside at some distance.

Both Helen Hannah Trantham and Paul Woody remembered when they were in school and there was a revival at the church, the school children would be marched to church to hear the preaching. Soon as it was over, they were marched back to school and given a quiz on the sermon. They both said you had to know what the preacher said. That was no goof off time.

People were serious about their religion and schooling. Parents disciplined their children and they expected the teachers to do the same. As a result, there were very few criminals, if any.

Beech Grove School

This was the third school in Big Cataloochee. No one would donate or sell land for the new school site. On April 2, 1906, the Board of Education arranged for the Clerk of Court to have appraisers locate and condemn a site for a schoolhouse on land belonging to the minor heirs of D.L. (Doctor) Caldwell, deceased. The appraisers were Elijah M. Messer, Mack W. Hannah, and John Hall. The value was set at $15.00 per acre. The school site was $23.25 according to the deed, dated November 14, 1907. The land was part of the Jessie R. Palmer tract, purchased from the Love Estate at $1.00 an acre.

The school was to be thirty-six feet long by twenty-four feet wide and from floor to ceiling, twelve feet. There was a portable sawmill set up at Uncle Harrison's place on Uncle Andy's farm. The shingles were made at Uncle Steve Woody's house. Alex Carpenter came from Jonathan's Creek and finished the shingles there.

On October 7, 1907, the board made a settlement with the committeemen in District #3 Cataloochee on the new schoolhouse as follows:

From the Building Fund	
Schaefer - for sawing lumber	$45.00
L.C. Reno builder	223.40
K.C. Boone Co., windows, doors, etc.	24.70
J.R. Morgan atty drawing up papers in condemnation suit	5.00
James Park - surveying lot	2.50
Paint	15.00

Cataloochee Valley

Land for site (J.F. Palmer)	23.25
Total	$338.85

From Local Residents
Lumber furnished by citizens	$56.50
Committee paid for district to treasurer	114.50
George Caldwell for work due from bid. (He wouldn't accept, told them to apply it to schoolhouse debt in county)	3.00
Shingles, nails, etc.	64.85
Total	238.85

Additional bills came in over a two-year period. On December 10, 1907 the board paid:

J.R. Boyd for registering deed	$1.10
J.K. Boone - Paint 12 gallons	1.50
Three gallons linseed oil @ .60 a 5 gal. can	.50
Total	$20.30

They also allocated $10.00 for the school from the Rural Library Fund.

Incidentally, J.K. Boone was on the county board, and apparently they were not as touchy about conflicts of interest back then.

- On January 6, 1908, the board paid A. H. Andrews Co. of Chicago $113.00 from the general fund for desks, some of which were for Cataloochee.
- On June 1, 1908, paid another $11.65 to Steve Woody for paint.
- July 1908 - A.J. Andrews Co. $73.00 for 70 desks, 20 were for Cataloochee.
- Jan. 9, 1909, paid Steve Woody $10.00 due for painting school.
- County School Board paid $431.10 including some desks and library books.
- Local committee and citizens paid $275.30.
- TOTAL for the new Beech Grove School in Cataloochee was $706.45.

Committeemen throughout the building period were, Steven L. Woody, George H. Caldwell, and George H. Palmer.

In 1904, schools were supposed to run for five months. Salary for the principal was $35.00 per month and the assistant was $20.00 per month. The principal teacher at Little Cataloochee received $30.00 per month.

In January 1928, the local districts were ordered to extend school terms to seven months. The following year, 1928-29, Big Cataloochee provided eight months of school while the other four districts in the township provided seven, but monthly salaries had been cut (due to the great depression)! The teachers clearly had to absorb much of the additional cost for providing longer terms.

It is interesting to note that an additional expense was incurred for a real innovation in the Big Cataloochee district 1928-29 school year–transportation for pupils. In May, 1927, M.H. (Hub) Caldwell had requested transportation on behalf of the district. The following month, the Board of Education awarded him a contract for hauling children from the bridge over Cataloochee Creek and returning for the sum of $40.00 per month. He was to furnish car, gasoline, oil, and all expenses.

Hub Caldwell rendered the service for two years and then in 1930-31 Jarvis Caldwell assumed the responsibility under the same generous contract.

The Compulsory Attendance Law was passed in 1911. Two years later in 1913, the first four months of a school term were designated as "compulsory attendance months" and attendance officers were appointed. Floyd W. Woody was the first such officer for Cataloochee. In 1919, a new school law required a levy for six months of school, and the board agreed to allow no more stopping children from school on account of the demands of farm work or homes. In 1920 the school board "agreed to suspend all rules allowed heretofore the parents to take their children out of school for work of any kind."[1]

Swimming Hole and School 1918

Gudger Palmer remembered that he and several boys started home after school one hot, autumn day. They decided to stop by

---
[1] Dr. Ray Carroll Historic Structure Report

Cataloochee Valley

the swimming hole. It was a nice, deep place in Cataloochee Creek out from the Nellie Post Office. They went out through the bushes to the edge of the creek and took off their clothes. They were in the creek just having a big old time. Then they looked up and saw their teacher, Lavada Palmer. She just stood there and looked to see who they were. She didn't say a word. The next morning when they came to school she lined them up and whipped each one of them. The teacher was responsible for the children until they got home. The children knew they were supposed to go straight home from school. They had disobeyed. In those days the parents and teachers believed in disciplining the children. Of course they believed in the Bible. Didn't it say, "Spare the rod and spoil the child?"

Floyd Woody had a wonderful, mischievous sense of humor and was always in trouble in school. He said, "If the teacher gave you a whipping at school, when you got home your parents would give you another whipping. Nowadays (1974) if the teacher whips a kid, the next day the parent goes and whips the teacher. That's wrong."

Gudger remembered one year they had Elizabeth Palmer for their teacher at Beech Grove School. She assigned them several words to learn how to spell. She would have them spell and pronounce the word while looking at the book. Then they were supposed to take their speller home that night and learn to spell every word she had assigned them. If they misspelled a word the next day, she gave them a few licks with an ironwood hickory.

Beech Grove school, like all others there, were grades one through seven. When Gudger was in the sixth grade there, his sister, Hattie lived in Charlotte, N.C. His parents had arranged for him to stay with her and go to high school there. One day he threw his cap out the window of the Beech Grove School. When his teacher made him go get it, he went out, picked up his cap, and never went back inside. That was his last school day in Cataloochee. He knew he was soon going to Charlotte to school. After finishing school there, he went to the University of North Carolina at Chapel Hill. After he graduated there, he came back to Canton and worked as an accountant for Champion Fiber until he retired.

Caldwell Fork Schoolhouse at McKee Branch, Cataloochee, N.C. long after it closed. Photo Courtesy of GSMNP.

Caldwell Fork School

The last school district created in the township was Caldwell Fork. In 1922 Miss Addie Sutton was paid $45.00 a month to teach in the new District #5 for six months in 1922-1923. An acre of land was purchased for a school site, and the schoolhouse was built in 1923 after she had already started teaching.

In an interview, Thad Sutton recalled his school days on Caldwell Fork. "The building was similar to the Beech Grove School. The desks were double and two students sat together," he said. "We liked to do devilish things, but we had a teacher from Crabtree named Letha Noland (Clay). She told us to be quiet, and when we didn't, she scolded us and warned us. A little while later we laughed out loud when she was talking, and we didn't pay any attention. But I'll tell you, she got our attention. She could really whip you with a big hickory. We found out she did not put up with any foolishness."

In another interview Thad also remembered the names of three other teachers who taught on Caldwell Fork. They were Clara Leatherwood from Lake Junaluska, John Howell from Cove

Cataloochee Valley

Thad Sutton recalled his school days on Caldwell Fork. Photo Courtesy of Hattie C. Davis.

Creek, and Mary Green from White Oak. Since there was no road up there, the teachers always boarded with some family near the school.

Letha Noland Clay remembered teaching at the Caldwell Fork School. She boarded with Addie and Huston Sutton. She said, "Yes, I enjoyed teaching there, and the Suttons were so nice to me. On those cold mornings some of the bigger boys would go to the schoolhouse early. They carried in plenty of wood for the day and built a big fire in the old pot-bellied stove. When I got there the room was warm, and a fresh bucket of water was carried in. Miss Addie was a real good cook and always had good hot meals. None of the children ever gave me any trouble after they found out I intended for them to listen and study. Yes, they were good people up there and good to me."[1]

---

[1] 3-19-91 Interview with Letha

6

THE TWENTIES

Second Improvement of the Cataloochee Turnpike

Finally in the 1920s the Cataloochee people voted bonds to modernize the Turnpike. They were to pay part of the cost, but since the lumber companies owned the biggest portion of the mountain land, they would pay the largest amount of money to get the road in better condition.

All agreed to hire Will Medford as the contractor because he had dynamite! He could get rid of the huge boulders and rock cliffs that were so large they could not be moved by manual labor. In the period between 1855 and 1860 the men worked hard to build the road by hand, using the bull tongue plow pulled by oxen or horses. Men used the pick, shovel, sledge hammer, prize poles, and employed rawhiding, and mainly strength and awkwardness in road building. Mr. Clark Medford described it as slash, drag, push, pull, heave, huff and hollar, beat and break, sweat and swear, and grub (dig out stumps with mattocks after the trees were cut). Try as they might it was impossible to remove the largest rock sticking out of the bank where the road bed should be. They had to make the road go down the hill under the rock, then back up, to get the road on grade as surveyed. This was the only way to bypass the rock cliff. Sometimes this detour would be awfully steep, but the men being expert horsemen, knew how to get their wagons through this kind of road.

Cataloochee Valley

Glenn Palmer and family arriving at the Nellie Post Office. They traveled from Crabtree to visit his parents.
Photo courtesy of Gudger Palmer.

Everyone was glad to get the rock dynamited and out of their way. You may wonder how a heavy wagon load could go down the steep mountain and not run over the horses. The wagons had brakes, which were big blocks of wood fastened on to a long wooden handle. One man drove and one pushed forward on the long wooden handle which caused the big block of wood to press back against the back wheel. That took a strong man applying great pressure to slow the wagon, but it would not hold the wagon back if the load was real heavy and the grade was steep.

Gudger and others have told how they would cut a good size tree and fasten it to the back of the wagon.

The weight of the tree would help hold back the weight of the heavily loaded wagon. Of course, when they started uphill, the tree would be cut loose.

Gudger Palmer remembered the Bennett turn was awfully steep because of a large rock protruding out of the bank, and they had to travel down under the rock and then back up, causing a steep switchback. The road was so narrow that if one met another, one of them would have to back up to find a place wide enough for the other to pass.[1]

---

[1] Interview with Gudger Palmer August 9, 1995

Making Hay Early Twenties

As customary when a man's hay was ready to be cut, dried, and stacked, several neighbors came to help, and later he would help them. Several of their wives would go to help cook for the big crowd of men working in the hay field or any other big job.

In the early days the hay had to be cut by hand with a scythe, a long sharp blade attached to a long wooden handle which was curved to fit their hands. This long handle had two short handles set on a different angle, one for the right hand, one for the left hand. They had to swing this scythe back and forth all day long, or several days, depending on the size of farm, to cut all the hay. They waited a few days for it to dry, using a pitch fork to turn the hay over, to dry it on both sides. When it was dry, it was picked up with pitchforks and packed on a wagon or sled and hauled to the barn loft. When it was full, the rest of the hay was hauled to the location where it would be stacked.

A stack pole would be cut from a small tree or sapling, the limbs cut off, but leaving some a foot or so long sticking out where they had grown from the tree. This helped to hold the hay. They had to dig a hole to set this pole in, then the haystack would be

Haystacks in Cataloochee. Photo courtesy of Gudger Palmer.

Cataloochee Valley

made by throwing pitchforks full of hay around the pole, one man standing on the stack, placing and packing the hay evenly, so that the stack would not be crooked. He was stomping and packing it as he went, the other men throwing on more and more hay. He kept on packing until it was fifteen feet or so high, then it was rounded off on top, so the rain would not penetrate into the stack and cause rotting.

That was quite an art, to form the haystacks perfectly, and lots of hard work from start to finish. They got sweaty and hot, and hay seed and dust stuck to them. When it got to itching them, they often went swimming in the creek because no one had a shower, not even a bathroom or running water. But they managed to keep themselves clean most of the time.

When they got their first horse drawn mowing machine, that saved them from much hard work of swinging that scythe all day. Lots of the neighbors came to help a certain man with his hay, but he had started drinking. He never got so drunk that he couldn't work. His wife was worried about him working with that "dangerous thing," (horse drawn mowing machine) and begged him not to drink, but it did no good. She argued he could get his legs cut off or mangled, maybe killed if he fell off it.

But he continued drinking and working while his wife and the other ladies were cooking dinner (noon) for the men, she told them, "If you can't beat them, join them." She told the ladies of her plan and they had so much fun, they helped her. When dinner was almost ready they took rouge and put it all over her face and neck until it looked fiery red. They took some of the pins out of the big ball of hair on the back of her head, letting her long hair fall over her face and string every which way.

Someone went to tell the men to come to dinner. When her husband came in, he inquired about her. One of the women pointed to the bedroom saying she was sick. He rushed in to see about her. He got the shock of his life. There she lay all sprawled out in the bed with her clothes half off and one shoe on, her hair stringing in every direction, her face red as fire and beside the bed sat a half gallon jar about half full. It looked like whiskey! (Actually it was water.) She talked with a slurred speech, and said, "Hunee husbon, you are right, that whiskey make me feel so good! I like to lay here and drink, I'm sooo relaxed. I think I'll do it every day. But I ain't much drunk now! I'll go fix you some dinner."

"No, oh, no! You stay right here, you can't be seen in such condition." He went back into the dining room where the others were just sitting down to eat. She staggered in and flopped down in her chair at the table. Early that morning she had brought in a big nice ball of butter from the springhouse to let it get soft. She had placed this ball of butter near his place. She said in a slurred loud voice, "Hunee husbon, pass me the butter." When he did, instead of her cutting off a serving of the butter, she just grabbed the whole ball in her hand and squeezed it so hard it squirted out between her fingers. At that her husband jumped up to help her back to bed! He was so embarrassed that he never again drank in hay season and a little later stopped drinking altogether because she threatened to get drunk if he did. He never knew she had fooled him. As a general rule, the women did not drink, nor even allow it in the house.

This man and the neighbor men were so shocked because this woman wouldn't take a drink for anything, but to see her like this, they couldn't believe it! The neighbor women were having a hard time keeping a straight face. After the men went back to the field, the women had a good laugh about her pitching a dry drunk. They could always think up something funny.

Divorce

There were very few divorces in earlier years, especially in Cataloochee. But there was a couple who married and after several children, the man started drinking and became rude and violent to her. When her last baby was born, as soon as she got strong enough, she took her baby and left. She went all the way to California, leaving her husband and several children. Some people said they didn't blame her for leaving. When her baby was nearly one year old, she brought it back to Cataloochee and said she had come for the rest of her children. Some of the older children heard what she planned to do. They saw the toddler walking about the yard, and they ran out and snatched the baby up and ran into the deep woods. They stayed hidden until she had to catch her ride back to California. They were hidden out on the Jim Ridge when the baby got to crying. They knew it was hungry, but they had no bottle. They could not go to ask their daddy what to do because they did not know if the mother had left.

They decided to go to a neighbor's house and tell her the truth and ask her about a bottle. Here came these children carrying their poor little baby brother, and he was crying. His mother had been breast feeding him. The neighbor was a sweet, compassionate mother of several children. When she heard their story she said, "Now don't you worry, I have been nursing this child of mine, but she is old enough to wean. I will wean her and nurse this baby."

So she weaned her child and continued nursing the little boy, and he called her Mother. She helped raise him. When he was older, he went to see his birth mother in California. He stayed a little while but came back home. Several of her children went to visit from time to time. Some stayed longer than others, but most came back.

Back in those days the mothers let the children nurse until they weaned themselves or until they were expecting another baby. These women always seemed happy and contented. It seemed the more children they had, the happier they were.

Old Age

One old fellow was getting so senile he couldn't remember how old he was. Some of the ladies thought they would go talk to him and perhaps help him remember something that might give them a clue.

After talking about old times and things they remembered, they could not even get a clue from him. One lady decided to ask, "Rass, how old are you?" He replied, "Well, if it will help you ladies any, I feel as old as hell." Always after that, when someone asked "How old are you?" if persons did not want to tell their age, they said, "As old as Rass."

Influenza

In 1918, the terrible influenza epidemic swept around the world killing more than 20 million people. Apparently it was 1920 when it swept into Cataloochee. Eldridge Caldwell was at the Round Bottom logging camp.

His parents, Hiram and Lizzy, both took the flu. Hiram sent someone to bring Eldridge home to take care of them. He came home as fast as he could to find them so sick neither one could get up. There was only a small fire and no wood in the house. He hurried to bring in more and made a big fire. Then he made them some tea and potato soup and fed them. As soon as he could leave them, he found another young man (I forgot who) who was not sick. They went from house to house, to build fires and make tea and soup for the sick. And nearly all the people were so weak and sick they had to prop them up in bed to feed them. He went up on Shanty Mountain to see about Uncle George and his family. They lived more than a mile from any neighbor. When he got there, he was quite relieved because Aunt Mag was up sweeping and saying it was the nastiest old disease in the world and how it nearly killed them. But there were families that lost two, three, or four members to influenza. Will Messer and Rachel lost two daughters in one week. Loretta had two children and expecting another when she got the flu. She went into labor and died, but they were able to save the two month premature baby. Loretta's sister who also died that week was named Vanalie. Another sister, Ollie, who was going to school in Newport, Tennessee also died during the epidemic.

There are many little graves with just a flat rock sticking up for a headstone. The reason for that was the smallpox, influenza or other epidemics were so contagious they had to bury the dead as soon as possible to keep the others from getting it. Those were terrible times.

Spring Tonic and Blood Letting

There were herbs for medicine, and most of the homemade remedies worked. Helen Hannah Trantham remembered her grandmother, Aunt Fannie Hoyle Hannah, mixed up sulphur and molasses every spring and made all the family eat some. She said it purified their blood. Aunt Fannie was not the only one to feed the family sulphur and molasses. It was practiced in lots of families, ours included.

Aunt Lizzie (grandma) and most of the folks of her generation, used to have "blood letting" in the spring, which was a common practice back them. They said a body's blood got too thick in the winter time, which caused them to feel sluggish. They used a straight razor to split a small place in their heel to let some blood run out. When they thought enough had run out they stopped it, and put a bandage on it.

When Homer Caldwell worked at a CCC camp, his son, Marshall, had asthma, and he had talked to another man at the camp about it. The man gave Homer some type of herb that was supposed to help the child. He brought it home and they made a tea of the leaves. Marshal's cousin, J.R., was spending the night with him. Marshall wouldn't drink it unless J.R. would; so J.R. took about a spoonful and Marshall drank about half a cup. Both of the boys went wild, plumb out of their head. It affected their speech and vision. Flora lit the lantern about two or three a.m. and took the boys to Jarvis Caldwell's house. He took them to the doctor but the doctor said it would just have to wear off. It finally did, but come to find out, they were supposed to crumble the leaves in a small container, set fire to it, and inhale the smoke. Marshall is still laughing about it.

Horse Saves Rider in 20s

People in Cataloochee treated their animals well and saw that they were well fed. In return the animals cared about their owners. In one instance, a man was drunk one cold winter night, and as he rode his horse on past a house, he passed out and fell off his horse. The temperature was hovering near zero. It was late, and the family in the house had gone to bed. They heard something pawing on their cement walk. The man and boys in the house jumped up, lit the lantern, and went to see what the strange noise was. It was a horse and he was telling them something. When they got close enough, they knew whose horse it was and wondered what happened and which way to go. While they were talking, the horse turned and went back up the road. They followed him, and there beside the road lay the drunk man. The man and his boys managed to lift him up and lay him across his horse. They took him back to their house. While they wrapped him in blankets and built a big fire, the wife made hot coffee. They had to pour it in him, his hands were so frozen, they could not bend to hold the cup. Finally, when they knew he was thawed and warm, they offered him a bed, but he said "no, just let me sleep here." They made him a pallet, put him on it, and covered him up. Next morning he was fine. He thanked them over and over, then went on home. If not for his neighbors and horse getting help for him, he would have frozen to death.–from Raymond Caldwell

Dog Saves Rider

When Eldridge Caldwell was a young man, he had gone to Waynesville and was returning to Big Cataloochee late at night. After he crossed the iron bridge, something in the woods spooked his horse, the horse snorted and reared up so suddenly it threw Eldridge out of the saddle but one foot was hung in the stirrup. The horse was frightened and was dragging him. He could not get the horse to stop. As always his ever faithful dog was with him. This was protection in case he passed a house where lots of dogs lived. They might try to attack his horse, but they laid low if another big dog was with the horse and rider. Here the horse was dragging this poor man by the foot which was broken, and he kept talking to his horse to quieten him, but he would not stop, at first.

Then Eldridge looked for his dog, but he was gone. He wondered where his dog was, and was really concerned about what had caused his gentle horse to act like this. Could there be a panther or wildcat nearby? He could only hear the rippling of the creek as it ran over the rocks. Then rustling of the leaves. Could it be the wind or was a panther stalking him? There was not enough light to see.

Finally the horse stopped for a brief time, long enough for him to get his broken foot out of the stirrup. He was in awful pain, with

Cataloochee Valley

no way to walk. He would just have to crawl on home.

Meanwhile his dog had realized his master needed help. He ran about three miles to where the family lived, barked and scratched furiously at the door until Hiram (Eldridge's father), who was ill, heard the dog. He knew immediately something had happened. He woke another of his sons, Dillard, who jumped out of bed, jerked on his clothes, lit the lantern, ran to the barn, got on his horse, and raced down the road to find his brother. The faithful dog got to him first. Dillard helped Eldridge on his horse and took him home, and his foot was taken care of.

Some years later, when Eldridge was riding in the mountains, his horse slipped and fell on him. He had a fine western saddle, which was deep, and he said he would have been crushed to death, if not for the well built saddle. This time his other foot was broken. This happened in late summer of 1927.

His foot was still in a cast when their house caught fire. All he could do was go on his crutches out to the wood yard where he sat on a log and held the baby. (This writer was the baby, only two months old.)

Caldwell Fork

To reach Caldwell Fork in Cataloochee you go across the footlog above the rangers station, near the campground and walk 3-3/4 miles. To get to the area called the Deading you have to walk five miles or more, crossing the creek fifteen times. That is where Thad and his family lived, in a two story log house that his father, Big Jim Sutton, had built. The park service had that house and others burned. Everybody was bitter about it, especially Big Jim and his wife, Pearl Rogers Sutton.

They never had a road up there that a vehicle could travel on. It was always walk or ride a horse. There was a rough old wagon road you could drive a two-horse team and wagon or a small sled on.

After the park got it, they built a narrow road for the ranger to go by jeep.

Thad talked of his mother being sick and needing a prescription refilled. He walked all the way to Waynesville, got the

Big Jim Sutton and his wife, Pearl Rogers. Photo Courtesy of Floyd Sutton.

medicine and spent the night with his cousin Bob Sutton in Waynesville, then walked back home the next day. He knew how to go across the Purchase (mountain) which made the distance shorter, but it was still two full days of walking.

Thad was born and raised on Caldwell Fork. He and his family moved out in 1936 due to the restrictions the park had imposed on people. Thad said there was a lot of good farm land on Caldwell Fork. He rented one hundred acres from John Mull Caldwell, up near the Deading and John had another one hundred acres farther down the mountain. Ira McGee had a good farm there. He moved out and sold it to Chris Long. Jim Evans and Carson Messer had good farms, too. Thad said, "Carson Messer built his house up against a bank where a two inch stream of water came out of the bank into his house, then ran out under the house. He was the only one with running water," Thad laughed. He said, "Lige Messer had a good farm. He always carried a walking stick with a cup on the top, so he could get a drink of water wherever he wanted to."

Thad said he was back up on Caldwell Fork a few years ago. It was all in woods. He could not have recognized the places he had plowed so many times, if not for the old rock fences. They

Cataloochee Valley

Big Jim Sutton and his pet deer. Photo Courtesy of Floyd Sutton.

were four feet thick, four feet high and 150 feet long. He did not know who had made these fences, but he knew the rocks had been moved off the land when they had cleared it to farm.

Thad had gone to school with Anderson Messer, son of Carson, but had not seen him for seventy years. Then he came to the Cataloochee Reunion a few years back. "Now he comes back to see me every year. He lives off down in Tennessee, somewhere, Leona, Tennessee, I think," Thad said.

Thad said fifteen or twenty years ago, a man came from South Carolina and wanted to know how to get to a cemetery on McGee Branch. He had bought a tombstone to put on a grave. He couldn't remember who the man was. Thad is now close to eighty years of age and has a very good memory considering that. The interview was conducted January 24th, 1996.

Thad told of his parents. Big Jim Sutton married Pearl Rogers, daughter of Herman Rogers of Stamey Cove. Her mother died when she was two years old. Jim and Pearl had eleven children, all born at home except one. They were delivered by Granny Annie Sutton, a midwife, who was very good at it, and delivered for anyone, wherever she was needed.

Their last child was born when the mother was forty-nine years old. As the time drew near she was having problems. They decided she should go to the hospital for this one when the time came. There had been a really big rain, and the creeks were up and swift at the fifteen crossings. Then she was having labor pains. Some of the children were sent to tell the neighbors. There were eleven men who came on horseback to help get her off that mountain. They filled the wagon with shucks and lots of straw. They loaded her in the wagon and started down the mountain. At the first creek these men on horseback tied ropes to the upper side of the wagon to hold it, to keep it from being washed down stream. The water was so swift, the wagon almost got away from them, even though they had the ropes wrapped around the saddle horns and the horses were doing their best to help hold it. They finally made it through that first creek, but they had to figure out some other way.

These wise men quickly devised another plan to safely cross the other fourteen times with this woman in labor. They put a lead horse several feet out in front of the wagon and team. They attached a long rope to the lead horse, running back under the wagon to another horse several feet behind the wagon. This way the lead horse could go through the creek, get up on the ground and have solid footing, while the wagon was being pulled by the team in the water. The horse in back had solid footing on the ground and with all the men on horses, with ropes attached to the wagon, managed to keep it from being swept downstream. This had to be done fourteen times to get her safely down to the road, where a car was waiting to take her to the hospital. Dr. Kirkpatrick delivered the baby, who they named Solomon for his great grandaddy Sutton and Kirk for Dr. Kirkpatrick. Both mother and son were fine.[1]

Helping Neighbors

Thad remembered how he used to go to the Nellie Post Office and General store. Maybe he would buy horse shoes and nails and other articles that would make his load heavy to carry back up the steep mountain. It was was less steep to go up by Jim Caldwell's

---

[1] Interview with Thad Sutton August 10, 1995

Cataloochee Valley

Barn built by Levi Colwell, later moved by his grandson Eldridge, who added more stalls and the hay loft.

on Fork Ridge then back across, up to the Deading where they lived. He said when he got up to Jim's, one of Jim's sons Burl, would say, "Just get on this horse, I'll load you up. Take your stuff on home, when you get there, just turn him loose and he will come on back home." Well, the horse went back home. I always appreciated it. And another thing, if Burl passed someone's house and saw little boys trying to cut wood while their daddy was working away from home or maybe on a cattle drive, Burl would stop and cut up a big pile of wood for them. "Yes," Thad said, "everyone wanted to help each other in anyway they could."

Farming

Long before daylight, the man of the house would get up and build a fire in the cook stove and wake up his wife to cook breakfast while he went to the barn to feed the horses. He would have to light a lantern to see how to get to the barn and feed the horses because they needed to eat and let their food digest before they were harnessed up and started a hard day's work. The man would go back to the house to a big hearty breakfast, then by the crack of dawn, be ready to start farming or whatever work was necessary.

Thad said, "We tended (farmed) about forty acres, and the rest was in woodland and some pasture." The farm work was awful hard. We had only crude homemade implements, a bull tongue plow, which was a regular plow with a point about the size of a man's hand. When the plow hit a root, it would bounce back and the mule or horse pulling the plow would back up too, right on top of me. My grandaddy Sol Sutton was a good blacksmith. He welded a very sharp point on that plow. The sharp point cut right through the small roots, making the plowing much easier. The plow handles were made of either oak or locust, the toughest wood."

Thad said, "They used a mattock to grub out stumps and roots in the new ground. Another implement they made was a maul. This was a long heavy stick sawed off at a knot, leaving enough of the limb for a handle. This was used to drive stakes in the ground or drive gluts (or wedges) in logs when they were splitting them for fence rails or splitting shingles. It had to be tough wood to take all that pounding. He said dogwood was best. Gluts were also made of oak or locust. Then he talked about making sleds to haul their crops on. Most of the sled runners were made of sourwood. We could climb the tree and find a limb that had grown out a ways then curved up. We had to find a matching pair, or as near matching as possible, then we nailed the bed on it.

"After we got the ground plowed, the big rough chunks of dirt had to be broken up. We did that with a metal disk harrow pulled by two horses. The harrow had sharp wheels that cut the clods. We had a flat double harrows with steel teeth sticking down in the ground. These harrow were attached to heavy six by eight timbers and pulled over the plowed ground with horses. This worked the dirt up well and soft so the crops could grow and we could hoe it. But first before the ground was turned under (plowed with a bull tongue or turning plow), we hauled all the manure out of the barn and spread it on the ground, along with corn stalks. That was to enrich the soil and make the crops grow."

Thad remembered the smallpox epidemic, which struck two

Cataloochee Valley

of his brothers. Big yellow blisters popped out on the bottom of their feet. They used needles to release the fluid. He slept between his brothers but never got smallpox. Later when he was in the CCC camp, they gave shots for smallpox. His was ineffective, and after three shots they quit.

Thad talked about native American chestnuts, the best nuts in the world. "We ate them raw or roasted them. There were always big crops and good money crops, too. One year me and my brother found these two big chestnut trees, close together with a gulley between them." He said they took bushel hampers and shovels up there and shoveled up sixty bushels of chestnuts. They had to make trip after trip to carry them to the wagon road. They loaded the wagon, came off that mountain, crossing the creek fifteen times then on up Cove Creek mountain to the top. It took all day with a loaded wagon. All the people coming up there with loaded wagons had to spend the night, sleep on the ground, and go on into Waynesville the next day. They sold the chestnuts for $3 a bushel–$180. "Boys we's rich!" he exclaimed.

I had an interview with Floyd Sutton, son of Essie and Thad. The Sutton family had lived on Caldwell Fork in Cataloochee, moving away in 1936. After the park service took over, they tried to stay on, but like everyone else, they couldn't make a living due to restrictions.

When Floyd Sutton was eight years old, he went to live with his grandmother, Granny Annie. She lived on Caldwell Fork, too. She was a widow. He went to help her with the farm work. He stayed with her until he was twenty-one years old. Floyd said stacking hay to make a nice uniform hay stack was not easy to do. The way some people stack them, one leans over in one direction, another one in some other direction; all crooked, but not Granny Annie. She could stack hay as straight as any man, better than some.

Granny Annie was a mid-wife and delivered lots of babies. She rode a horse and carried saddle bags with her supplies in them. He said, "She would go day or night no matter what the weather was."

Floyd said, "There were about one hundred people living on

Caldwell Fork before the park took over." Granny Annie knew the old-fashioned remedies and lots of people came for her to help them. She could stop blood if someone got cut. She would read a verse from the Bible and say something, and they would soon stop bleeding.

If someone got burned, she could take the fire out. Floyd had an injury to his leg, which set up blood poisoning. Granny put fat meat on it and bound it up. She cured him because the fat drew out the poison and infection. For croup, she made them take a spoonful of groundhog grease. It tasted awful, but it sure helped.

She made a salve of mutton tallow, sulphur, and crushed buds of a tree called Balm of Gilead. It was good for cuts and bruises. If someone got a broken bone, they tried to pull it straight as possible, then use oak splints and wrap it until it healed. Sometimes they didn't get it lined up properly, and the leg healed a little crooked.

Floyd said one of his calves broke her leg, and he used the oak splints and wrapped it real well. Today the cow is walking around just fine.

He said Granny Annie could cure thrush (blisters in a baby's mouth). Sometimes they would get so bad, the baby couldn't take its bottle. After several trips to the doctor, they took the child to Granny to cure. She opened the child's mouth and blew in it, said a verse in the Bible, and next day he was taking the bottle.

Thad Sutton talked about all the hard work he had done when he lived on Caldwell Fork. At fourteen years of age, he helped survey the fifty-five miles of the mountain tops surrounding Big Cataloochee and Caldwell Fork.

He remembered splitting chestnut rails for fences. They had to cut the tree then cut it in ten foot lengths and drive wedges in each end and pound away with a go-devil (eight pound hammer) or a wooden maul, first on one end then the other until it was split. This had to be done over and over to make enough rails.

The rails were used to build fences near trees. If a tree should fall on it, there would be a short section broken. They could repair it at no cost but with plenty of hard work. If they had a woven wire fence and a tree fell on it, then there was a long section of it to

Cataloochee Valley

Jessie McGee house on Caldwell Fork. Later lived in by John Caldwell (son of Levi) who married Nicie McGee. Last to live here was Thad Sutton, wife Essie and family, until 1936. Photo Courtesy of GSMNP.

replace. Thad said he only got twenty-five cents a day for splitting the rails. His young son said, "Tell us another joke." Of course he could not realize how scarce money was in the depression. He said having to carry the rails up hill was tougher than splitting them.

When he was older, he worked with the CCC camp. They paid $30 a month. Then he was made a leader and received $45 a month. The great depression was still on. He considered that he was real lucky to have a job. But in spite of the hard times, he still longed for the good ol' days. He was getting all choked up with emotion and said, "There is a real good country song about country roads lead me home." Big tears poured down his face, a sob caught in his throat; he had to stop a minute to compose himself so he could go on talking of all the roads he had walked in Cataloochee that were so dear to him.

Thad Sutton talked about helping survey for the railroad for the logging companies. He said they surveyed from Palls Gap to the Wooly Head of George Ira Creek, on around to Shanty Mountain, then to Cove Creek about fifty-five miles, but the government stopped them. This railroad would have circled Big Cataloochee on top of the mountains. There were law suits but the government was only paying $3 per acre for many thousands of acres to the lumber companies, as remembered by Thad.

Reminiscing

Eldridge Caldwell related fond memories of growing up in Cataloochee. Later in life there were good times and tragic times. He spoke of playing Indian ball with the Indians who came to show the Cataloochee boys how to play their stick ball game. He said it was fun, but too rough. The roughest games he ever knew of, the Cherokees won.

Always on Sunday after church there would be a large crowd to eat dinner. All afternoon the children and young folks played games. Pitching horseshoes was a favorite. Town ball was their ball game. It was similar to baseball, but the girls could play it too. As he grew older a group of them would ride horses and picnic and play other games and swim in the creeks.

The young men liked to train young horses to ride or work.

Eldridge Caldwell said, "Sometimes on a moonlit night these young boys would get together and ride steers to see who could stay on the longest. Oh, it was exciting all right, but them steers could buck you off. You sure knew you had been throwed hard on the ground!

"We weren't supposed to ride the steers; so we would light our lantern and say we were going possum hunting. We got away with it a while, but we got caught and thought we would be lawed. So we didn't do that again.

"Everybody went courting on horseback. Big groups of us would ride up to the musterin' ground on Cove Creek Mountain or up to Spruce Mountain tower. We always took food for a picnic and had good times. We would play tricks on each other or tell clean jokes, and sometimes have horse races.

"We could catch all the fish we wanted and carry them on a forked stick. Once when the string of fish got too heavy, we put them in the edge of the creek with a big rock on the stick. We thought they would be safe. We were fishing close by and caught a few more. We decided that was enough.

"When we picked up our string of fish, half of them were gone,

Cataloochee Valley

Pearl Valentine, Mail Carrier and future wife of Eldridge Caldwell. This picture was taken just before she married when she carried the mail from Little Cataloochee to Big Cataloochee. Photo Courtesy of Ken Caldwell.

and we got the glimpse of a snake, which had eaten most of them.

"Most everyone my age liked to dance. We square danced and did the Virginia Reel, sometimes round danced.

"We had a big time, sometimes had a little whiskey to refresh ourself between dances. At other times we had cake walks and box suppers."

Then he courted over on Little Cataloochee. Pearl Valentine was his sweetheart, since he met her at a bean stringing, then at the Post Office. While they were courting, his father, Hiram, passed away in 1922. A year later he married and brought his bride to live with him and his mother, Aunt Lizzie.

Pearl Valentine and her sister, Ressie, had moved from Tennessee with their mother Emma, to help take care of their brother Claude's children. Ressie went to school in Little Cataloochee. Pearl had attended the Caton Grove School in Tennessee. When the children of Loretta and Claude got big enough for Emma and Ressie to take care of, Pearl went to Newport, Tennessee to work in her Uncle Press Valentine's hotel for a while. When she came back to Little Cataloochee and was a substitute mail carrier Eldridge saw her and talked with her. She liked him and pretty soon the neighbors, Mercius Hall and his wife Alice, gave a big bean stringing party and invited the people from Big Cataloochee. This was customary and many people attended. They all pitched in stringing the beans, laughing, and talking until it was lunch time. Then the Halls served up a feast, all kinds of good food. After they ate they sat around and finished the beans. Then the music, fun, and games started and ended up with dancing. This was how boy met girl in those days in Cataloochee. Or it may have been corn-shucking or other work where they got together and started courting. Pearl and Eldridge courted for about two years. They got married in 1923 at the courthouse in Newport, Tennessee and lived at Big Cataloochee until March, 1934.

They were happy, and their first child was a little girl named Nell. Three years later they had another child, named Hattie (after Eldridge's sister). When she was only eighteen months old she became very sick. Eldridge rode his horse as fast as he could to Waynesville to get Dr. Able to come see what he could do for this child. Eldridge hired a nurse, Mrs. Stiles, to come and stay to help take care of the baby. Dr. Able drove his car and brought the nurse with him. This was 1928.

The doctor examined the baby and told them she had double pneumonia and also scarlet fever. He said it was doubtful that she would live. Mrs. Stiles stayed on, caring for the baby until the child finally got better; she had lost a lot of weight. The skin peeled off her feet and hands.

They noticed that every time they cooked meat, this baby would cry and scream and gnaw her fist. They knew she was hungry because the milk and other food she was getting did not satisfy her. But they were afraid to feed her meat. Eldridge could not stand to see his child hungry; so he saddled up his horse and rode over to Waynesville again to explain to the doctor and ask his advice.

The doctor listened and then told him the child's body had been depleted of certain things she needed. He advised him to go back home and have them boil a piece of fat meat until it was falling apart, feed her a few tiny bites at first, then increase it a little every day until she quit crying for it. When he fed her, he laughed

Cataloochee Valley

The back of Eldridge Caldwell's house where he saw a coal fall off of the roof.

and said, "She smacked her lips like a little pig." She screamed and grabbed the spoon when he stopped feeding her. She loved the fat meat they fed her and soon began to gain weight and was a contented child.

A few months later tragedy struck. The first born child, Nell, became ill, running a high fever. Eldridge hurried back to get the doctor and the nurse again. The doctor examined Nell and discovered she had spinal meningitis, and there was little that could be done for her. She was only five years old, and she had been the sunshine of their life. Pearl was making Nell some new dresses for spring. She had finished one, and had another one that was almost finished. Nell had tried them on and was happy with her new clothes.

Now Nell was sick and dying, and nothing could be done. Pearl and Eldridge were crushed and heartbroken. Nell died January 4, 1929. They were expecting another child, who was born two months after they had to bury their first child. She was named Helen, and then in 1931 they had a son named Ken.

Even though Pearl lived to be ninty-one years old, in her last days she talked of Nell and how hard it was to give her up. Pearl kept that little dress of Nell's that she never finished, she never put it on either of her other two daughters when they grew to size five, but kept it in a trunk. Not long after we had moved to Maggie Valley, a neighbor sent someone to see if Pearl would make a dress for them to bury their little girl in. The depression was still on and people couldn't buy much of anything. Pearl took this little pale pink dress out of the trunk and finished making a row of deep pink rose buds across the top of the hand smocking. She sent the dress to those people. They were so pleased that they walked up and carried the little casket two miles to Pearl's house and set it on the front porch and opened it for her to see how beautiful the child looked in that dress she had made. They said it was the prettiest dress she ever had. Pearl was pleased too, for she knew she had done another good deed.

She worked in the church and community affairs, helped to get a lunch room in the Maggie Elementary School. She was an expert seamstress and an excellent cook. She helped with many church suppers and other needs.

House on Fire 1927

When you look at the Hiram Caldwell house, just think, it caught fire in November, 1927. How in the world did they get the fire put out? Certainly there was no fire department there. They did not even have running water or water hoses.

At the time, Eldridge and Pearl Caldwell, Eldridge's mother, Aunt Lizzie, Pearl's sister, Mae Miller, and her children Polly, about twelve years old, and her son Ernest about fourteen or fifteen years old, and this writer, a two month old baby, and Nell lived in this house. Eldridge's foot was broken, and he was on crutches, but as was customary he had built a big fire in the fireplace. There had been a lot of rain for several days and now this cold November day the ground had frozen with an icy glaze on it. After Eldridge had the fire going and he got warmed up, he went out on the back porch to shave. That is where is the shaving table and mirror were. Someone brought a kettle of hot water and fixed his shaving water for him, since he was on crutches and he could not do that.

He had himself propped up on the crutches and was about half finished shaving. As he was looking into the mirror, he

Cataloochee Valley

caught a glimpse of something falling off the house. He got over to the edge of the porch to see what it was. Well, he was just shocked because it was a coal of fire! "The house is on fire! The house is on fire!" he shouted.

He hollered for everyone to get out. Pearl told him to try to get out to the woodyard and sit on a log. She ran in the house, grabbed up the baby, told the Miller children to run as fast as they could to tell the neighbors. Eldridge had made it out to the woodyard and sat there in despair. Pearl took the baby and a quilt out to him. She said, "Here hold this baby. Wrap both of you in this quilt." And off she went running to get a long ladder that he told her was at the barn. As she ran across the footlog, a Mr. Price was running down the road to tell them he could see the roof of their house was on fire. He had been walking down the road and a young boy (Ernest Miller) came running past him hollering "fire! fire!" and out of breath he kept on running. Mr. Price ran down to the barn and got that big long ladder and helped Pearl carry it over to the house. Meanwhile Ernest had got to Charlie Ray Caldwell's (nearest neighbors) hollering "fire, fire! The house is on fire!" There were several men there, fixing to kill hogs. They dropped everything and came running to help. Polly had run across the field to Tommy Caldwell's, and here came a big group of people. Some chopped a hole in the ceiling to pour water on the rafters so they wouldn't burn. Some set the long ladder up on the edge of the roof where it was not on fire A man stood there, another a few feet below him, and another a few more feet away. They lined up all the way to the big branch where there was a trough made of two planks nailed together in a V shape. It had a big sluice of water running so swiftly, it would fill a big bucket immediately. They set up a bucket-brigade, passing buckets of water from hand to hand on up to the top of the ladder, where the water was poured on the flames. Some were carrying buckets of water, passing them up through the hole in the ceiling. The man in the attic was keeping the rafters and ceiling wet. They were successful in getting the fire put out.

The roof caught on fire because the roof was made of hand rived oak shingles which had been on more than twenty years.

The moisture from the nearby branch and many trees that kept it shaded had encouraged some moss to grow on the shingles. With the big fire in the fireplace some sparks had gone up the chimney and fallen and ignited the moss.

Now it was November and the roof was gone; it had to be replaced. This time it would be metal shingles. Eldridge got Jim Caldwell to measure it, then go into Waynesville and order the shingles and nails.

We don't know where the shingles were shipped from, but it would be two weeks before they could go back to get them. While they were waiting, all the frame work, some rafters and other damage was replaced and repaired, except a gable end on the top story.

It was time to go for the shingles, which would take three days. One full day to take the wagon with four horses pulling it empty. They hoped to get there in time to load the shingles before dark, so they could start back to Cataloochee as early as possible next morning. They knew they would do well to get as far as the top of Cove Creek Mountain and camp out for the night. It would take all day the third day, just to come down into the valley and up to Eldridge's house.

Now they had the shingles, and next morning early they started putting them on and they knew they would have to hurry because they could feel a snow coming soon. They had almost finished when the snow started. They had decided not to take the time to put the gable back on top. They just got the roof on in time, because it snowed for days afterwards. We don't know who the workmen were or who went for the shingles. We think that it was Jim Caldwell, his sons, and others. We just know that Eldridge had the broken foot and was on crutches and the house was saved.

Gold

Gudger told of a gold mine on Big Cataloochee. He said, "During the 20s some man came over there and somewhere between Creek George's place and Turkey George's house, he dug a really large hole into the mountain and had the mine in

Cataloochee Valley

Daddy Bryson wreck, Elkmont, Tenn. Photo courtesy of GSMNP.

operation. There was not enough gold to be profitable. The man finally abandoned it. Gudger said the last time he was there, there was still evidence of where the mine had been.[1]

Timber and Railroads

In 1927 it was estimated that there were 360,000,000 board feet of timber standing in the forests of Haywood County. Before that year the estimated value cut and sawed amounted to $200,000 annually. Some think this is too high, but possibly it is not too high. The North Carolina Park Commission has taken most of this stumpage and also some of the virgin tracts into the Great Smoky Mountains National Park.[2]

When the lumber companies discovered the big, fine virgin timber in the Cataloochee Township, and in Swain and Jackson Counties, they came in and bought up the mountains, and built a whole network of railroads. They built crude logging camps and hired everyone they could to cut and haul timber. Clay McGaha said people don't believe how many railroads were in these mountains.

[1] Interview with Gudger Palmer March 19, 1995
[2] Mr. W.C. Medford, The Middle History of Haywood Country. P. 22-23

Larry Caldwell confirmed that. When he was sixteen years old he was hired to help survey for a railroad to go from Cove Creek Gap on around to Turkey George Palmer's land. Larry says he thinks it was eighty-five miles. He said the miles really add up when you go down one mountain and up another, mountain after mountain. They were trying to build it on a one and a half percent grade. This track never got finished because they were in a law suit then with the government over sale of land for the national park. Larry thought the lumber companies only got fifty cents an acre for the thousands of acres they had; but they had put up a long hard fight with the government, and like everyone else they finally had to pull out.

Larry said the lumber companies had camps at Crestmont, at Big Creek, and one at Walnut Bottom six miles up from Big Creek. There were also camps at Round Bottom and in Swain and Jackson Counties, and their railroads were coming into the headwaters of Big Cataloochee, above Uncle Steve Woody's from Swain County. They came by way of Pin Oak Gap, out Beech Ridge Creek on to Indian Knob. There was a Ravensford Lumber Company at Smokemont above Cherokee. Suncrest had a large camp in Jackson County operated by the Sunburst Lumber Company, sometimes having 500 men working for them. Sunburst also had a large

Logging team at Elkmont. Photo courtesy of GSMNP.

Cataloochee Valley

operation on the Pigeon River. They also had a large sawmill in Waynesville on Richmond Creek in the area called the Band Mill Bottom. It included all the areas where Winn-Dixie and Taylor Motors are all the way around to Shoney's and all the way up to the old road into Waynesville, Highway 276.

The trains brought the logs there to be sawed, stacked to dry and to be shipped. The Sunburst Lumber Company had a railroad in the Black Camp Area and were planning to build out through Polls Gap to Woody Creek on to Spruce Mountain and Brushy Gap. Sunburst had a big sawmill up on the Pigeon River. There was also a sawmill at Big Creek, which shipped sawed lumber to Tennessee.

All of this timber operation was going on in the early twenties and maybe a little before. It was late twenties when they started in Cataloochee, but they were stopped in a year or so by the park service.

When logging was done with horses, there was not much damage to the surrounding timber. Larry said today (1996) there is no sign that it was ever logged. But where the lumber companies came in with railroads built on top of the mountains and ridges, they had overhead skidders, which could reach down the side of the mountains and pick up the large sawed logs, then lift them onto the train. In doing that, they broke off and crushed every tree and everything in their path. Nothing was left standing that was over six feet high. Taking only the largest trees, they left an awful mess of brush and limbs. Larry said there is still evidence of all their destruction. That was the reason the park decided to make it a National Park, before it was ruined. [1]

Whiskey

Before prohibition, there was not much of a market for whiskey in Cataloochee or elsewhere. They only made what they needed. The first settlers brought their know-how from the old country for making their spirits, and it was said to be so fine and pure that a man could drink a glass full of it and next morning get up feeling fine, with no hangover at all. They used it for several ailments as well as drinking.

---

[1] Interview with Clay and Larry Caldwell, March 16, 1996

I have been told they could not have worked as hard as they did, if they had not had the whiskey. When they got tired they could go over and take a big drink, rest a few minutes, then get back to work. There was so much work to do they could not spare the time to get drunk. It was used as a remedy for several ailments. Jud Palmer spoke of his grandfather, Turkey George Palmer, and his father, Charlie Palmer, using whiskey to doctor the kids when they got sick. The whiskey was poured in a cup, then a match struck to it. That burned the alcohol off. Jud said, "What was left was drunk by whoever was sick. You know that was like penicillin, but we didn't know it then. We just knew it would help us."

Whiskey was used for toothache, especially if the tooth had to be pulled. It was used for all sorts of pain. If someone got bit by a poisonous snake, and if they could hold a bottle of whiskey to the bite, it would draw out most of the poison. A man got bit on his little finger, he turned a bottle of whiskey up over his finger, and as he sat there with his finger in the bottle, he could see the whiskey turn green. Later the end of his finger turned black. In about a year it fell off at the first joint, but he considered he was lucky because he was up on a mountain by himself when he got bit.

Hiram Caldwell had gone to Waynesville one day. He had left Big Cataloochee before daylight so he could get there and back in one day. After he had transacted his business, he was on his way back up Cove Creek mountain. The temperature suddenly dropped and fog moved in, and it was getting dark. The farther up the mountain he went, the thicker the fog got. Finally he could not see the road anymore. He thought if he just let the horse go where he wanted, that by instinct the horse could find his way home. The horse was walking slowly. Hiram felt sure he was taking him home, but about that time the horse stopped. When Hiram put his hand out, there was a big limb, and he knew they were both lost in the woods. He got off the horse and tied him to the tree he had stopped by. The fog was so thick that he had no idea of where he was, and he was freezing. His overcoat and his beard were wet and freezing in ice. The only thing he could do was to walk around and around the tree to keep his blood circulating. He had a flask of whiskey in his saddlebags. When he got so cold he couldn't stand it any longer, he took a drink of the whiskey and kept walking all night long, around and around that tree. It was a long, miserable night. Finally, about daybreak the fog started to rise barely enough to see. He was able to go home. He told his family he would have frozen to death if he had not had the whiskey.

Hiram always kept a half-gallon of whiskey in the closet. He took two tablespoons of it before breakfast every morning. He said it made his food digest. They say that's all he ever drank, and that he did not make it, but had someone who could furnish it when needed.

It was passed down through the family to me, that in the early days, when they went to the fields to work that they would carry a water bucket full of whiskey and a dipper. This would be set in the shade and when they were exhausted they could refresh themselves with it and get right back to work. Two older men have told the same story.

A businessman from Waynesville came over the Cataloochee and found what fine whiskey they made. He sent his friends some in New York, and then there was a big demand for it. It had been served at some of New York's finest parties; also in Washington, D.C.

Since there was a big demand, they would pay big prices for it. This was after prohibition.

There was a woman who became a widow with no means of support for her and several children. Two or three of the boys were big enough to help her make whiskey (a very hard job). This was the only way she could raise her family.

The same man from Waynesville was known to be somewhat dishonest. He arranged to buy some whiskey from the widow. After they got it loaded in his car, he said, "I'm going on up the road to get some more. I'll pay you for it, when I come back." She pulled a sawed-off shotgun out from under her big, long apron. She said, "If you don't pay me, you won't go up that road." Needless to say, he was glad to pay her immediately.

There was another woman whose husband had died, leaving her with four children to raise. In those days there was no help available, no social security, no welfare, nothing. Usually some of the family would take some of the children to raise or they would have to go to an orphanage. In this case two of the boys were sent to Cataloochee to live with their grandfather and grandmother.

The oldest boy felt like he should earn money to help his mother and the smaller children. When he was about seventeen years old, he talked to one of his grandfather's renters there on the farm, who told him, "Come help me make liquor. They say them folks in New York will pay big money for this good whiskey we can make." He said, "Son, we can get rich." The boy knew he would be in big trouble if his grandfather found out, but he knew his mother was having a hard time and needed the money, he decided to risk it. "That was awful hard work, and we were farming, too," he said, "but we managed."

"We had found the perfect place to hide our still while we operated it. There was a waterfall with a cave in behind it. We could go in right beside the waterfall. It was tough to carry all our supplies up that mountain. We had to build a furnace. We used rock. We had to hang a lantern and have it lit to see what we were doing. The corn had to be soaked in water to sprout, then had to be coarse ground, put in water and cooked and stirred. You had to keep stirring. The only thing handy that we did not have to carry up that mountain was the water. The waterfalls were real handy. After the corn and water is cooked, let it set a few days until it ferments, cook and stir, and let it alone to ferment some more. But we had to go up every day to stir. Then it cooked some more when it was ready to run through the copper tube (called a worm). We had barrels to catch it in. We had cases of half gallon glass jars. We poured the whiskey in the jars and sealed them. We had to carry it part of the way down the mountain, then put it on the sled to get on down the mountain to the wagon. We placed our cases of whiskey in the wagon bed, then put in a big load of apples, which covered our whiskey. We told grandpa we were going to sell the apples.

"It took one whole day to get to the top of Cove Creek with that heavy loaded wagon. We slept on the ground, same as everyone who hauled a load up that mountain. That was as far as you could go in one day with a load.

Next day we went on down the mountain, on into Waynesville, arriving about dark. There was a livery stable on Depot Street. (It is now attorney offices.) This was where everyone traveling came

Cataloochee Valley

to feed their horses and leave them for the night, and to unload produce or whatever they had brought to sell. When we got there, it was dark enough to unload the apples without anyone seeing what we had in the wagon. The same man who had bought whiskey from the widow, came to the livery stable and paid for the whiskey. He arranged to get it shipped to New York by rail. Of course he tasted the whiskey before paying for it. He said, "Boys, this is good stuff, better than anything they can get up there."

This young man was quite proud to have this money for his mother and the young children. He soon went to visit her in the small town where she lived. He had made up a story about where he got the money, but he couldn't fool her. She made him tell her where he got the money. She and his grandfather put a stop to his enterprise. He laughed and said, "That was the last time I ever fooled with it. It was too much hard work. I'd rather farm."

There were many who did not make whiskey or even allow it in the house, but most of the men would take a drink. Farming and raising livestock was easier than making whiskey, and there was no danger of being sent to jail. Those who had enough land and were well established did not make whiskey, but there were others who had to make it to survive.

There was another family that moved into Cataloochee as renters. After years of hard work, they bought a small farm and were happy and doing well. Then came the word the government wanted their land. They would condemn it and pay what they thought it was worth. But it was not near what it was actually worth. That was unbelievable. No one wanted to leave this place. Most had never lived anywhere else.

Finally, they realized that they must leave. This man who had worked so long and so hard to own his homeplace, knew they would never pay him enough to replace it. They had already sent men in to evaluate their property. Everyone felt cheated. He decided the only way to own another place was to make whiskey, even though it was risky. The revenuers were always coming over there looking to cut down someone's still. A few had been caught. He would just have to outsmart them.

The man got his still set up where he thought it to be safe. He sent one son along the road up Cove Creek. He was to watch for any stranger who came down the mountain. If he saw one, he was to fire three shots in the air, rapidfire. His daddy was on an opposite mountain and could hear the shots and immediately put out the fire because the smoke would have been a tell-tale sign. As soon as he got the fire out, he hurried down off the mountain, brushing out his tracks. One of the other boys would hitch the horse to the plow. The man came down and started plowing, just like that was where he had been working all day. When they were forced out of Cataloochee, they had enough money to buy another farm with the money he had made and the small amount the government paid them. He also put some of his children through college.

One man said he hauled his still out in a truck covered well with hay.

Not everyone was so lucky. There were many stills cut down by the revenuers. Sometimes they caught the operators of these stills, but most of the time they got away. It was a big loss when stills got chopped up or hauled away. The stills were made of copper. It was expensive. They bought big sheets of it, then had to construct the still or have someone do it for them.

If the man was caught and sent to prison, leaving his wife and children at home, usually one of his brothers and their wives would move in with her and help out with all the work until he was released. Absolutely everyone helped each other anytime they were in need.

One man had a small still, just to make whiskey for his own use. He didn't drink very often but when he did, he would be drunk four or five days. His wife got tired of him lying around drunk while she had all the work to do. She had several children, the cows to milk, crops to make, and cooking and washing to do.

She started watching which way he went. She saw he went up a trail where logs had been pulled off the mountain. When he came back she could smell the whiskey on his breath. She didn't say a word about it, but she had a plan working. When her oldest son came home from school, she told him to come with her. They went up the same trail and across Deer Lick Creek. The son wondered why his mother was carrying a double bit axe. He

Cataloochee Valley

Arriving at the Caldwell's house in the twenties.

thought they would get some stove wood. As soon as they crossed the creek, she told him to wait there. She went on into a laurel thicket. He could hear banging and clanking of metal. Then he knew his mother was cutting down his father's still. After that, his father straightened out and did not drink again. He later became a deacon in the Baptist Church.

Judge Alley wrote, I repeat: there are comparatively few moonshiners and drinking is by no means as universal in the mountains as it has been in the cities of this state and others!

Paul Woody remembered when some of the park surveyors were way back on a mountain on Little Cataloochee, someone came to their house to get help. One of the surveyors had fallen and broken his leg. Paul's father, Carl, said yes he would go get the man and bring him out on a mule so he could be taken to the doctor by car. But first Carl went by a neighbor's house to get some whiskey, for he knew the man would be in great pain. It was about 1 a.m. when he got to the surveyor. He asked the man if he took a drink. The man said no. Carl asked if he was in pain. The man said, "Oh yes." Carl told him, "If you drink some of this, it will ease the pain," so the man drank it. When they got down into the settlement where someone had a car, he said to Carl, "How much do I owe you?" Carl said "It's no cost

Ola Messer Palmer, daughter of the late Will and Rachel Messer at the Big Cataloochee Reunion 1993. Ola Post Office in Little Cataloochee was named after her. She now lives in Hickory, N.C.

to you, but if the government pays it for you, it's $10." Soon after that he received the $10.

The Model T

In 1929 or 1930 Jarvis Palmer bought a Model T Ford, but couldn't drive it. He got out in the pasture in back of the house, got it started and began circling around and around and headed toward a big pile of cinders. He began to yell, "Whoa! Whoa!" When it got stopped, he got out and said he would not try to drive it again. Uncle Harley learned how to drive well enough to drive us to church and back without wrecking us. We kept it about two years then sold it.[1]

Post Offices

Talking with Gudger Palmer, he said the first post office was in Young Bennett's house. Then there was one at Frank Palmer's. He had a store near the iron bridge and the post office was in it. The third post office was in the Jarvis Palmer house (which now houses the small museum). Aunt Maria Palmer was the postmistress, and it was called the Cataloochee Post Office. It was in operation several years, along with the fourth post office, called Nellie.

---
[1] As told to Dr. Roy Carroll by Jarvis Linton Palmer, Jr.

Cataloochee Valley

Nellie Post Office and general store, Aunt Milia operated the Post Office, and Uncle Dillard operated the store. An old Indian passing through painted the sign, making the N backward. Aunt Milia thought it was unique and left it as a tribute to the Indian. Photo Courtesy of Gudger Palmer.

Sometime later the Cataloochee Post Office was discontinued. The Nellie Post Office was named after a daughter of Turkey George Palmer. It was located just below the Palmer's Chapel. The post office was in one side of her general store. It was in operation from the early 1900's until June, 1937. The park had come in and many of the people had left. Aunt Milia closed her store and left on June 8, 1938. Gudger Palmer had the last letters postmarked there.

Postage to send a letter was two cents. Later the postage to send a letter was three cents. A post card was one cent. The first class mail was carried in a big bag made of tough cloth. It was three or four feet long. It had a leather strap attached to it. The mail was put in and a lock put on. Only the next postmaster or postmistress had the key to unlock it upon arrival. Third class and other mail was carried in the same type of bag with a draw string.

The post office in Little Cataloochee was named Ola, for the daughter of Mr. and Mrs. Will Messer. They had a store there with the post office in it.

The mail was carried from the Ola Post Office before 8:00 a.m. to the Nellie Post Office for Aunt Milia to add any mail she had going out. Hub Caldwell was the carrier that we can remember. He would pick up the mail bags and throw them over his horse or in a buggy and go up over Cove Creek mountain, down the other side to the foot of Cove Creek, to the post office where he delivered the outgoing mail. Then he would pick up the mail for Cataloochee, ride back to the Nellie Post Office, a twenty-four mile trip. He would arrive late in the afternoon. Aunt Milia would sort the mail, all the Little Cataloochee mail would have to lay over night, to be taken to the Ola Post Office next morning by the carrier who had brought over the outgoing mail. This was called a star route. There were no mail boxes, so everyone had to go to the post office to get their mail and maybe buy something and socialize a while.

The mail carriers bid for a contract for a certain period of time. The lowest bid got the contract. One carrier was Mercius Hall on Little Cataloochee. He got the contract to carry the mail from Little Cataloochee to Big Cataloochee. He usually carried the mail on horse back, but in the early spring he needed to take his cattle out to range on the grassy balds, or needed to get crops planted or plowed, then he would send his daughter Ella to carry the mail as his substitute.

Later when she went away to school, Mr. Hall hired (my mother) Pearl Valentine to be his substitue. She was a close friend of Ella's and a close neighbor. She was about eighteen years old and loved riding the horse. She had no fear of riding alone through the woods about four or five miles. She had a horse named Little Mag, a good jumper, and she would just sail across logs or deep ditches.

Pearl was a beautiful young lady. She made her riding clothes,

Cataloochee Valley

with a nicely fitted jacket. One day when she brought the mail to the Nellie post office my father (Eldridge Caldwell) saw her. He had already heard how pretty she was with long flowing black hair, perfect complexion, and beautiful blue eyes. He would go to the post office to meet her, then ride his horse along with her part of the way. Later he gave her a ruby engagement ring, and about two years later they were married, in Febuary 1923.

Pearl and Ella had been friends, but Ella was older. When she passed away, we said Pearl (Mother) was the last of the pony express. She carried the mail 1920-1922.

Hub Caldwell also had a substitute. She was Myrtle Sutton (Fitzgerald). Hub had got a new horse to pull his buggy. One day when he was on his way back to Cataloochee, he got up about the Cove Creek gap when something spooked his horse. It ran straight down that mountain, never mind going around the curves, he just tore off, taking a short cut, down through the woods, brush, briars, and all. Hub couldn't stop him, the wheels flew off, he didn't stop. He had up his speed, dragging the buggy body, Hub and all. Mail flying all over the place, the buggy finally broke loose with Hub still sitting in it, and mail scattered everywhere. He gathered the mail up as best he could and walked on home several miles. There stood that horse with nothing left of his buggy except the shafts still hanging on the horse. This is just one of the funny stories told by two of Hub's sons, Ray and Gilmer, at the Cataloochee Reunion last year (1995).

The Little Cataloochee Post Office was in Will Messer's store. The stores usually sold about the same kind of merchandise. Uncle Dillard Caldwell operated the store at Nellie. Gudger remembered they sold horse shoes, horseshoe nails, mule shoes, snuff, tobacco, cloth by the yard, coffee, salt, sugar, men's work shoes and boots, twine, ropes, buckets, and candy. They had fifty-gallon drums of kerosene (called coal oil) and sold it for five or ten cents a gallon. This was used in the oil lamps for light.

Gudger remembered a tall glass showcase, taller than his head. He said it had women's hats in it. "Real fancy, with big plumes and things on them." In pictures, you will see they dressed very stylish, and the women wore hats to church, etc., but not for every day.[1]

---

[1] Interview with Gudger September 2, 1995

7

THE DEPRESSION

Civilian Conservation Corps Camps

When the stock market crashed in 1929, people lost millions of dollars. The manufacturing plants closed, there were no jobs, stores closed. Banks closed, many in bankruptcy. No one could get money to buy with. Many committed suicide over their great losses. People all over the United States were starving to death.

We were lucky to have President Franklin D. Roosevelt and others who saw our nation falling, come up with a plan that saved our nation. They set up the Civilian Conservation Corps. The CCC had camps all over the nation, most with makeshift housing and in some areas with tents to live in.

These CCC camps were set up by the government during the great depression to employ men of all ages. There were thousands of young men willing to work, who were lucky to get into the camps. They were paid $30 per month of which they could keep $5, and the remainder was sent to their family. Many people were starving, there were almost no jobs and very little money in circulation. The government had set these jobs up and these men were happy to get work. They earned their pay. The jobs saved many lives.

These men did hard, manual labor building bridges, roads, and trails in the park, building fencing in certain areas, building fire towers and part of the Appalachian Trail. In other

Cataloochee Valley

A typical Civilian Conservation Corps camp in the mountains. Photo Courtesy of Flora Burgess Caldwell Laws.

states they may have done other jobs. These men came from all over the U.S.A. Those from big cities did not know what a crow bar was or a peevy or any other tool they had not seen. All of these local fellows knew what these things were and how to use them.

Some of the poor fellows from the city had never been in the woods. They didn't know what to do, had no experience. These local fellows wanted to get them out of their way, so they would send two or three of the most helpless ones off the mountain down several miles to borrow a bank stretcher or some other made-up tool name. It was all a big joke. Lots of the young men were far from home and were sad and homesick. Daddy (Eldridge) had a heart of gold and would bring several home with him on weekends—until they got over being homesick and became used to our southern ways.

When the Civilian Conservation Corps was set up in Big Cataloochee in the 30s Eldridge Caldwell was a local leader. He was in charge of his crew, and one day when he had the men working along the road they discovered a thin vein of gold running through a large rock. It was somewhere near the iron bridge, but now it was government property and nothing could be removed.

Palmer's Chapel In The Early Thirties

The little white church sitting near the creek on the original road is Palmer's Chapel. People came for the service on Sunday riding on horses and hitched them to a hitching rail on the right side of the church, in the shade of the trees. Some people came in wagons loaded with children. Some came in buggies, and of course lots of people walked. Very few had automobiles in the 30s.

They all gathered in the church yard to visit with each other. Then the bell rang and echoed out over the valley, signaling time to go inside. They had Sunday school every Sunday and the circuit riding preacher came to preach the fourth Sunday of each month.

Aunt Lizzie Caldwell was the superintendent for twenty-six years. Aunt Eleanor Palmer was also superintendent at one time, as was Magnolia Caldwell Palmer and others. They sang in the choir, read the bible, prayed, and taught class.

Gudger Palmer remembers teaching the adult class at one time. He said, "They had literature from the Methodist publishing house. For the adults, they had quarterlies. And for the children, they had cards with pictures and words printed on them. The older adults class was on the right side of the pulpit, the young adults on the left for Sunday school class. There were two or three children's classes in separate places in the back. Gudger said, "They would sing, then teach Sunday school, then sing some more and pray lots. Jarvis Caldwell always stood up and led the singing.

"Jarvis Palmer could sing well, and he always came in on the bass part. There had been a Mr. Long at Cove Creek who came over and taught singing in the summer in the school house.

"There never was any complaint about all the Sunday school classes being taught at the same time," he said, "Seems like everyone paid attention to their teacher but no attention to the others."

Gudger recalled the funeral of his father, William Palmer (High Sheriff of Haywood Co.) as the only funeral he could remember being held in the Palmer's Chapel Church. Folks

Cataloochee Valley

usually had graveside services. But his father's was held there and Rev. Hall from the Hall place held the service, and (Creek) George Palmer got up and spoke of "what a fine man Mr. William Palmer was."

Then we talked about when church was over every Sunday how everyone gathered in the church yard to visit with each other again, maybe fifteen or twenty minutes, catching up on the news and inviting people to come and have dinner (noon) with them. Before they had a church bell (1929) the men sat outside talking about their cattle, crops, etc. until someone went outside to tell them it was time to go in.

Aunt Lizzie (my grandma) always wore her dresses down to her ankles and buttoned up to the neck like all the older ladies her age. She made all of her clothes. Her Sunday dresses were made of black satin or black taffeta, and she always made and wore a bonnet to match. She made her everyday dresses, bonnet, and apron of tiny checked gingham, navy and white or black and white. She even made her winter coats.

One very cold Sunday as she came from church, she met a woman who she knew was sick. She and her family had moved to Cataloochee a short time earlier as tenant farmers. This woman did not have a winter coat, and Lizzie took off her coat and gave it to the woman. She had some wool broadcloth at home to make another coat, which she did soon after that. (Info from Mrs. Pearl Caldwell 2-10-92.)

Gudger and I talked about how the circuit riding preachers always came on Saturday to spend the night, then preach and visit different families on Sunday, spend the night again, and go back over the mountain on Monday. Everyone felt it was an honor to have a preacher or school teacher spend the night with them. The Cataloochee people had so much good food, and always set a good table, but Sunday was special. Some used white damask table cloths, but the rest of the week, oil cloth.

Eldridge and Pearl Caldwell, as well as others, had large crowds to visit them on Sunday, partly due to the fact that Eldridge was a good barber and Sunday afternoon was the only day he cut hair. Pearl was an exceptionally good cook, as was her mother-in-law, Aunt Lizzie, and her sister, Mae Miller, all of

Palmer's Chapel

whom lived with them. Saturday was spent doing some extra preparation for the Sunday dinner, baking, getting in extra vegetables, and dressing chickens, etc. All of this in addition to fixing three hot meals each day. Everybody either went somewhere to have dinner or had a house full to eat with them. They all enjoyed it. Because there was so much work to do, they would be busy until next Sunday. They would not take much time to visit unless a neighbor was sick. Like the Bible said, work six days and rest on the Sabbath.

Pearl Caldwell (my mother) said that in the 30s with the terrible depression on there was very little money. They all had plenty of food because they farmed and raised livestock to sell, but people couldn't afford to buy much. They didn't have much money at Cataloochee and sometimes could not get enough to pay the preacher's salary. She said, "Jarvis Palmer was really a good man. Him and his family had a tourist business. Lots of doctors and people came there to fish, rest, and relax and enjoy the good food cooked by Velma and Maria. Even though business was off some, Jarvis could always come up with the balance of the

Cataloochee Valley

preacher's salary. And people really appreciated that. Everybody believed in paying the preacher, but just couldn't at that time.

Most all of the women went to church, and for this they dressed in the style of the day. Some ordered from Sears Roebuck and Co., but Dr. Carroll gives an account of two dressmakers living in Cataloochee in 1870. Of course, they taught their daughters everything they knew. By 1926-1930, many women had sewing machines and there were several fine seamstresses. They could buy cloth, real pretty Calico print, twenty-five cents a yard, and other material which cost more. All was available at the general store which was in the Nellie Post Office.

Saturdays were spent by most of the ladies and children getting shoes polished and dresses starched and ironed for Church. There was also some cooking done. They baked a cake, gingerbread or cookies. The frying chickens were killed and dressed, then kept in cold water in a crock or some vessel in the springhouse until time to fry. Sometimes there was a big fat hen cooked with dumplings. These Cataloochee women prided themselves on their cooking. They were glad to share their recipes with each other.

Praying was also an important activity that was shared. Aunt Lizzie was a very religious person. Before breakfast was served, everyone gathered in the living room (guests and all) while we read from the Bible and prayed on our knees. At dinner (lunch) after everyone was seated, she asked the blessing while everyone sat with bowed heads. After supper was finished and the dishes washed, everyone sat and listened to her read the Bible, and then we knelt for a long prayer.

After we moved to Maggie Valley, Aunt Lizzie had a place where she stopped to pray every time she went to the garden, and she took me with her. It was such a pretty place in the woods on the side of the road. It was cool and shady, with a log lying on the ground and covered with soft green moss. There was a small babbling branch running by. While she would kneel beside the log and pray, of course, I was kneeling too and listening. After her long prayer, she always finished with the words: "Dear Lord, when thou art through with us on earth, give us a home in heaven. We humbly beg and pray and ask it in your name, Dear Jesus. Amen."

She still prayed three times a day in the house. I asked her why she prayed so much. She said, "Well, after losing our home in Cataloochee it just seems like the load is too heavy to carry by myself. I have to ask the Lord to help me carry on." Her son Eldridge and his wife Pearl Valentine Caldwell lived with her and took care of her until she died at age eighty-two in 1937.

These Cataloochee people were serious about their religion; it was unifying and strengthening. They had compassion for each other and taught their children to be kind to each other, especially if a child had a physical ailment or an impediment of speech. They were taught to never make fun of the unfortunate, but to be sympathetic with them.

Indians Spend the Night 1930

Molly Running Wolfe and her husband, both Cherokee Indians, were walking through Big Cataloochee one day as they and others had for centuries. They were closest neighbors and friends of the Cataloochee people. Many of the first and second generation of Cataloochee people spoke the Cherokee language. This particular time it was about dark and there appeared to be a big winter storm coming in. Eldridge Caldwell was at his barn on the edge of the road when they came along. He was concerned about their having to go six more miles to their home. He invited them to spend the night. They said yes, but seemed to be discussing it as he hurried on to get his animals fed before the storm moved in. In the meantime they had decided to go on to Cherokee.

About a year later the same two Indians came upon Eldridge's front porch and sat down in the swing. Zeoma McGaha (Rich) happened to be there. She was sent out to ask what they wanted.

They said they felt very honored to have been invited to spend the night and now they were ready to do so. They were brought in and given supper and a room upstairs to sleep in. But after they ate, they sat in front of the fire with the family. They held the two little children, petted them, and warmed their feet by the fireplace. Molly talked at length, telling how she would go into the woods alone and have her babies. After Aunt Lizzie read the Bible and prayed, everyone went to bed.

Cataloochee Valley

Fox Hunt

Lots of times a group of young courting folks got together and went up on a mountain at night. They took some dogs to chase foxes. They lit their lanterns, took some food and maybe a guitar or several instruments to make music. They built a big fire and sat around on moss-covered logs, told stories, made music, and listened for the fox chase. Later when they got hungry they cooked over the fire. Listening to the hounds bay as they chased the fox was exciting for them. They probably had some refreshing drink too, but they enjoyed life.

Cataloochee Ranch

The Cataloochee Ranch was founded by Mr. Tom Alexander and his wife Judy. Tom was from Atlanta, Ga., and Judy was living in Asheville, N.C. at the time of their marrage. They came into Big Cataloochee to start a tourist business of horseback riding, fishing, and hiking. They soon made friends with the Cataloochee people, hiring a few to help get the place ready. They leased the Preacher Hall place at the lower end of the Valley below the iron bridge.

They learned the Cataloochee people made music and had lots of square dances. They invited them to come dance at the lodge. That was good entertainment for all. Some of the tourists learned to square dance, and everyone had a good time. The Alexanders got their business opened in 1933. Several families had moved out before that, due to strict rules imposed upon them by the park service. More were leaving all the time, and it was very sad to see them go.

Tom Alexander saw them leaving and expressed it so well in his book "Mountain Fever." Here is part of what he wrote:

> The Cataloochee Valley was occupied by nearly a hundred find old time mountain families. During the five years we lived there, we saw many fine mountain families, our good friends forced to move away as the federal government consolidated its holdings in the new National Park. It was heart-rending to see these excellent people,

As in the days of Tom and Judy Alexander's Ranch, the Cataloochee people make good music and dance. Hannahs, Messers, Tranthams, and Woods are pictured playing on the Jarvis Palmer house porch during a Cataloochee Reunion.

some crying, with their household goods piled in wagons, leaving their beautiful valley.

This miniature trail of tears was comparable to a disgraceful episode that had occurred a century earlier, when the Cherokee Indians were forcibly relocated from the southern Appalachians to Oklahoma.

The nineteenth-century Cherokee were driven from their ancestral mountain homelands because outlanders wanted to farm their lands. The white mountaineers were forced out because outlanders wanted to hike and fish in their mountains. Just as the government representatives deceived the Cherokees, state agents negotiating in the name of the national park, deceived the whites. They promised the Cataloochee people that they could live in the valley for the rest of their lives. But no sooner had the mountain people deeded their lands than officials began instituting restrictions that forbade hunting, grazing of livestock, cutting green timber, or planting gardens on sloping land. Fishing was only permitted under rigid restrictions. The Park Service, in short, made it impossible for these self sufficient people to earn a living in the only ways they knew, despite the "lifetime" tenancy.

Cataloochee Valley

Not long after taking over Cataloochee, for instance, they systematically and arrogantly began burning or dismantling the human dwellings, log cabins, frame houses, barns, smoke houses. These amounted to rare relics of nineteenth-century frontier life which had virtually vanished from America. A few buildings remain at Cataloochee. The Park Service is now belatedly trying to conserve the artifacts as valuable and interesting in their own way as the park's natural glories. The genuine character of an utterly self-sufficient human community is gone.

Over five generally happy years at Cataloochee, we too, grew increasingly hampered by Park Service restrictions and the year by year lease arrangement that discouraged us from improving and enlarging Cataloochee Ranch.[1]

The people in Cataloochee liked the Alexanders and welcomed them into the community. Mr. Tom had a warm personality and got along with everyone. Miss Judy was admired by the women because she could drive a car (very few Cataloochee women even tried, due to the steep crooked road), and Miss Judy did not act like a city slicker. She canned food and made gardens like they did.

The Alexanders operated the ranch for five years and were well-established when the park kept imposing stricter regulations making it impossible for them to keep operating their business. They had to move out, too.

Mr. Tom's book "Mountain Fever" is very interesting. It tells of the Alexander family, their life and times in Big Cataloochee, being forced out and eventually getting reestablished in the present Cataloochee Ranch.

Aunt Hattie and Uncle Verlin Campbell had a twelve hundred acre farm on the top of Fie Top mountain, three miles above Maggie Valley. The Alexanders bought this property from the Campbells, and named it Cataloochee Ranch. The property line joins the Great Smoky Mountains National Park. In the summer time they have trail rides, and ten-day pack trips into the park and into Cataloochee. In the winter they have skiing, fine dining, and other things.

---

[1] Material from the book "Mountain Fever" by Tom Alexander used courtesy of the publisher Bright Mountain Books, Inc.

8

THE PARK

Heartbroken

After 100 years of hard work clearing the wilderness and making it productive, the Cataloocheans heard that the government wanted this land for a park, but no one believed it. They thought it must be just a rumor. A park did not make any sense to them. It sounded foolish.

The Rev. Pat Davis was preaching at the Palmer's Chapel in 1928 and announced that the government would buy all the land in the area, to establish the Great Smoky Mountains National Park. Rev. Davis said, "You would be scattered all over the United States, and part of you will be here no more." None of the people could believe it, but the preacher had said it, so it must be true. They expressed utter amazement, then fell into depression and anger.

It was 1933, and a big crowd of our neighbors had gathered at our house. At first they did a lot of talking, then all of them got worried looking. Some started to cry. Some were sitting on the porch, on the steps, and others were sitting in the grass. They were so sad saying, "Where will we go? What will we do? We can't bear to give up our homes, our land, and our good neighbors. Oh Lord, what in the world will we do? We can't leave here."

I can still see them. Some of the women were large and held babies in their arms the tears running down their cheeks. Some dipped snuff which was running out the corners of their mouths

Cataloochee Valley

and down their chins. One woman was crying so hard, the big ball of hair on the back of her head was shaking and hair pins falling out. Lots of small children were playing all over the yard, but when they saw their mothers crying, they all started crying too. I was about five years old and crying also. I was scared for I had never seen adults cry. This had always been a happy place with people laughing and singing. Now it was a very emotional thing for everyone. The men shed silent tears. They soon moved over to the other side of the yard and continued to discuss their plight.

Most of the men were mad and wanted to fight anyone who would dare take all of this from them! They said, "NEVER! We can shoot better than any of them fellows. We know this country, every trail, every cliff, everything about it. We could cut them off at Cove Creek Gap and the only other way to enter the valley is to come in from the Tennessee side, across Mt. Sterling.

"We know them men over there on Mt. Sterling and down on Big Creek will help us fight. We have heard them government fellows want to take their homes and land too!" One man said, "Boys, I tell you. We can get us some dynamite and blow up the roads, yeah we could! We will, too! We don't need that outside world. Never, no Never; we will never give it up! We could never find a place as good as this. We have the sweetest, coldest water in the world." Some said they'd rather be dead than to leave here.

Another man said, "Boys, we'll show 'em this is our land. Us and our forefathers have earned it by the sweat of our brow. Why, our daddies and grandaddies would turn over in their graves if we give up! We'll show 'em. We ain't no cowards."

Daddy (Eldridge Caldwell) and a few others said, "Boys it won't work, no use to fight," but tempers flared. They were hot. They said, "Yes we will fight and fight to the end!" One said, "We have worked too hard and too long to build good farm land. We will not let them take it from us. We have a good life here–good homes, good fishing, good hunting. Yes siree, we'll fight!"

Finally the meeting broke up, Eldridge and the wiser ones knew they would have to wait for another day to reason with the others, if indeed they ever could convince them not to fight, for it was a shame to have it all taken from them. They did not want to lose all of this, either.

After all, it was the height of the great depression. Cataloochee people knew of the hard times people in the outside world were having. There were no jobs, no way to get money for food. Many were on starvation, while here in Cataloochee people could raise all the food they needed and had everything except a few basic items and could make the rest.

The Sad Exodus

Yes, our ancestors had worked one hundred years to convert the rugged wildernesses of Cataloochee into good farm and pasture land. They did not mind the hard work because they had pride in all they did. They were a unique breed of people (mostly Scotch-Irish) who had a spirit of independence and resourcefulness. Their accomplishments were not so much for themselves, as for their descendents. This beautiful place was to be their children's inheritance.

They had been very successful cattlemen and farmers. They had earned this place by the sweat of their brow. They lived in peace and friendship. They had nice homes, churches, and schools.

Then the government stepped in and wanted to put the people out, right in the middle of the great depression. The Cataloochee people got mad and some planned to fight the government or anyone else who would dare to take Cataloochee from them. How could they make such a sacrifice? This had been home to them, their fathers, and grandfathers. Some of the men talked about murdering both of the appraisers. It took a long time to get them cooled down. Some of the more sensible ones said, "Now, fellows, you may as well go on, do the best you can and not disgrace us all."

Now the government wanted the land for a park, and everyone was upset. Where would they live? What would they do? Then they were promised that they could lease the land and live like they always had for the rest of their lives, if they would sell it to the park. Cataloochee people were honorable and had made business deals with a handshake many times. Their word was their bond. Perhaps they believed those park men were equally honorable. They were badly deceived. Soon as the deeds were signed, everything changed. Cataloochee would never be the

Cataloochee Valley

Jarvis Palmer's place.

same again. At first a few families left, but most stayed on four or five years. When they realized they would have to move out, they went looking for another farm. The awful depression had been on four or five years, and all the farms and homes were in poor condition outside Cataloochee. No one had money for paint or repairs, not even fertilizer for their crops, and as a result the farms were run down, and worn out fences had fallen down. While at Cataloochee they had fared better, but now they would have to buy some old place and fix it up, best as they could.

They were so heartbroken to have to make such a great sacrifice that words can't describe their anguish and hurt. They were filled with such sorrow when they moved away their health broke; some soon died. Others grieved about it as long as they lived. They felt that they had been cheated and failed their ancestors and the future generations. Many just suffered in silence. As a result their children never heard lots of stories, history, and experiences.

In most cases they bought farms with decent houses, but they worked the rest of their lives trying to make good, productive land. Some worked themselves to death, dying of the stress of losing good farms and trying to build up old run down farms.

Cataloochee people felt like they had been robbed because

they were not paid enough for the homes and land. Some sued and received a little more money, but they had to pay lawyers. Most did not sue because they said no one wins except the lawyers.

Cataloochee men had kept their soil built up by spreading manure and cornstalks on it, then turned it under. They rotated the crops, so as not to wear out the land. They used some fertilizer and lime, and had good, productive crops. They had put their heart and soul in everything they did, so they could have a home, live well, and leave a legacy for their children.

Now that they had been forced to sacrifice all of that, they mostly just moved around the outer edge of the park, to various places in Haywood County. But the soil was different. Some would wash out in big gullies during the rainy season. Some farms were red clay soil, and they had to learn new methods of farming.

As Paul Woody said they had a brotherly love and you just couldn't walk away from that. They missed their friends and neighbors.

Linton Palmer remembered their moving day, September 9, 1938, when they left Cataloochee. He said, "I was almost six years old. Vincent Palmer had a two ton truck to move us. It took several trips to get us to Jonathan Creek where we were going to live. I was going to ride with Aunt Maria across the mountain and she had the old family wooden wheel clock which she took great pride in. She wouldn't let anybody pack it in the back of the truck. She was going to carry it in her lap across that mountain. I knew when I climbed up in that truck, it was the biggest truck that I'd ever seen, but I was doing pretty well until Aunt Maria started crying and said, 'Vincent don't break this clock going across the mountain, for I hate to leave bad enough, I sure don't want my clock broken.' She cried most all the way with the clock on her lap and fussed at Vincent that he was going too fast and was going to break it. (Linton still has the clock and several pieces of furniture made by Will Messer.)[1]

Jarvis (Linton Palmer's father) was paid for his land by check (from the government). He wasn't at home when the mailman brought the check. He was upset when he found out he had missed a ride with the mailman to go put the check in the bank. He

---
[1] Dr. Carroll's interview with Linton Palmer, July 11, 1977

Cataloochee Valley

Nancy Jane Colwell Palmer

worried that if the house burned down or something he would lose it all, but next day he did go to the bank. When he arrived he was told that was the morning the bank closed (due to the Great Depression) and if he had gotten there the day before he would have lost the money.

Jarvis used the money to buy a good farm on the lower end of Jonathan Creek. For five years, Aunt Maria, his wife Velma, and family continued to live at Cataloochee. He operated the farm at Jonathan Creek during the week. Restrictions became tighter and less tolerable; so they moved out of Cataloochee. Within a decade of the purchase of the Jonathan Creek farm Jarvis made it into one of the prize registered Hereford beef cattle farms in Western NC.

Dillard Caldwell, Herb Caldwell, and Jarvis Caldwell had trucks. So did some of Uncle Will's boys by 1930 or later. They helped move the people out of Cataloochee. But many of them moved out in wagons.

Several relatives came to live with us in Cataloochee during the great depression. Two of Daddy's nephews from Detroit, Hiram and Wayne Caldwell, one of mother's cousins from Tennessee, Sam Killian, also Mother's sister, Mae Miller, and her

Aunt Maria and Aunt Velma outside the spring house.

two children, Pauline and Ernest Miller, besides Grandma Lizzie Caldwell and sometimes Grandma Emma Valentine, and our family of five, and lots of visitors.

There was always plenty of food because everyone worked to make it. Most of the people in Cataloochee said they never felt the depression until they had to move out of their paradise.

It would be hard for everyone to give up this beautiful, peaceful, happy place. They felt like they were letting down their forefathers, who had built sturdy log cabins which were still standing straight and handsome with their handrived wooden shingles. They had aged to a beautiful silvery gray and so had the split rail fences that surrounded cabins and crops. Some fences were covered with red rambling roses.

By 1900, the population had grown to 700, according to the census. By the time the park service wanted to buy the property, several people had built large beautiful weatherboarded houses. Others had put weatherboarding over their log houses and added more rooms. All the houses and yards were neat, clean, and well kept.

The yards had lots of flowers. It was truly a picturesque place, with gladiolas, roses, lilacs, dahlias, hollyhock, and wisteria.

Cataloochee Valley

The house built by Lige Messer. Later Lush Caldwell's family lived here. Photo Courtesy of GSMNP.

Many homes had picket fences. Some had rail fences.

The women said, "Oh, Lord! How can we give up all this. Our homes built with such loving care, hard work, and sweat?" One man said, "Well, you ain't gonna have to give it up, cause we'll fight and we will win!"

I'll never forget how mad some of those men were. Their faces flushed red with anger, their eyes were watery and you could see the hurt in them. I was scared. I had never seen such sadness and so much crying.

The women had almost stopped crying. They were still mournful, saying, "Oh, Lord, help us. Where will we live, What will happen to our good neighbors?" Someone said, "No matter what happens or where we get scattered to, we should always come back to our church every year. We can worship, visit and bring plenty of good food. We'll have a homecoming. We can come back to our homes for one day."

Again they cried as they thought about coming home for only one day each year. But it was agreed on. Every August for more than sixty years, a great number have returned from as far away as California, Texas, and many other states.

Goodbye

Several families moved out of Cataloochee before we did. I can see those wagons yet, piled high with their belongings. Sometimes there were two wagons filled with all kinds of things, and along behind came another wagon full of children and the parents. They had the longest, saddest faces in the world, every family along the way standing beside the road, the women holding babies and a crowd of children were there to wave goodbye. As soon as the wagons came into sight, the crying started. They were saying, "There's our good friends leaving. Law how can we stand it? Oh Lord this is a sad day. We never thought such a thing would happen." As the wagons came nearer, they were overcome with sadness to have to say goodbye, and the crying got louder and louder. The man driving the wagons didn't stop. They had tears in their eyes as they waved good bye to their good friends and neighbors. It was truly heartwrenching. This happened each time a family moved out. Some were moved in trucks, but it was a sad scene as they kept looking back at home they could never live in again.

Yes, it was truly the end of the valley. The families moved out, a few each year, until no one lived there except the Park Ranger and his family, the maintenance men and families, Turkey George and his family, and Uncle Steve Woody, who was not about to leave. He stayed on, keeping some family to live there with him. He stayed until just shortly before his death in 1944. Most all the families were gone by 1937. The Alexanders at the Ranch stayed until 1938.

Much Elizabethan Speech

Mary Elizabeth Howell Caldwell spoke lots of Elizabethan words which were proper in Shakespeare's time and most of the Cataloochee people used some of the same words. As children we did not know the difference.

When we moved to Maggie Valley and went to school, we carried our lunch in a poke. I got laughed at for saying poke. I had never heard of carrying anything in a bag! It was always a poke or a tow sack. Grandma said fetch in a bucket of water. She referred to food as victuals (vittles.) We all said tote instead of carry and many other Elizabethan words.

The people of Cataloochee had been mostly isolated for one hundred years, and they retained the old fashioned speech, moral standards, and customs, teaching their children religion and manners. When we moved out of Cataloochee, it was like moving to another world, not only in speech but many other ways. We saw our first electric lights and telephones in 1934 (some moved a few years earlier, some later) and other modern conveniences.

Deceived

Oh, the promises they made! The government men promised fair and square that everybody could live on in Cataloochee just as they always had, that they could farm and raise cattle, hogs, and sheep and just lease their farms from the government for a small sum. They were promised "Yes, you can live here a lifetime; nothing will change."

They finally convinced the people of these promises and people sold to them. But once the government took control, nothing would ever be the same again. If a man's animal got out, he lost his lease. John Caldwell on Caldwell Fork had some sheep get out of the pasture, and he lost his lease. They imposed very strict rules about fishing, and no hunting was allowed. If they needed to cut firewood, they had to get permission. They would not let a man cut a nearby tree; they would require him to go to some mountain top and cut a dead tree. Then if a limb hit a green tree and knocked a limb off, he automatically lost his lease.

When it was time to plant crops, Cataloochee men had to get permission and could not plow and plant in the best soil. They would be told by a government man where to plow. These fine intelligent men did not need someone telling them when, where and how to farm because their grandfathers, fathers, and they, themselves had very successfully farmed this land. For a while Cataloochee people put up with all these strict rules because they loved their homes, and their neighbors, and their land.

Now that the government owned it, they stopped the free

Home of Avie and Jim Caldwell, built by Uncle Harrison. Photo Courtesy of GSMNP.

ranging of cattle and hogs on the grassy balds. That is what had brought the people there in the first place and had been their major source of income. Now they were limited to very few animals.

The top of Mt. Sterling was not included in the park boundary.

In order to keep his cattle and not break their rules, Eldridge Caldwell bought 100 acres of good pasture land on top of Mt. Sterling from Glenn Palmer. It was a long, hard trip up the steep mountain, more than 6,000 feet high, for him to go check on his cattle, and it was a real hardship on him. He had a family living up there to keep check on the cattle, but he would often go to salt the cattle and count them.

It was only a few years until he would go find several head slaughtered and strewn all over by the bears. Since the park did not allow hunting, pretty soon bears multiplied and traveled all over, killing as many cattle as they pleased. Finally Eldridge gave up and sold "High Top" to the park.

The park people would promise anything to get a fellow to sell. They promised Eldridge Caldwell that he could have the beautiful log house he was born in. Oh yes, they said, even if you decide to move out, you can take it with you. Well, he believed them and sold his property to them. The house was built before the Civil War by his grandfather Levi in 1858. It had the original

Cataloochee Valley

Home of Tommy and Ella Caldwell. Photo Courtesy of GSMNP.

split shingle roof on it, and one side was getting some leaks. Eldridge said he was going to get some shingles like the originals to replace the shingles on the leaky side. The park people said no repairs, but he could move it, if he moved out.

After his parents Hiram and Lizzy had built the large house, the old log house was used as a school until the present Beech Grove school was built. Then it had served as a blacksmith shop and was used to store feed in. When Eldridge asked to move it out of Cataloochee later, the answer was, "No, nothing could be moved off government property."

Well that was it! He would not put up with this any longer! He began making plans right then. This would be the last time in his life that he would ever harvest his crops in Cataloochee Valley and the next spring he would move out. It broke his heart, but his decision was made; he couldn't stay there and see the buildings rot down.

Judge Alley wrote that Miss Marley got it right when she wrote that while the rest of the world was rushing to some unknown goal, these mountain people were happy and content living in their peaceful world. (This applies to all mountain people, everything that Judge Felix Alley wrote defending all the mountaineers in his

Tommy and Ella Caldwell. Photo Courtesy of Lloyd Caldwell.

book "Random Thoughts and Musings Of a Mountaineer," published in 1941. At that time, many outside writers had nothing good to say about the mountain people.)

Lord, how our ancestors loved Cataloochee; to most it was the "Garden of Eden." Offering more than they dreamed of–food, fish, game, and all kinds of berries. Nature provided so many wonderful things, there were blackberries, huckleberries (same as wild blue berries) cranberries, raspberries, and large, delicious strawberries.

They had many kinds of apples, which grew without any sprays. Insecticides were unheard of, and so was cancer in Cataloochee except two people (all we have found). One man, Dan Cook, who grew up in Tennessee then moved to Cataloochee, died of cancer of the throat. A Grooms woman had cancer of the stomach when she moved there. They were tenant farmers, and we don't know where they came from. But that proves that doctors knew what cancer was back then.

Their control for bugs was to give all the children a little bottle filled half full of kerosene and send them to the garden to pick the bugs off and drop them in the bottle, killing them. It was a contest to see who could catch the most bugs.

Cataloochee Valley

What the Park Purchased

The following information was found in the North Carolina Park Commission Report on Audit (31 Oct. 1925 through 30 June 1933) to Governor JCB Ehringhaus.

Money They Were Paid For Their Homes and Land

Name	Date	Purchased Acreage	Amount
Suncrest Lumber Co.	2-07-33	32,853.53	$300,000
J.L. Caldwell	10-26-29	213.16	7,700
C.M. Long	6-12-29	98.47	3,500
Caldwell Fork School	3-06-30	2.16	500
W.M. Sutton, heirs	4-18-32	48.45	850
Maria L. Palmer	9-30-29	101.61	3,600
Mrs. Lou King	5-22-31	182.14	5,000
B.J. Sloan	7-29-29	60.13	4,300
D.W. Caldwell	1-17-31	68.98	4,350
James Caldwell	2-17-30	155.82	5,800
Jonathan Woody	7-18-31	151.49	11,165
Mrs. S.L. Woody	7-18-31	46.74	812
F.W. Woody	7-18-31	116.18	3,552
Floyd W. Woody	7-18-31	45.00	1,000
Thomas Caldwell	12-21-31	93.85	4,850
Charles R. Caldwell	10-28-29	199.00	7,000
Eldridge Caldwell	6-10-29	122.98	10,300
George H. Caldwell	10-29-31	150.58	4,000
J.R. Hall	2-28-29	121.44	4,000
Indian Creek School	3-06-30	1.25	1,325
Palmer's Chapel Church	12-16-29	1.47	1,150
V.A. Campbell	9-16-29	145.66	9,700
H.R. Palmer	4-21-30	163.29	8,500
W.H. Palmer	9-06-29	111.21	5,265
M.H. Caldwell	12-27-30	134.35	11,500
Linton Palmer	8-10-29	47.55	1,425
Jarvis Palmer	1-14-31	558.93	25,000
Guy Pease	5-17-30	38.67	2,755.50

Name	Date	Amount	Value
W.M. Hall	5-22-31	105.00	14,500
Sidney H. Nelson	7-20-29	46.32	1,600
J.G. Strikeleather	10-01-32	930.11	20,501.46
Rainbow Fish Club	1-22-31	33.75	1,500
M.N. Hall	12-16-29	39.47	2,800
Ola Church	12-20-29	.29	1,200
W.G. Messer	1-08-30	343.32	35,405
George Bennett	7-20-29	41.63	3,890
W.B. Bennett	7-20-29	39.36	3,670
J.W. Burgess	7-20-29	35.25	3,250
Mrs. J.R. Woody and children	1-11-32	73.61	3,400
Laura Eggleston, Arthur Ford, et al.	4-18-32	170.00	3,708.50
Carl Sutton	1-17-31	44.62	1,800
S.C. Caldwell	1-17-30	71.20	1,200
D.H. Burris	1-28-30	117.78	4,500
George N. Palmer	10-31-29	187.64	5,600
V.A. Campbell	9-21-29	35.31	875
C.L. Palmer	12-12-29	65.35	2,600
J.B. Lockman	1-17-30	42.32	650
I.B. McGaha	10-14-29	10.58	400
John M. Palmer	8-15-29	171.14	7,210
J.M. Conrad	9-16-29	108.58	3,450
J.M. Conrad	9-16-29	20.53	1,285
D.B. Nelson	9-16-29	62.83	1,605
J.A. Conrad	10-31-29	27.91	500
J.S. Woody	4-18-32	149.19	4,500
Ola School	3-06-30	1.55	1,700
James H. Hannah	1-11-32	32.44	1,650
J.B. Hannah	6-23-30	51.54	2,000
Mack W. Hannah	4-18-32	152.06	11,023.80
W.D. Messer	11-15-29	53.96	2,500
L.N. Hall	10-31-29	65.42	6,000
I.V. Hannah	9-03-29	21.27	1,250
W.R. Hannah	9-16-29	11.19	610
Jethro Hannah	9-30-29	12.24	870
J. Oss Smith	7-07-30	33.79	931.67

Cataloochee Valley

A.R. Hannah	6-26-30	133.92	6,046.54
A.C. Bennett	2-17-30	141.81	5,000
W.C. Woody	9-16-29	48.13	2,480
Thomas R. Byrd, Estate	4-29-33	20,190.40	81,453.22
L.A. Hopkins	4-23-32	51.36	2,027.20
T.H. (Bud) White	9-08-30	43.72	650
J.C. Hopkins	4-23-32	61.41	5,235.95
I.H. Hopkins, Estate	6-26-30	80.02	3,720
R. Prince	4-23-32	85.50	2,000
J.M. Caldwell	10-29-31	39.20	925.98
George Phillips	4-23-32	45.47	1,500
Presbyterian School	16-29-31	42.46	2,500
Walter Grooms	8-18-30	1.23	200
Mrs. Maggie Jarvis	2-12-30	141.21	2,000
J.L.C. Messer	5-13-29	50.26	2,700
E.M. Messer	6-22-29	73.50	1,935
G.M.D. Messer	8-15-29	27.48	1,525
Robert Partin	11-15-29	32.97	1,100
Robert Palmer	8-12-29	235.53	5,055
B.H. Sutton	10-31-29	22.00	320
Mrs. Addie Sutton	3-03-30	82.24	1,450
Dee Clark	5-06-30	40.33	650
D.J. Boyd	7-26-29	131.84	5,000
P.W. Mehaffey	4-16-32	12.00	192
R.T. Boyd/C.M. Moody	4-09-32	27.70	692.50
G.C. Clark	7-23-32	5.22	325
C.M. Moody	4-09-32	17.40	435
C.A.Campbell/J.R.Boyd	4-18-32	9.80	453
W.A. Early/wife	7-20-31	12.80	300

Trade Hound Pups for Land

Carl Woody on Little Cataloochee bought fifty acres of land. Originally this land was bought from the Love family for two hound pups, this deal was made between the Love heirs and Tyne Woody. He raised the pups, put them in a wagon and took them to the Loves in Waynesville who made him a deed for the fifty acres. They were land speculators and were required to get all the land in the Cataloochee township homesteaded. Tyne Woody sold these fifty acres to Blaine Hannah for $300, then he sold it to a Mr. Sutton for $600, then he sold it to Carl Woody for $900. Carl had $700 saved up, which he paid down on the land, then got the crops planted and left his wife to tend the crops while he went to work at Smokemont in the timber business. That summer he was able to save $200 more and pay it off. When he first bought the land, there was a stack of good lumber, and he got Vic Smith to build the house and traded him a seven dollar calf to build a chimney.

When Carl's wife was in labor and they knew the baby would be born, Carl went to get Aunt Fannie Hannah to deliver the baby. Uncle Mac went to the barn to saddle the horse and brought it to her. He said "Hurry, Fannie, hurry." It was a big red horse with a white face.

The baby was born, and Aunt Fannie stayed a week or ten days. She cooked, washed, and looked after baby and mother. When she was ready to leave, Carl asked her how much he owed her. In her kind gentle voice, she said two dollars.

When Carl sold to the government, he received $2,480 for the fifty acres, a house, barn, and other buildings.

Twins

Paul Woody's mother, Lou White Woody, was expecting twins. The other babies were born at home, but this time she went to the hospital in Waynesville.

Two weeks earlier she had gone to stay with her sister, Aunt Laura, in Waynesville. Carl knew she was in good hands; so he went back to Little Cataloochee to take care of Paul and Clay

Cataloochee Valley

Carl and Lou White Woody with baby Paul. Photo Courtesy of Paul Woody.

and to tend to the crops and livestock. When the babies were born, Holbert Franklin, who lived at the Kerr place, heard about it from someone passing through. Probably they had sent word by the mailman. Holbert walked all the way up to Carl's to tell him that he had twins. There was a boy and a girl, named Frank and Frankie.

Carl got Willie Messer, who had a car or truck to bring them home. When he drove to the end of the road, the mother and babies were loaded on a sled to ride the one and a quarter miles to the house.

Tint Woody, also of Cataloochee, was a twin to Margaret Black, there were other twins in the Woody family–Cary and Lary also Lem and Clem.

Carl Woody moves out of Little Cataloochee

Paul Woody was ten years old when they had to leave Little Cataloochee. His father, Carl, had gone to look around Haywood County for a place to move his family and start over, trying to get a productive farm.

The place Carl decided on was up on Little East Fork of the Pigeon River, remarkably like Little Cataloochee in the lay of the land and plentiful water.

The Woodys moved in December 1931. There was not a road to the Cataloochee house, only a narrow wagon road. All the household furnishings were loaded on the wagon and hauled one and a quarter miles down to a road where Willie Messer met them with his big truck. There they had to unload all the furniture off the wagon onto the truck. He took it on to Little East Fork, unloaded it, and charged eight dollars.

Carl had a big load of corn in his barn loft, which had to be loaded in the wagon, but it would take a long time and lots of hard work to load it ear by ear. He planned an easier way. They backed the wagon into the barn, chopped a hole under the corn pile, and let it fall into the wagon. They drove the wagon back down to the road to where Carl had arranged for Dillard Caldwell to bring his truck to haul the corn, they had to unload it from the wagon and onto the truck. They had put their plows and farm implements on a sled and had hauled them there to load on top of the corn. Dillard hauled it all to Little East Fork for eight dollars also.

Then Carl had arranged for Eldridge Caldwell to haul him and the family to their new place. Carl had torn the fences down from around the hay stacks so the cows and mules could eat until he could get settled and come back for them. He would drive the livestock out on foot. What a long trip that was. He started out just at the crack of daylight, from Little Cataloochee driving his livestock all the way to Waynesville, near the Barberville Baptist church, to Virgil and Dare Sizemores, his brother-in-law and sister, who had a barn to keep the cattle in. He spent the night there and started out early next morning.

This would be another long hard day to drive the cattle all the way to Little East Fork. Of course, they had to walk on the paved streets of Waynesville, and as they got near Ray's Deptment Store, one heifer saw herself in a long glass window of the store, she made a run for the image. Carl made a run for it too, just barely in time to keep her from running through the window. Carl had bought 240 acres in Little East Fork. After

Cataloochee Valley

a while, he realized he could not pay for all of it, due to the depression. He said he never knew there was a depression until they moved from Cataloochee. He knew it, but it had been easier for him and his family at Cataloochee. He had to sell off part of the East Fork property in order to pay for the rest of the land.

As soon as his two oldest sons, Paul and Clay, grew up and got jobs, they bought back the portion of land that their daddy originally bought. They still own it today.[1]

Virlin and Hattie Campbell on their wedding day in 1902. Photo Courtesy of Ernestine Edwards Upchurch granddaughter of the couple.

[1] Info from Paul Woody-Little East Fork, Mar. 1996

9

THE PARK IS DEDICATED

Mr. Hiram Wilburn and The Museum Collection

Mr. Wilburn was sent to survey all the land in the Cataloochee valley in preperation for the creation of the park. He was a very fine man, and everyone liked him. First he surveyed Big Cataloochee, and Eldridge Caldwell and others helped him. In Little Cataloochee Mark Hannah and others helped him.

Mr. Wilburn loved the area, its people, and its history. He was a self-appointed historian, interviewed many people, and faithfully made notes about everything. He hoped the government would preserve this beautiful valley. It was an historic place with its hand hewn log homes and barns, rail and rock fences, spring houses, carriage houses, and corn cribs. The old mills and water wheels, old mill stones, quaint little one and two room school houses, the little country stores and post offices were beautiful. Then there were the large weather boarded homes. Yes, it was truly a picturesque place. It really should have been preserved. Mr. Wilburn did all he could to have it preserved. But the government wanted a wilderness and ordered all the buildings burned. Mark Hannah had to comply with their rules, as he was the ranger, but it was a sad time for him, then and ever after. Mr. Wilburn was so furious with them that he would not give them his notebooks and he had many. It has been difficult to find some of his work. He gave them to various libraries, colleges, and scattered archives.

Cataloochee Valley

Through Mr. Wilburn's notes I have been able to document many of the stories I had heard.

President Roosevelt Dedicates the Park

Our dear Mr. Wilburn was truly a friend of the Cataloochee people. He knew the park would be dedicated by President Roosevelt. Mr. Wilburn began writing letters more than a year before dedication trying to persuade some of the officials to let him bring some of the old settlers from the park area to have honored seats and be recognized in some way. If they could only be mentioned and referred to by the master of ceremonies, that would be sufficient.

His letter stated that, this group would be representative of some 3,000 or 4,000 persons who were called upon to give up their homes in order that we might have the park. This would also be representative of "mountain culture" and historical setup, both of which are to be stressed in our museum and historical program.

(letter dated June 8, 1939)

... Here follows a list from the North Carolina area that I suggest as being suitable and given preference.

1. Alden Carver, aged 94 yrs.
2. Mrs. George Caldwell, age about 95
3. Dock Conner, about 87
4. George Bennett, 68
5. Steve Woody, 88
6. Dock Burris, 75

Of course it would be up to Carlos Campbell or some other in Tennessee to designate representatives from that state.

If the idea can be worked into the program, I could arrange for the transportation and care of these old people.

Thanking you for your consideration, signed,
Very Truly Yours,
H.C. Wilburn

Franklin D. Roosevelt at the Newfound Gap ceremonies dedicating the Great Smoky Mountains National Park, September 2, 1940. Photo Courtesy of GSMNP.

President Franklin D. Roosevelt signed the bill authorizing full operation of the park on June 15, 1934, but it was not dedicated until September 2, 1940, when ceremonies were held at Newfound Gap. They claimed President Roosevelt had one foot in Tennessee and one foot in North Carolina as he dedicated the park.

The Great Smoky Mountains National Park is unique. It is the first of its kind, created by the acquisition of land and donations from the private sector. As the result of a five million dollar contribution from the Laura Spelman Rockefeller Memorial Foundation, it became a reality.

Governors from Tennessee and North Carolina were speakers at the dedication. In 1984 there was a fifty year celebration of the park. Governor Hunt of North Carolina and Governor Alexander of Tennessee, made speeches, proclaiming the year of 1984 as the "Year of the Great Smokies." There was a commemorative coin struck for this golden anniversary of the park.

Mr. Wilburn had put great effort into getting recognition for the old pioneers, but his efforts and pleas were ignored. Relatives who were there cannot remember if any kind of honor was paid to them. Evelyn and Kimberly Parham and son Richard, Gudger Palmer and his mother Milia said it looked like most of the Cataloochee people were there and thousands of people were there from both Tennessee and North Carolina.

Cataloochee Valley

Museum?

At first when the Park Service took Cataloochee in the early 30s and for many more years they did not see the historic value in preserving the beautiful old structures.

Cataloochee could have been one of the finest museums of the American pioneers, showing a transmission of cultural values over a period of one hundred years.

Some park officials collected spinning wheels, flax wheels, hand made furniture, beautiful hand woven coverlets, mill wheels, buggies, old guns, bear traps, hand made tools and farm implements, and many more things, always promising we would have a museum. Finally there is a small museum with some pictures and a few tools. It is still only a dream that all of the old antiques and artifacts could be displayed there in Cataloochee where they were made and used.

Mr Hiram Wilburn tried to get the Park Service officals interested in a real museum. Following is a portion of a letter to Mr. Ned Burns, Acting Chief, Eastern Museum Division, National Park Service, Washington, D.C., but got no results.

(Letter dated March 30, 1937)

March 9 I collected a spinning wheel, a loom complete, and several objects illustrative of domestic activities in the Cataloochee area. In connection with this donation, I was permitted to take a copy of a photograph made in the year 1902. This picture is of George H. Caldwell family, each member of which, but one, was clothed in garments made "from the sheeps back" by the mother in the family who is familiarly known as "Aunt Mag." She is still living (1937) and donated the material. Aunt Mag stated that her oldest daughter who had grown to be a young woman felt that she had to have "store bought" clothes. A print copy of this picture is enclosed, and one that I made of Aunt Mag, now 80 years old.

Wilburn II 3

The photo refered to in Hiram Wilburn's letter. George Caldwell and family in a photo taken in the year 1902. Photo Courtesy of GSMNP.

Mr. Wilburn collected museum quality articles. He very carefully numbered and identified each article so it could be displayed accurately.

Note number 335
    Nellie, NC Collected by HCW at Cataloochee:
    #1486-1-handmade trowel found at MW Hannah place
            on Little Cataloochee
    #1487-2-handmade shuttles
    #1488-3-handmade shuttles
    #1489-4-coffee mills, crank, cup

Note number 4.26
    Mrs. Callie Bennett of Candler who sold the Jessie Palmer loom to me for $5. She wants one of the shuttles – Palmer will give the cord out of old bed. Bring out bed and chair and carry to Mrs. Bennett.

Cataloochee Valley

Note number [141] 253

    The old chair, Mrs. George Caldwell sat in it, first time I ever saw her. She gave it to me and I practically raised my children in it. She wove many clothes and coverlets on the old loom.

Note number [120] 217, At Big Cataloochee

    Aunt Mag Caldwell, 79 years, 11th Jan. 1937. Loom was made and first set up in 1881 was used to supply the entire family until about 1912. Loom was made by Elijah (EM) Messer. $6 was the price of loom, wheel was brought in by a man from Tennessee. Price of wheel was $3.50, chair 75 cents, six got at this time probably 1882. Soap trough was made by George H. Caldwell about the same time, dry double wash tub with legs and a hole in the bottom.

Note number [195] 337, 9/25/35, Collected on Little Cataloochee:
#1492-1-handmade shuttle
#1493-2-eye hoe
#1494-3-eye hoe
#1495-4-accessory to old loom.

    Hiram Wilburn also collected a grass root's history of the Cataloochee people. He wrote down the stories and tales that he was told. Through Mr. Wilburn's notes, a past generation speaks to us today.

Note number [195] 337

    Sitton complained that on account of isolation, he could not live in Big Cataloochee, so the Loves employed John Mull to come in and build a mill and a sawmill. He built a tub mill and was not satisfactory at Jessie Palmers place, then a regular size grist mill and a sash saw mill was built, first mill was 60 yards above present location.

Notebook [63] P. 28

    Ira McGee caught a very large bear in a big trap, on Caldwell Fork 1891. Ira buried the trap above the house where we lived. It was found by CCC workers in 1935 and is in the museum collection.

Notebook [60] P. 25
A long gun was donated by Mrs. Price, now of East Orange, NJ. It had belonged to Eli Arrington of Saunook. He bought it from Joe Miller 1910 when it was nearly new. It was a Lemon-Lancaster gun. Eli Arrington used this gun in a shooting match. He told Mr. Wilburn "I drunk about a pint of liquor and put three balls in the same hole. Then I used Austin Arrington's board, and I centered the target on it. This gun was originally purchased from George and Clarence Miller about twenty years before I got it. I think it was the last gun of its kind sold in Waynesville." NOTE: this gun is catalog number 5727 in the park collection of guns now at the ranger station.

Mr. Wilburn has listed many articles collected for museums; they are listed at random throughout many of his notebooks. It would be interesting to know what happened to these items and where they are now: maybe stored in some government building?

Corn Mills

Mr. W.C. Wilburn was fascinated by mill stones, and there were many on Cataloochee. He counted and numbered and measured them, giving location, when they were cut, where and by whom. Also, he noted where they had been used, and the date if possible and complete measurement of diameter, thickness, and eye measurement. His notebooks contain much information about the Mill stones, as you will see in the following story:

Notebook [63] page 28.
Sept. 24, 1937. In Cataloochee one mile below the Kerr place, mill stone XXVII(27) was found. This was the Vick Smith mill at the mouth of Little Cataloochee. The stone was washed down with the timbers, when the mill was

washed away. The stone is six inches diameter, three inches thick, with a three inch round eye.

Vick Smith says, "He built a mill for Thomas Palmer at the Jesse Palmer place about 1908. Also, he built a mill for Bill Noland on Davidson Branch about 1906. I cut these stones about one mile below the Kerr place. This was the first time they had been used. They were later carried to the Carson Messer place.

Note: Raymond Caldwell says Jessie Palmer built the mill himself.

These mills were important because cornbread was a staple then and still preferred by most Cataloochee people. One man speaking of bought loaf bread said, "That lightbread is just something to fool a fellow. IT AIN'T NOTHING BUT AIR."

Aunt Mag's Buggy

Raymond Caldwell talked of his family moving from Big Cataloochee when he was fifteen years old. He drove a wagon loaded with some of their belongings. It was quite a job for a 15-year-old boy to handle the team of horses and the wagon piled high. He had to drive up the steep, crooked Cove Creek Mountain and down the other side, and all the way to a farm on Iron Duff that his parents Jarvis and Bonnie had bought.

A big truck had hauled several loads of household goods and farm implements. The livestock had been driven out on foot. When the family arrived in Iron Duff, there was much work to be done, get the house furnishing set up, get the farm implements stored, fences mended, crops planted and much more.

Raymond's grandmother, Aunt Mag, lived with them there at Cataloochee and she, like other ladies, traveled by buggy. She had a nice old buggy, but when they moved, there was not room enough to take it. They would come back and get it. Well, there was so much work at Iron Duff, and they were to busy to go back. Finally they got caught up with their work and went back to get the buggy.

Jarvis and some of the boys loaded it on the truck and were

about half way up the mountain when they met the park ranger John Needham. He told them to turn around and take the buggy back, that it belonged to the park. Jarvis did as he was told, but they were mad about it and still are! The buggy stayed in the (Jarvis Cataloochee) barn for awhile, then disappeared. The park service collected many, many things, that were supposed to be put in the museum. Today there is pitiful little in the tiny museum in Cataloochee. They even took Cataloochee buildings out and reassembled them in other places.

They took Jim Caldwell's springhouse from Big Cataloochee and Will Messer's applehouse from Little Cataloochee and reassembled them both at the Oconaluftee rangers station above Cherokee. They took a barn from Little Cataloochee and reassembled it on Big Cataloochee, near the ranger's house. (Which was originally Hub and Maude Caldwell's house built in 1916.)

These pioneers were very gifted and could make many things. We know most of their furniture was homemade before the Civil War. They made straight chairs and used oak strips for the seats. They also made chairs chopped out of logs. Tables were made of maple or walnut and put together with wooden pegs, and sometimes with square homemade nails.

They usually made a long dining table and made peg leg benches for each side. Most of the benches were made of pine. (See Levi Caldwell's table at the Museum of North Carolina Handicrafts, 307 Shelton Street, Waynesville, N.C.)

Dock Caldwell, grandson of Doctor, remembered their beds were hand carved poster beds, some almost as tall as the ceiling. Most had ropes laced through holes in the sides, and ends, the rope was laced back and forth like squares. That rope was drawn real tight and served as the springs. Many people used straw or finely shredded shucks as the mattress. When the weather got cold, the feather beds were put on for warmth. All the quilts they made were padded with clean, puffy white wool from the backs of their sheep. There were wool blankets too, that they had woven, or in some cases, they sent the wool to the Chatham Milling Company and received blankets from them.

Yes it would have been a treasure if all these hand made articles could have been preserved and have a place in history.

Cataloochee Valley

Mark Hannah, who was born in Little Cataloochee, worked for the Park Service while the Great Smoky Mountains National Park was being built. Photo Courtesy of Lowell Hannah.

Mark Hannah who was born in Little Cataloochee and grew up there, applied for and got the job of Park Ranger for the Cataloochee area. He and his wife, Verda Messer Hannah, and their family moved from Little Cataloochee to Big Cataloochee. They lived in the Jarvis Palmer house, which now houses the little museum. The Hannahs lived there for more than thirty years and raised a large family.

Mark often talked about how much he hated to have to burn those fine old houses and beautifully well-constructed log houses. He had been friends and neighbors with these people all of his life. Now he was told if he did not burn the houses, that he would lose his job; so he had to do what he was ordered. He often talked and agonized about it after his retirement. He well knew the hard labor these neighbors and relatives had done to have a home they loved and had taken such pride in building. Mark would look so sad and shake his head, and say, "Nothing left now, just the chimneys and they fell down."

Mark's son-in-law, Dick Stokes, became the park ranger in the Big Creek area. He said he begged the park officials for tar paper to nail on the leaking roofs, some years after the people had moved out. But they told him they had to be burned, not preserved because they planned for it to be a complete wilderness.

The Park Service now realizes the historic value of the few buildings left standing. We appreciate their help in restoring them in the 70s and 80s.

Although the museum is small, we think it has a place of considerable importance to the history of Cataloochee, and we have hope that it can be completed, and the valuable antiques put back where they were made and used.

Locations They Moved To

Families from Big Cataloochee moved to areas around in Haywood County.

Turkey George Palmer's family moved to Clyde after his death in 1939. He was 81 years old. (Source: Headstone Palmer's Chapel Cemetery)
Jim Caldwell to Ironduff
Tommy Caldwell to Jonathan Creek
Hub Caldwell to Jonathan Creek and later to Waynesville
Charlie Ray Caldwell to Bethel
Dillard Caldwell to Bethel
Eldridge Caldwell to Maggie Valley
Homer Caldwell to Waynesville
Steve Woody did not move until 1942
Jarvis Palmer to Jonathan Creek and later to Howell Mill Rd., Waynesville.
William Palmer died and was buried at Big Cataloochee, Palmer's Chapel Cemetery, Feb. 2, 1916
George Caldwell to Maggie Valley
Hiram Caldwell to Maggie Valley
Lush Caldwell - stayed on at Big Cataloochee and worked for the government until about 1960 then moved to Maggie Valley
Mark Hannah - moved from Little Cataloochee to Big Cataloochee into the Jarvis Palmer house, then he moved to Maggie Valley after retiring as park ranger
Norman Caldwell to Maggie Valley
Aunt Milia Palmer to near Lake Junaluska and later moved to Canton
Gudger Palmer to Canton
Vaughn Palmer near Mooney Cove, Waynesville
Glenn Palmer to Crabtree

Cataloochee Valley

Turkey George Palmer never moved out of Cataloochee; however, he purchased a farm for his family to move to in Clyde, NC. Turkey's family remained at Big Cataloochee until his death in 1939. Photo Courtesy of Bob Palmer.

Will and Elenor Palmer to Bethel
Kimsey Palmer to Ironduff
Charlie Palmer to Waynesville
Vinson Palmer to California
Arlo Palmer to Lenoir

Paul Woody remembered where most of the families in Little Cataloochee moved to when they were forced to leave:
Eldridge & Bartlett Bennett moved to Franklin
Tyne Bennett to Sylva
George Bennett to North Georgia
Weaver Bennett to Cander
Burl McGaha to Waynesville
John Connard and Dave Nelson to Newport, Tennessee
Carl Woody, Jonah and Bob Brown, Little East Fork
Will Messer his family and three Valentine grandchildren moved to Lenoir
Cal Messer to Costy, Tennessee
John Burgess to Lenoir

Steve Woody, who stayed on his land until 1942. Photo Courtesy of GSMNP.

Rev. Will Hall to Clay County
Kimsey Palmer, Jarvis Caldwell, Flora Palmer Medford to Ironduff
Sherman Woody to Dutch Cove, near Canton
Dock Burris to Lenoir

Locations Families from Caldwell Fork Moved To
Lige (Elijah) Messer to Lenoir
Mack Messer to Lenoir
Bob Parton to Lenoir
Addie Sutton to Jonathan Creek
Jim Evans to Hemphill
Harrison Sutton to Cove Creek
John Caldwell to Jonathan Creek
Jim Sutton to Jonathan Creek
Thad Sutton to Jonathan Creek
Robert Palmer (deceased, sons listed below) Bill, Ed, & Dave Palmer moved to some western state[1]

---

[1]Interview with Thad Sutton 3-20-96

Cataloochee Valley

Myrtle Bennett, daughter of Mr. and Mrs. George Bennett, a friend of Pearl Valentine Caldwell.

Claude Caldwell and his wife, Gazzie McGee Caldwell, shown with their children (l to r) Hazel, George, and Evelyn.

Martha Russell Palmer, the wife of George (Creek) H. Palmer. Photo Courtesy of Ethel Palmer McCracken.

10

MEMORIES

Hattie Caldwell Davis Remembers

Every time I go back to that old Caldwell (1903) house, memories come flooding into my mind. I close my eyes, my imagination plays tricks on me, I think I smell the warm, freshly baked gingerbread or the stack cakes filled with spiced apple sauce, made with dried apples, stacked ten thin layers high. I think I can smell cinnamon, nutmeg, cloves, and ginger. Another time I almost get a whiff of the good sugar cured country ham they are frying or the good hot cornbread or biscuits.

The house always smelled of something good cooking. How I wish I could sit on the old peg leg bench at the long dining table and eat with the family again. (The same table and bench which are in the Museum of N.C. Handicraft in Waynesville).

There were three good cooks in our house, Pearl (my mother), Aunt Mae (her sister), and Aunt Lizzie (grandma). They cooked three hot meals each day, always biscuits for breakfast and cornbread for dinner and supper.

It was not unusual to have a big platter of delicious fried ham, fish, and chicken along with all kinds of fresh vegetables and delicious cobblers made of strawberries, apples, blackberries or huckleberries (wild blueberries). Chicken and dumplings were a favorite. Always hot bread and fine yellow homemade butter, honey, jams, and jelly.

The spring house served as our refrigerator. There was a

Cataloochee Valley

The daughter of Eldridge and Pearl Caldwell, Hattie Caldwell Davis, at age six.

cement trough in it where the cold water ran through it. This is where the milk, butter, cream, and leftover food were kept until needed.

The cows had to be milked in the evening and morning. The milk would be strained through a clean bleached flour sack, then carried to the springhouse where it would be set down in the cold water. This would cause the cream to rise to the top. When the milk was needed part of the thick cream was skimmed off into a crock, the rest of the cream was stirred into the milk. This was fine, wholesome, fresh milk for every meal (adults drank coffee for breakfast). The children drank milk.

The cream that was skimmed off was added to the crock (pottery jar) each time more milk was needed. The crock was kept in the cold water until enough cream was collected to churn, then it was brought up to the house, poured in the wooden churn which had a wooden dash. Someone (lots of times a child) would sit there lifting the dash up and down, up and down over and over until the butter collected and rose to the top. Next the dasher and lid were removed and the butter taken out and dressed.

How in the world would you dress butter? Well, that was the terminology used. It meant to pour cold water over the butter and put your hand in it and squeeze the butter and rinse and squeeze some more until all the milk was washed out, leaving pure fine butter. Then the butter was packed into a wooden mold. Our mold printed a beautiful shock of wheat on the butter, looked like it had been handcarved on top of this round, half pound of rich golden butter. These were truly a thing of beauty. There would be several balls of butter depending on the amount of cream that was churned.

Cleanliness was the rule in everything. After the milk had been strained through the flour sack, it would be rinsed, boiled with soap, and rinsed some more, then hung in the sun to dry. The milk buckets (some were eight-pound lard buckets made of tin) were washed, scalded, and hung out in the sun each time they were used.

Many times there were extra people at our house at meal times. The long table and bench would seat twelve to fourteen people, depending on the size of the children on the bench. Most always on Sunday the table had to be set two times, sometimes three times with adults first. The children were told to sit on the porch and wait for the next seating. Grandma Lizzie usually saw to it that the children ate as well as the adults. She set aside some of the fried ham and chicken legs and our favorites, and maybe slip us some of her good homemade cookies while we waited. She called them tea cakes, and they had granulated sugar sprinkled on them before they were baked.

I feel the women had to be somewhat engineers to fire those old wood cook stoves just right, not too hot, not too cold to bake cakes and things. Otherwise the cakes would fall.

It also took special knowledge to keep the stove fired up for cooking other things and for canning, which took four hours of constant boiling. In those days, many of the canning jars were green or blue. There was a flat rubber ring put on the can and can tops were lead-lined with glass. It was the women's pride and joy to have her cans all filled with beautiful, green, yellow, red, and other vegetables, and lots of canned pork and sausage and soup mix and all sorts of things.

After canning season was over with, I remember the women inviting the neighbors to come out to the can house or upstairs wherever they kept them, to see her pretty canned stuff. When the neighbor or visitor was departing they were usually given a gift of some kind, maybe a bucket of fresh cold buttermilk, or a ball of butter, maybe something from the garden or a can of something.

Cataloochee Valley

If a neighbor had several children and needed food, they would be given more.

I guess there was never a group of people who extended their hospitality and cared so much for other human beings.

In the winter time they sat around the fire, and often told stories of their pioneering forefathers and of their own experiences on cattle drives, hunting, fishing, and many other things.

In the summertime after supper, everyone came out on the front porch and sat around resting and talking about the day's work and planning what and how they would do the next day. They were always joking and laughing.

As dark was closing in, Aunt Lizzy came out and called everyone in for Bible reading and long prayers, then off to bed. When the lamps were blown out I remember smelling kerosene.

Yes, it's true, we took baths in a large wash tub on Saturday night (and other times). First we had to carry in lots of water and heat it, some in tea kettles and the reservoir on the Home Comfort stove, and keep the fire going. The baths were taken in the kitchen because it was the smallest room and was cozy warm after heating all that water. At all other times, there was always a large washpan, warm water, and soap; we got scrubbed and washed often.

There was a table on the back porch where a bucket of water, a washpan, soap, and towel were kept. That is where everyone went to wash up before a meal. There was also a small mirror where the men could see to shave and comb their hair. The women and children could wash their hands there. Some had wash stands with a large bowl of water, pitcher, and mirror inside the house, where they primped and combed their hair and washed up.

The back porch was where we churned butter and peeled and prepared food to cook or to can. In the winter, stove wood and firewood was stacked in a neat row to keep it handy and dry.

The wood house and meat house combined, was just a few feet from the back porch. The meat house did not have a window in it. In the center of the damp dirt floor is where Aunt Lizzie would build a fire of hickory wood and keep it smoldering for days to cure the hams. Aunt Lizzie (grandma) and Daddy made a sugar cure for some of the ham too, they used brown sugar, salt, and

Ella Caldwell and her girls washing. Photo Courtesy of GSMNP.

pepper. After the hams were cured, they were washed to get the salt off and placed in clean white bags and tied to a pole which ran across the room in the smoke house.

Beyond the wood house about fifty feet, was the wash place near a bold stream. Usually the laundry was done Monday, weather permitting. There were three large wash tubs of water sitting on blocks of sawed logs. They were the proper height to bend over and rub the clothes with homemade soap on the wash board. The big black wash pot was sitting nearby with a fire under it. After the clothes were scrubbed, they were put in the pot and boiled with lye soap then rinsed two or three times and hung on a clothes line to dry, except the shirts and Sunday dresses which were dipped into homemade starch, made by boiling water and flour. When they were dry, they would be sprinkled to dampen, then they would be ironed with flat irons heated on the stove or in hot coals in the fireplace.

No one would think of going to church without having their dresses and shirts starched and ironed to perfection and shoes polished. Some starched and ironed all their clothes.

Over to the right of the wash place was the wood yard where many logs were pulled after the trees had been cut and sawed in

Cataloochee Valley

lengths. They hooked a horse to each log and pulled it there to be sawed with a cross cut saw. This was a lot of hard work; as was splitting all of that wood for the fireplace and the cook stove.

Much less wood was needed for summer, just enough for the cook stove.

I was born in the Hiram Caldwell house, which is still standing. I was six and a half years old when we had to move out of Big Cataloochee. I have many happy memories and I can close my eyes and visualize how it looked, where the houses were and how nice they were kept up. Sometimes the yards had grass and some were barren of grass, but they were kept clean by sweeping and always pretty flowers bordered them. Today as you travel there, you will find a short strip of pavement, which was put there long after people had moved out.

Memories of Music

Music was an important part of life in Cataloochee. They had teachers come in to teach singing lessons. This was for religious songs. There were others who knew and sang the old time ballads and love songs. I remember a group of musicians coming to our house one night to play and sing. They sang several songs, but the one I could remember was "The Red River Valley." (lyrics-From this valley they say you are going.) It was a beautiful song that brought tears to everyone's eyes because the park was taking over. No one wanted to leave this beautiful valley. I could feel their pain. (I think I still can.)

The very first song I remember was "The Sweet Bye and Bye" at church sitting on Grandma's lap. She sang in the choir.

Some families were so gifted in music that they could play several instruments. Then when their children were big enough to hold a guitar or other instruments, in a short time they could play too. I wish I could remember who all could play the harmonica. They could make a sound just exactly like a steam engine train, puffing along and blowing the whistle, then rumbling on down the track. I heard this before I ever saw a train. Another thing these harmonica players could play was the fox chase. There was music, but there was also the sound of a dog barking, telling which ridge the dog was chasing the fox over. Loud sounds when near, then fading away as the hounds chased him over the ridge. Sometimes they were calling here Blue, here Blue. All of these sounds were musical. I doubt if any of those harmonica players are left. Hopefully some of the younger ones will take time to learn it.

Those musicians were truly gifted. All of Mark Hannah's family, several Suttons and Messers, maybe others posessed this talent. They were always glad to come and play for any occasion.

Dr. Robert Woody, who was born on Little Cataloochee, said the first money he ever earned as a child was for dancing at a wedding. (Dr. Woody was a history professor at Duke.)

I remember sitting on the front porch in the swing, in the quiet of the day, listening to the cooing of turtle doves, sometimes the call of the whippoorwill, the tinkle of a far away cow bell, the clear-flowing creek softly humming in the background, and then a gentle breeze carried the sweet fragrance of lilacs to my nostrils.

One day I went past the springhouse, into the edge of the woods. There we had a playhouse (not a house) all lined with rocks, a short stump for a table. We had made mud pies, pretending to cook and so on. We had a big moss-covered log we could sit or lie on. As I lay on the log, I could hear the creek and most of the sounds I had heard on the porch and here I could smell the spicy clean fragrance of the pines. I longed to stay here and not go away. Pretty soon they were calling me to come to the house. I was about six years old and promised myself that we would have another playhouse when we moved away, but no, there was never another place like Cataloochee.

Daddy (Eldridge Caldwell) bought his first car, a Model T Ford, about 1930. I can remember riding in it up across Cove Creek Mountain and down the other side, going to Waynesville to see Uncle William, daddy's brother, and Aunt Sally Teague Caldwell.

I don't know which side of the mountain has the most curves, but going around all of those caused me to have motion sickness. I vomited all over myself and others. We had to stop at the next branch and try to clean up. That is the first time I can remember going over the mountain. I don't know how old

Cataloochee Valley

I was, but I probably had never been out of Cataloochee before.

My second trip across the mountain, I got motion sickness again. There were places along the road, where the branch came down in the hollow. Someone had put an iron pipe here, so it would be easy to stop and get a drink of water. That is where we stopped this time, they cleaned me up, we got a good cold drink of water and went on to town, but after that I stayed home with Grandma and others. I never left Cataloochee again until we moved. I had only left Cataloochee twice in my six and a half years that I can remember.

Both times while we were gone, there had been a big rain, and the creeks were up. The road in the valley ran beside the creek in those days. The creek was up and overflowing while we were gone.

Daddy said, "The creek was down some. Now maybe we could drive through it." He meant Indian Creek (now called Palmer Creek) near the Beech Grove School. There was no bridge and we had to ford it.

Daddy drove about half way through the creek, and we got stalled on one of those slick moss-covered rocks. Daddy got out of the car, and said, "Just sit still. I'll get some help. I'll be back soon." He waded through the creek and went on up the road. Well, we were not scared because daddy would be back. We just sat there in the middle of the creek and entertained ourselves looking for fish and talking. We were sitting in the rumble seat, my sister and I.

Daddy walked to his barn (the Caldwell Place, 1903) and put the harness on his horses, walked back and waded into the creek with his horses. He turned them around and backed them up near the car. He hooked to the bumper and they pulled us right out of there. Then he had to take the horses back to the barn, and walk back to drive us home.

The next trip was our moving day, March 1934. Daddy's nephew, Kyle Campbell, had a big truck. He came the day before we moved. He spent the night with us. They loaded part of our furniture and things on the big truck so we could leave early next morning. Everyone was up at 4 a.m. We ate a big breakfast, got loaded up in the truck and left before daylight. Some of us rode with Kyle; I sat on Grandma's lap. This time I didn't get sick, probably due to darkness. As soon as we got to Maggie Valley, fires were built in the fireplaces, everything unloaded, and Kyle and others were on their way back to Cataloochee. It would take several trips to bring furniture, household things and farm equipment. Most of the livestock were put on pasture on top of Mount Sterling, which was not taken in by the park at that time. They would be driven out on foot at a later date.

We never heard people grumbling or self pitying about having to work. Everyone accepted whatever job that needed to get done. They tackled it with great enthusiasm and pride. Their homes and farms looked much like an Amish Village, all neat and clean. They loved the good land and the good things they could grow. They helped each other, laughing and joking as they worked. The big jobs seemed small, with everyone working together.

This work ethic was instilled in them when they were small children. When the adult went to carry in a big load of wood, the child went along. He or she would be given a few sticks of kindling wood to carry. The child would then be told that he was such a big help. If the adult went to carry in water, the child was given a small bucket to help. Or if they went to the springhouse to carry a big bucket of milk to the house, the child got to carry a ball of butter.

The children were included in most of the work, and they were made to feel important for helping. As they grew older, their jobs became bigger, but they did not mind.

This writer has helped with all of the chores listed here, also helped Aunt Lizzie pick down (tiny feathers) from chickens, ducks and geese for feather beds and pillows, and cure hams, dry apples, stir lye soap, stir hominy, and punch down clothes boiling in the big wash pot. I even tried to wash clothes on a washboard, but at six years old, I did not do very well.

It was not all work, we played tap hand, ring around the roses, hide and seek, all kinds of games. We had playhouses and a grapevine swing. We had so many cousins and visitors that we always had plenty of children to play with. I liked the grapevine

Cataloochee Valley

swing best of all. Up in the woods beside the springhouse, there were several logs lying on the ground, all of them covered with soft green moss.

Some older cousins had cut a grapevine, making a swing. We could climb up on a log, grab the grapevine and swing away across the hollow to the next ridge, then grab another vine to swing back.

The big room upstairs was great to play in on cold or rainy days. Sometimes they let us make a few stitches on the quilts when they were quilting.

Aunt Lizzie liked to cook the food the big black iron kettles in the fireplace. There was an iron hook on an arm that she could swing out, to hang a pot of raw food in, then swing it back into the fire. There was one on each side. Hiram had ordered her a new 1904 Home Comfort cook stove, but she preferred to cook on the open fire as she had been doing for years. She would have a big pot of fresh pork on one side and vegetable, on the other side in another pot, and a big dutch oven on the hearth baking cornbread, the best in the world because it had a nice crispy crust on it. The dutch oven had three legs. She put hot coals under it and on the lid. She would put potatoes and apples in the hot ashes to bake. She could cook a fine meal on the open fire. She mostly used the cook stove to cook breakfast and bake cookies and cakes. The first words and letters I learned to spell were "Home Comfort 1904." That was long before I went to school.

When Aunt Lizzie made a big batch of sugar cookies (she called them tea cakes), she would fill her long apron, and come out in the yard where we were playing. She sat on the steps and everyone sat with her and ate all the cookies they wanted. I have never tasted another cookie as good as hers.

When I was a small child, Daddy came into the living room with his leather saddle bags. When he opened them, I could see the rich brown shiny chestnuts. He said, "I want you to remember this because a blight has killed most every chestnut tree. I walked many miles trying to find some, and I just found a few here and there. I know these are the last American chestnuts we will ever see." He roasted them in the fireplace, and we all enjoyed them. This was probably around 1931.

I can remember the first car I ever saw. It was a yellow roadster convertible with the top down. The car was full of young folks, all singing and having a good time. In recent years I have inquired whose car it was. Someone said it was some Allison's from Jonathan Creek.

The first radio I ever saw was at Charlie Ray and Eulala Caldwell's. There were only a few radios in Cataloochee when the park took over. We went up to Charlie's to hear Edward R. Murrow report the news, then stayed to hear the Grand Ole Opry and Amos and Andy.

I can also remember the first airplane I saw. They said it was carrying the mail. I thought it should stop at the Nellie Post Office and wanted to hurry down there to get a better look at it.

Beech Grove school was not too far to walk, but if it snowed Daddy would take us. We rode horseback also, and sometimes he would have one of the cousins to take me on the horse or to come pick me up if the snow was deep.

Our cousin Ernest Miller lived with us. He was a teenager. He was going to take a sack of shelled corn to the mill to have it ground into cornmeal. He was on the horse and someone put the sack of corn on the horse behind him and he went down the road. After a short time the horse came back to the barn with the corn still on his back. What happened to Ernest? They went looking for him. The neighbors joined in the hunt. They looked and hunted and searched for him all day and with lanterns at night. They could not find him. They could not figure what happened to him. There were no tracks to follow. The next morning some adults let me go with them to hunt for him. I must have been four or five years old, and as we were walking across the foot log, I looked down into the creek. There on the creek bank lay Ernest with blood on his head. I screamed, "I see him." They had to bend down to see him because the laurel was so thick, hanging over him. Something had spooked the horse, and it threw him into a thick laurel patch, causing him to strike his head on a rock. He was knocked unconscious and lay there that day and all night. He probably had a concussion. They got him back to the house, and after a short time he was back to normal.

Cataloochee Valley

I was afraid of thunder storms. Grandma put me in the bed and told me I was safe because I was in a featherbed. She said, "Lightning never strikes anything that has feathers on it."

The children often sat on someone's lap, mothers, daddies, aunts, uncles, or whoever was around. When the babies were sleepy they would be rocked to sleep, usually by their mother, who sang a lullaby. "Rock-a-bye-baby in a tree top, when the wind blows the cradle will rock. When the bow breaks, the cradle will fall, and down will come baby cradle and all."

In winter time they all sat around the fireplace talking, children in their laps. Before they were put to bed at night, the children's feet would be warmed real well, then carried to bed and tucked in. The children said their prayers and said good night and the kerosene lamps were blown out.

There were no electric blankets, or even any insulation in the walls, only the fireplaces for heat. Most everyone had feather beds, ticks filled with down (tiny feathers). Those were cozy for sleeping. When the weather was real cold, flat irons were heated by placing them close to the fire in the fireplace. When the iron was hot, a thick cloth would be wrapped around it, then it would be placed in the bed near their feet. Some people who didn't have ducks or geese to pick the down to make feather beds would use straw or very finely shredded shucks for their mattress. Some folks used all three kinds of bedding, especially those who had large families or lots of company.

All the quilts were handmade and padded with wool and hand quilted. Quilting was a pastime for the ladies in the winter time when there were no gardens to hoe or canning to do.

Flora Caldwell Laws

We have really enjoyed interviewing all of the Cataloochee people. We interviewed Flora Burress Caldwell (Laws) daughter of D.H. Burress and Mattie Lockman Burress. She is eighty-four years of age. She remembered living on the head of Indian Creek near Stiff Knee Mountain when she was a child.

They lived in an old log house. It was a typical old log house with two separate large rooms connected by a dog trot. One room

Flora Burress Caldwell Laws at age eighty-four.

was used for cooking, one for sleeping. Her parents slept downstairs. There was a ladder nailed to the wall, and all the children slept upstairs. She said they had six or seven beds up there in one big room for eleven children. Where the chinking had fallen out of the cracks in some places snow would blow in on their beds. They would jump up, shake the snow off the covers and jump back in bed real fast.

The most amazing thing to me was that they did not have lamps. They used rich pine knots for light. She was born in 1911. She remembered they used the pine knots until she was about five or six years old. That would have been 1915 or 1916.

We inquired how they lit the pine knots. She said people back then didn't ever use a match. We kept a fire in the fireplace all year, just mostly live coals and a little fire in the summer. We would just get a stick of kindling wood and stick it in the coals. It would soon blaze, and as soon as you stuck it to the rich pine it would light up. When asked how they held the torch, she said, "Oh, just stick it in the mud dobbin between the logs. We had to watch it very carefully so as not to set the house on fire. Most knots had a long limb where they had grown from the tree. One would last a week or more, depending what it was used for. We used to carry the torch (same as pine knot) out at night to do our chores, feed the stock and have one of the kids to hold it while others milked the cows."

Where did they get the pine knots? She said, "Oh, we would

Cataloochee Valley

go out in the woods, find an old pine tree that had fallen and mostly rotted away, we just dug away the soft rotted wood and find the knots where the limb had grown out.

How many people used the pine knots? we asked. She replied, "Well just the poorest families. Later on daddy took all the oldest kids to Gastonia. They all worked in the cotton mills. They saved their money, came back to Cataloochee and bought a pretty good farm and a nice house with kerosene lamps." She laughed, "Yes we got modern." We wondered if all the early pioneers used the pine knots. "Why, yes, they must have because the first old road was too rough to carry anything glass; besides they had to bring in the necessary supplies."

They probably worked all the daylight hours so hard that they did not need much light at night because they went to bed so early in order to be up early next morning and back at work.

"How did you start a fire if your fire happened to go out?" we asked.

"Just get some flint rocks and strike them together over some dry moss and kindling wood, or if it had rained and everything was wet, we kids would be sent to a neighbor's house with some kind of pot. Most of the time, an iron pot with a bail to carry it by. We would borrow a few coals of fire and cover them with ashes, then hurry home to get a fire started with dry kindling wood."

After that interview I talked with Raymond Caldwell about the early pioneers using pine knots, and he remembered his grandmother, Aunt Mag Mooney Caldwell, telling him they used pine knots.

She told him of her husband, Uncle George, going hunting late one afternoon while she was cooking supper. Suddenly it got dark in the house, and she rushed over to close the shutter. As she reached out for the shutter she stuck her hand into a furry black bear's side. She rushed across the kitchen, found the torch, and stuck it in the fireplace until it blazed. Soon she found Uncle George had killed a young bear and had it draped across his shoulders and had backed up to the only window opening. Since that was the only window, he knew it would make the room dark and scare her when she stuck her hand in the fur. He did it for a joke. He must have been a mischievous fellow.

Flora told me when they bought the better farm and home that it was also on Indian Creek up near a mountain, called Alice's Butt. She said a big, fat woman had lived there before, and they had named the big round mountain after her. We both laughed at the comparison.

At first they did not have a clock, but they could all tell time by the sun.

Flora said they finally got a Big Ben wind-up clock, and her older brother showed her how to tell time before she was old enough to go to school. She was taught to tell time by the sun and her shadow, before they got the clock.

Flora and her siblings had to walk two miles to school each way. She said there were so many of the children (eleven) the parents could not buy shoes for all of them. Sometimes they would get caught in the snow at school and have to walk home in the snow barefooted. Their feet would get so cold that when they came to a branch they would stand in it to warm or thaw out their feet. Then hurry to the next branch.

In spite of the hard times, she and her sister Callie had lots of fun, swinging on gingervines and grapevines in the woods. They made playhouses, using rocks stacked up to make tables and chairs. They were covered with thick soft moss. She said there was not much clay around, but they found some and made plates and jugs, other dishes, and sometimes formed the clay in shape of man, woman, or child. They outlined the playhouse with rocks and made a carpet of the soft moss.

Sometimes Flora and Callie would slip out and get on the horse to ride. Once when they were riding, the horse went under a chestnut tree and they fell off, landing in a big pile of chestnut burrs. She laughed and said, "We both got our rear end full of stickers. We had an awful time picking the stickers out of each other's rear. We couldn't let our parents know because the horse had to be worked, plowing and all kinds of farm work, not pleasure riding."

Flora laughed again as she remembered how she and Callie would go hide out behind the house. "It took us two or three days to pick the stickers out of each other. Them things stung like a bee," she said as she recalled her childhood and laughed.

Cataloochee Valley

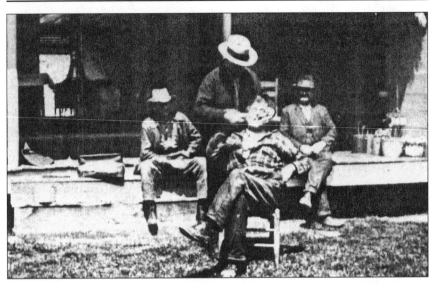

Pulling teeth the old-fashioned way with whiskey as a painkiller and a stout pair of pliers. Photo Courtesy of GSMNP.

Flora said she and her sister thought they were cowgirls. They would put a rope around a steer's neck, jump on and ride until he threw them off. They also competed with their brothers in barrel riding. Each one would get in a barrel and roll down the hill to see who would go the farthest and the fastest.

When we talked of pulling teeth, Flora said, "We did not have anything except whiskey to deaden the pain. When someone got the tooth ache, they would be given enough whiskey until they passed out, then take them to Hub Caldwell's, and he would pull their tooth." She thought he used pliers to pull them.

Jim Caldwell was another one who pulled teeth. He was a good blacksmith. He could make anything he wanted to. He made an instrument to pull teeth with. He had seen the forceps that Dr. Liner used when he came over to pull teeth, and Jim made his almost identical.

Dr. Liner often came over to Big Cataloochee to fish and rest up a few days. He brought along a little black bag with his instruments in case someone needed his service.

Flora said, "Once I was working in my garden until nearly dark, then went to milk, but the cow had not come in. I had to go hunt her. I took the .38 Smith and Wesson revolver, went out and got on our horse, Ol' Fred. As I rode up the trail, I looked up in a tree and saw a huge hoot owl. Well, he's the one that had been diving down into an apple tree near the kitchen window and grabbing one of my big fine hens. He had caught two or three of them, then flew away so quickly I didn't have time to get the gun and shoot him. Now was a chance. I patted Ol' Fred on the neck and told him not to jump, not to be scared, I was going to shoot. I shot the owl and Ol' Fred just stood there and shook. I patted his neck and told him everything is O.K. I got off the horse, threw the owl out of the trail, got back on Ol' Fred, and continued on up the trail.

"Another day I saw a hawk. It dived down and snatched one of my frying chickens. The rifle was handy. I grabbed it and fired, hitting the hawk's wing and broke it. He fell to the ground. The chicken got away and ran off. The dog finished killing the hawk.

"Once when my husband, Homer, was away from home, my Aunt came to spend the night with me. Sometime late that night the dogs were barking, and woke me up. Looking out the window I saw two men come into my yard. I could hear them talking. I grabbed the .38 pistol and fired right through the window. Next morning we could see tracks, looked like they had jumped twenty feet and ran down the road.

"Another night some man was hollering for help. I had seen two men go up the mountain that afternoon, and I knew something had happened. The man said, 'Somebody come help me get a rock off my friend.' These two men had built a fire near a large rock to cook and camp out up there. It was pretty cool and got colder that night. Evidently the rock had gotten very hot, and while the men slept the weather turned much colder, causing a big slab of rock to break loose and fall on one of the men. It mashed him flat as could be. It took lots of men to lift it off him. They hauled his body out in a wagon next morning."

House Flies

As a child, Flora remembered seeing lots of people seated at the long dining table eating. There would be two adults, one on each side of the table, slowly waving a limb with lots of

Cataloochee Valley

leaves on it over their heads of those eating. This was to keep flies off the food, since there were no window screens. Some summers there were more flies than others. Some people said it was a plague.

Sometimes they would cut newspaper like fringes, glue it on a stick, and used it to wave around over the table to scare away the flies.

Flora said, "Everybody used some kind of white powder. They would sprinkle it on the floor, then close the door for two or three hours, then go in and sweep up the dead flies before putting food on the table and serving. This was not used when they did not have the time. Sometimes they were out working in the garden, or picking vegetables and preparing for lunch."

When it was rainy and cold, the flies were worse, all trying to get in. Everyone, kids and all, would be given a white cloth. Someone would hold the door open while the others waved the towels in the air. The flies would be driven out. There were no window screens.

About March or early springtime, they started cleaning out the stables and hauled the manure out on the farm land and plowed it under. The manure was valuable fertilizer. Farmers learned that by spreading lime in the stables the flies mostly left or died. There were not so many after they practiced this every spring and the manure was hauled out on farms and turned under.

Flora recalled her early childhood days. They usually had a holly Christmas tree with berries on it at Beech Grove School. All the presents would be tied on the tree. At home they hung their stocking up, and next morning they would look really full. "Me and my sister Callie would run with excitement to see what we got, only to find our brothers had took out whatever was in the stockings and stuffed them with corncobs. They were mischievous and thought it was funny."

Most everyone said they got one orange, a few sticks of candy, and a few nuts. That was customary. Flora and her siblings made most of their toys. We made sling shots, whistles, wagons, and rag dolls. We made the dolls out of road monkey sox and used a black fire coal to draw the eyes and mouth. Sometimes their brothers tore up the dolls, then the race was on!

Candy pulling was a favorite time. When molasses was made in the fall some was put aside to make candy. The rest of it was put in five gallon tins, maybe some put in glass canning jars. To make candy, they boiled the molasses until a hard ball formed when dropped in cold water. Then the pot would be removed from the heat. When it was cool enough, everyone put butter on their hands, started pulling, stretching, and pulling with both hands. When it got stretched out long, they buttered their hands again, pulled and folded, each time using more butter. Finally it got creamy white and stiff, and it was twisted and cut in lengths. It was real good stick candy.

Food and Remedies

Flora discussed food. "Why, yes, we all had plenty of food, but the best and easiest to get were those big fine sweet strawberries–best I've ever tasted.

"There were wild berries that grew on the mountain behind our house. We would burn the broom sage off one year and the next year the mountain would be covered up with big red berries." Flora and others have talked about picking a ten-quart bucket full in just a short time.

A wagon load of family members would come to pick. Whole families came in buggies, with wash tubs to haul the berries home in. She said, "Oh, yes, there were plenty; why, the whole side of that mountain was red with strawberries." People took the berries home and made preserves and jelly. They canned lots of them to make pies and cobblers. They sure were good. Eldridge Caldwell always said he would not trade a pint of those wild Cataloochee strawberries for a gallon of the hybrid berries. They were canned in half gallon jars. We had mighty fine strawberry cobblers all winter long.

We pulled the cabbage out and buried them root up in a deep ditch. The potatoes, turnips, or rutabagas would be buried separately in a deep round hole covered by straw then mounded up with dirt and tar paper to keep them dry. We canned or dried fruit and berries for winter treats. Vegetables were pickled or canned and soup mixtures were prepared. Hog killings provided many servings of meat and sausage and ham bones for the soup mixture. Chicken was a favorite.

Of course there was always plenty of wild game, pheasant, bear, coon, turkey, squirrel, and groundhog. Some grew cane and made molasses for biscuits and sweetener.

Home Remedies

Flora remembered when people were seriously ill with influenza someone in the family would ride a horse across the mountain down to Cove Creek to get Dr. Bob Medford to come over to care for the sick. Since this was a contagious disease he protected himself. He asked for a quart of whiskey, and he always said the only thing he would eat was a big onion with cornbread and buttermilk. This was a successful remedy for him. It prevented him from catching the disease.

We talked about home remedies. Flora said, "Oh, everyone knew lots of remedies and most of them worked."

Mullin root was boiled to make tea for pneumonia and whooping cough. Sometimes this was used when a child had measles and he would not break out. If a child had red swollen eyes due to cold and sinus, someone would boil Lynn bark, and fold a cloth over it to make a poultice. This would be put on the child's eyes at night, and next morning the swelling would be gone and the eyes clear.

Then there was a woman who had seven or eight small children. She had very delicate skin and blond hair. In those days, cloth diapers were used and it took lots of washing to keep them clean, especially if two babies were wearing diapers in one family at the same time. This lady had washed diapers and her hands became cracked and sore. She went to the doctor several times, and they said she had eczema. A kind of cream had been prescribed for her, which did little or no good at all. Sometimes she would wake in the morning with her hands cracked open and bleeding. One day an old lady from Tennessee came to Big Cataloochee, and when she saw the terrible condition of that lady's hands, she said, "I know a cure for your poor hands, but you probably won't use this cure."

"Oh, yes! I will," She replied. "I will do anything; just tell me what it is!"

"Well," said the older lady, "just go out in the cow pasture and find a fresh warm cowpile, coat your hands with it, then go to the creek and wash them." Right then she ran out of the house to the cow pasture, and she saw a cow in the process of making a pile. She ran up behind the cow and caught both hands full. She said that relieved her raw hands immediately, and after a few treatments her hands were completely healed and she could have her hands in water without their getting sore. She was so happy, she thanked that old lady every time she saw her.

When Clay McGaha was about ten years old, he cut his foot wide open with an axe from his big toe almost to his ankle. His mother, Ethel, put a handful of sulphur in the cut and bound it up with a piece of a bedsheet. Today he has a very thin neat scar, and his foot has never given him any trouble.

Clay said in May each year everyone in the family had to take a spring tonic made of cat nip, molasses, and sulphur.

Ground ivy was made into a tea to make babies sleep, also to make the hives (a rash) break out. For asthma, they boiled the leaves of mullin and wild cherry bark then strained it and sweetened it for a tea. For croup and congestion they gave a child a teaspoon of groundhog grease. They all said it was terrible tasting, but it was very effective.

Grandma Lizzie made a salve with the buds of a tree, balm of Gilead (she pronounced it bama gilin). She crushed the buds and mixed this with mutton tallow and sulphur. It was used on cuts, scrapes, and sores, and it healed many injuries. She doctored with onion poultices and mustard poultices for pneumonia, croup, congestion, and flu.

She made worm medicine for the children, which really got results. She made it by boiling the seeds from a weed called Jerusalem oak, then straining it to leave a bitter tea. She knew she would never get the children to drink it, so she put stick candy in the liquid and stirred until it melted. When cool, she broke it into pieces for us to eat. It sure got good results.

Probably Granny Pop made it the same way, except sweetened it with honey or molasses and flavored it with peppermint which grows plentifully along the branches.

Soap was made by leaching lye out of the ashes of hickory

Cataloochee Valley

wood. This was added to grease or lard and sometimes meat skins and put into a big black iron wash pot with some water. They would build a big fire under it. The pot had to be stirred often, and Grandma let me help her stir it. She used a green sassafras stick to stir with, and when the bark began to peel off, that would indicate it was finished. It would be dipped out of the pot into a large pan or wooden box. When the mixture got cold it would be cut into blocks or bars.

This soap was used to wash clothes with a rub board. After the clothes had been lathered and scrubbed on the board they would be rinsed and then put in that big wash pot with more soap and boiled and punched and stirred and lifted out with that stick and rinsed through twice more. Then they were ready to hang in the sun to dry. Monday was always the wash day.

The big black wash pot was valuable to the people. They used it to make soap, boil clothes, make hominy, make applebutter, and boil water to pour over a hog they had killed so they could scrape off the hair, to dye thread and wool yarn, and many other uses.

Granny Pop grew the flax she used to weave a very strong linen cloth to make their clothes. She also grew a plant called indigo, which was used to dye clothes blue or black if used full strength. She also used black walnut which made a brown dye.

Mary Davis Palmer

I taught my first school at Big Cataloochee 1930 thru 1933. I was scared. It was my first experience at teaching, and there were twenty students and all their parents. Now they were interested in their children and they told me to let them know if their children didn't mind. Parents really encouraged me, really the parents were very nice to me.

Nobody ever missed a day, never thought of staying out because of bad weather. Some lived two miles or more away. Classes started at 8 a.m. Recess was 10 a.m. to 10:15 a.m. I would send some of the students to the spring for a bucket of fresh water, which was set on the table where everyone could help themselves. The big boys carried it from a spring across the road and across the creek.

Everybody brought a basket or bucket of lunch. Those who brought buckets usually had cornbread and milk which they placed in the creek to keep it almost ice cold. Others had biscuits with ham, jelly, eggs, etc. We all got together and had lunch, sometimes swapping food. We had one hour for lunch. We played ball and ran all over and climbed trees. I guess I climbed as many as the others did.

Sometimes they would bring their little brothers and sisters, three or four years old, to school with them and everyone wanted to sit with the little ones.

We didn't have holidays, but the men had one in particular, bear hunting. Mrs. Jarvis Caldwell (Bonnie) said she would be up at 2 a.m. to fix ham and biscuits, etc. for the men to take bear hunting. They were all excited getting their dogs together for the big hunt. I went on one hunt, walked four miles and carried a .30-30 rifle and had never learned to shoot. I was so frightened. They put me in a stand but no bear was killed that day. When they did kill one, they turned school out. Jarvis Caldwell, one of the commissioners, sent for me to send the children up there to see it. Mr. Hutchins from Canton, a great bear hunter along with Mr. Bill Bradley, Dr. Medford and others from Waynesville were there. Really, it was a festive time when the bear hunters came. Of course, I went with the children up there to see the bear and hear the exciting story.

Every parent expected the teacher to spend the night with them sometime in the school year. So I went everywhere. It was really great, the teacher spending the night and eating with them. We had a good time and the families were thrilled.

Dr. Carroll says families were dominated by men, but I'll tell you right now, the women did the work. Men did have some outings. They could go fishing, hunt wild hogs, go up to the Ledge, be gone two or three days, and so on, but the women who bore all the children took care of everything. They made a big garden so they could eat well in the winter, canned and make wonderful preserves, milked the cows, hunted the cows—all this time with a small child and expecting another. This was a really hard job for them. Another thing, it was so isolated, the trip out was so hard they just stayed over there. Maybe the women would go to town once a year.

Cataloochee Valley

They made a list of things they needed, and the men would get them when they went out, but they didn't have to buy much because the women did such a good job of canning and preserving the food.

They would take a stick and measure each child's foot and cut it the length of the foot, plus some to grow on. The men carried these sticks to town and bought the shoes accordingly, then would come back in with half a dozen pairs of shoes and see whose foot they would fit.

I have many pleasant memories of Cataloochee and it was the greatest thing ever to happen to me to live there, for that is where I got my husband, Gudger Palmer.

The Beech Grove schoolhouse was closed in 1964, and later was used by the Haywood Trail Riders as a horse camp in the 1960s and later. They installed a large old cooking range in there. It was vented, where once a big pot-bellied wood heater had stood. They slept on cots, sleeping bags or some makeshift sleeping arrangement.

The schoolhouse once had thirty to fifty children in school. In addition to the pot-bellied stove, there was the teachers desk and chair, the blackboard on the wall on the right side and on the left there was a table. There was always a bucket of cool fresh water on this table, and a dipper in the water. Everyone who wanted a drink could quietly go get a drink anytime, just so long as they didn't go too often. Everyone drank out of the same dipper, and no one seemed to get sick from it.

This water was carried in by some of the bigger boys. It was quite a distance to go out through the school yard, cross the road, go up a ways, cross the footlog that is there now, to the cold spring, which had been fixed with a cement box around it, and covered with tin or a plank to keep the leaves out. Usually two boys went to fetch the water. One would carry it a ways, then the other. This was done before school started, then at the recesses.

The horse camp has been discontinued and the little desks have been replaced to try to restore some of its historic value. Thanks again to Mr. Ed Trout, park Historian for his willingness, dedication and hard work it took to find the desks and try to restore them.

Clay McGaha

Clay McGaha's parents lived on Little Cataloochee. After the Park took over they had to move to Big Cataloochee in order for their children to go to school. The park service had closed the school in Little Cataloochee. Most of the people had moved away. The MaGahas wanted to live in the area, so they moved to the Uncle Will and Aunt Elenor Palmer's house on Big Cataloochee.

We talked about many subjects. His school days had been great fun. He said, "We played basketball at recess, but mostly us boys liked to play bear. Three or four of us played 'bear,' four or five of us played 'dogs,' then two or three played 'men with guns.' Us bears took off running, the dogs came after us, yapping and barking. You never heard the like! When they were about to catch us, we would climb a tree, and they treed us. You see, the dogs couldn't climb; so we had to stay in the tree until the 'men' came. The men would pretend to kill the bears. We built us a bear den, by making a wall of rocks and putting poles across it, then piled pine limbs and laurel over the top. We could crawl in there to hide, maybe some in different trees, some in the den, but always had to wait for the hunters to come and get us. But when that school bell rang we knew our game was over. We got in the school and to our lessons."

All seven grades were taught in the same room. They received and discussed what the lesson was about in all the grades. Clay said, "I learned more there at Beech Grove School than all the other schools I went to. I was just amazed to see how advanced we were compared with other schools when we finally had to move out. I was in the seventh grade when we went to other schools, and I knew all the lessons and was away ahead of the others. What made it so good was that all the different grades had discussed the lessons before at Cataloochee. I never really needed to study until high school, and several others have told me the same thing."

I asked, "Why did you pay so much attention to other classes?"

Clay laughed, "The teacher had a hickory that got you to pay attention to all the lessons."

Cataloochee Valley

I asked, "Did you get many whippings?"

"Yes," he said, "all the time, for mischievous things and fighting with the boys, but the roughest fight I ever had was with a girl. I don't remember what for, but I tell you, she beat the socks off me. I had never seen anything like it. I stayed out of her way after that. Then the teacher whipped us both for fighting. I didn't mind the teacher whipping me, but I sure hated for a girl to whip me. I thought I was tough before that." He smiled and looked off into space as though he was reliving the past. He said, "Yeah, that was a real life."

He talked about bringing his lunch to school. "We had a lard bucket full of good, rich, creamy milk and cornbread, which we would put in the creek. The creek was like ice water. Most of the children brought about the same thing. We had to watch for rain, and go quickly to get our buckets before the creek rose and washed them away. We had boiled corn on the cob, baked sweet potatoes, and ham or sausage biscuits. No one ever went hungry."

He talked about going to school one morning when it was cold and cloudy. After a while it started to snow, and it got two or three inches deep. The teacher turned school out early because half of the children were barefooted. When we were about a quarter mile from home we met Poppa on the horse coming after us. "Oh, how good that felt. I clamped my feet against that old horse's good warm sides," Clay said. "The next day Poppa went to Harwell's store on Cane Creek and bought us all shoes."

"Lots of people away from here thought we were ignorant and so dumb that we couldn't learn anything," remarked Clay, "but my brother Gene belonged to the 4-H club and won first place in a national contest. President Kennedy made the award of a large silver platter and Ford Motor Co. gave him a four-year scholarship to the University of North Carolina. Then he went to the University of Florida. He has his master's degree in English and math, and he teaches math at N.C. State and has taught at Brevard Junior College and the University of Florida."

Clay talked about how all the people pitched in to help each other. They would gather up in early spring and take their livestock out to pasture, then come back and get the crops planted, go back to the Ledge and salt the cattle, maybe camp out a day or two. Then they would come back home to plow and hoe the corn, then back to the Ledge to see about the cattle. Finally, they went back home to cut and put up the hay.

While they waited for the crops to ripen, they got up a winter's supply of wood, because there was no time to be wasted before the crops would have to be harvested.

Clay said, "At one time there were thirty-seven of us up at Uncle Steve Woody's getting wood. We had four or five crosscut saws going, and three or four wagons hauling it. Everyone was joking and laughing as they worked. We worked hard, but it didn't seem like it. We knew several women were in the kitchen cooking up a real feast. They never failed. I'm telling you, they really had good food at every house, and when we finished at one farm, we went on to the next. We made the rounds, saw that every one was ready for the winter. Most everybody had fireplaces, and took an awful lot of wood. They said the winters were so much worse then—more deep snows and severe cold. They could take the horses and sled across the creek on the solid ice, never worrying about the ice breaking. They knew it would not thaw until spring."

Clay looked sad as he talked of all the homes that were destroyed by the park service. His father, Burl McGaha, bought the Will Palmer house, the springhouse, can house, two barns, and the blacksmith shop for seventy-five dollars. Lee McGaha, brother of Burl came from Green Corner (Cocke County Tennessee) and bought the Carl Woody house. Lee took the lumber home and built a barn.

Kyle Campbell

"For me to tell my part in this story, I have to include Maggie Valley and Cataloochee Valley. I'm part of both places. I'll start out about my parents.

"Verlin Campbell was my daddy. He taught school over there in the late 1800s. That's where he met my mother, Hattie Caldwell. Papa always liked to fish, and Cataloochee Creek was probably the best trout stream in the world. He went up there to ask grandpa, Hiram Caldwell, if he could fish there. He said, 'Mama was working in the barn, and she looked up at him with

Cataloochee Valley

them brown eyes, like that and I thought, now there's the woman I want.' Papa tried to get her to marry him. Mama said she would when she was twenty-five. He tried to get her to marry him sooner, but she wouldn't. She would wait until she was twenty-five like she told him. They were married in 1900. I have their wedding picture.

"The first time I can remember going to Cataloochee, I was five years old. My daddy took me and Hiram and Lizzie (Elizabeth, his sister and brother), we walked across Fie Top. Papa said he had to play with me to keep me from giving out, and I walked from here (Campbell Creek in Maggie Valley) to Grandma Caldwell's house on Cataloochee.

"Papa had a big store down here in the Valley (just below the Methodist Church)—a big country store, the only one this side of Waynesville. I'll be 81 years old in March. After I got old enough to know what I was doing, I used to go over there and lay around at grandma's and Mrs. Milia Palmer's house. The reason we were acquainted with her was that my daddy boarded with her when he taught school there (in the first Beech Grove School).

"Granddaddy Hiram died when I was small, and the only thing I can remember about him was he had a pipe with a rooster on it. I used to sit on his lap while he smoked it. He was the only grandpa I ever knew because the Campbell grandparents had died before I was born.

"I loved to go to Grandma's. I never went there but what she had sugar cookies in the corner cabinet. She called them tea cakes. I looked forward to them cookies. Of course I was starved to death when I got there.

"When I was about fifteen years old, Papa bought me a Chevrolet roadster, and we would go over there in it, but before that we rode horses from here to Cataloochee across Fie Top. I rode behind my sister Elizabeth. We all had to double up, ride double on the horse. Hiram, my brother, you know, was named after Grandpa. Brother Hiram took Eula Green home to where she boarded and taught school at Beach Grove. Hiram, he come down with pneumonia while he was there at Aunt Milia Palmer's house. Me and Mama went over there to take care of him, and it was two weeks before he was well enough to come home with us.

"I really enjoyed going to Cataloochee. See, my mother was

raised in Cataloochee Valley and my daddy in Maggie Valley; so I belong to both places. It took about four hours to go on horseback up across Fie Top, down Double Gap, and up across Fork Mountain.

"I got a good story to tell about my flying over Cataloochee. This old fellow worked over there on the maintenance crew in the park. His name was Pilkington. I had this super cruiser. It would cruise (or glide) along–not make any noise. I was flying along by myself, just gliding along. I had a radio in it you could hear on the ground. I saw his truck going along in the Milia bottoms with the windows down. I took that mike and said, 'Hello Pilkington.' Well that truck stopped, both doors flew open. About two weeks after that I was over there. Pilkington said, 'I gonna kill you, Kyle Campbell.'

"I said, 'What have I done to you?' He said, 'I heard my name. I knowed it was coming from the elements. I was scared and jumped out of the truck. I just happened to see the tail of that little ol' airplane going around the mountain.'

"Major Woody was the finest ol' fellow. He stayed at Aunt Milia's. We were there two weeks when Hiram was sick. They always growed plenty of popcorn. Me and Gudger and some of us would pop it over the fire. The grains that didn't pop, we took them and ground them up in the coffee grinder. Man, that was good. We ate the meal. It had a good parched corn flavor.

"Back then there wasn't no roads much. Mama took us from here over there in a buggy that went around by Cove Creek and over the mountain that way. Certain times of the year, Grandma's cow would be dry. She wouldn't have any milk. I remember Mama put a big churn jar full of milk in the back of that buggy and when we got there, it had a big ball of butter in it. Going over that rough rocky road had churned the milk so the cream had turned to butter.

"First rattlesnake I ever saw, we were going down the mountain in the buggy. Hub Caldwell was coming up the mountain in a buggy. A big rattlesnake was laying across the road. Hub got out and took a big stick and killed it. It was about as long as the road was wide, a really big one.

"One time me and Sarah, my wife, (I've been married to her

Cataloochee Valley

sixty years) were riding horse back and we went to the big poplar for her to see it. We got back on the horses, and I heard a rattlesnake. We rode on down a little ways and there he was, coiled up. Them rattlers were really rattling. We looked over at him, and I sent Sarah on a little ways with the horses. I didn't know if the horses were afraid of a gun shot. Then I shot that snake with a .25 automatic. The snake had sixteen rattles and a button. I've still got it. That snake was as big around as my arm, the biggest one I have ever seen. It has been at least thirty years ago.

"Everybody on Cataloochee knew who you were. Anytime anybody needed help they were right there to help you, everybody helped each other. Of course, there were a few people who made a little whiskey. It was made from corn. They didn't have sugar or anything to put in it— it was pure corn liquor, very mild, very good.

"Old man Tommy Coldwell raised a big family, and they are fine people, every one of them. Lots of them live right around here. Cataloochee was a wonderful place, everybody was friends. I still think it's a shame the park took it. In a way maybe it ain't because they would have a pretty hard time over there now. But I love that place. I go every year. Grandma's house, Woody's house, and some look like they did. I walked across Fork Mountain. Brown Caldwell was raised there on Caldwell Fork, you know he married Fannie, my wife's sister. She is ninety-three. Brown died years ago. Brown's children had never been over there where he was born. We drove there and parked where the road is blacked, just up above your daddy's barn. We walked across Fork Mountain and down Long Branch. You know, he went on to become a very successful evangelist and had a radio broadcast from Greenville, S.C., for many years.

"There are seventeen foot logs from the Caldwell Fork down to the campground.

"I remember Ethan and Thurman Evans. They were raised on Caldwell Fork. Then later they worked on Fie Top for Papa. They were really good, hard workers. When the depression hit, my daddy had that big country store here in Maggie Valley. No one could find any work. If they did, they were lucky to get fifty cents a day. But they couldn't buy the necessary things. I mean they were good, honest people from all around here. Papa gave credit to them, but they just could not pay their debts. He kept on letting them have credit until he went broke, too, finally closed the store. Mama, Hattie Caldwell Campbell, would see some children who were barefooted and nearly naked, and she would go unlock the old store and try to find what they needed. She helped lots of people but never mentioned it. She saw they had overalls, shoes, boots, clothing, hardware, all sorts of things. Well, that was the way them Cataloochee people were. They helped each other. I would say they come the nearest living the "golden rule" of any where.

"And what kept us going during the depression was that Papa had bought $500 worth of Plow Chemical stocks in 1925 and all through the depression Mama looked for that check, just like I would look for a payroll check, and it wasn't but a few dollars, but it helped a lot. That's when they would say a dollar looked as big as a wagon wheel. We lived right here in this house. (Verlin Campbell house, Campbell Creek, Maggie Valley.)

"Old man Major Woody at Cataloochee was always awful good to us young ones. I would go over there and he would take me fishing. Now he could catch fish. He was crippled, but, buddy, he could catch them fish. Then Boone Caldwell, he was a real good fellow. One day I was at grandma's he come over there and said, 'Son come and let's go catch Aunt Lizzie a mess of fish.' We brought back a long string of fish."

Ethel Palmer McCracken

March 15, 1995

Today we had the pleasure of talking to Mrs. Ethel Palmer McCracken about Big Cataloochee. She was born there in 1894. She is now 101 years of age. Mrs. McCracken is very alert and clear of mind and looks younger than her age.

She attended school first at Beech Grove, and when it mysteriously burned down, she went to school in the log house Levi Colwell built in 1858 until the present Beech Grove was built. She had a two-and-a-half-mile walk each way.

When asked about snow she said, "Oh no, we never thought

Cataloochee Valley

Mrs. Ethel Palmer McCracken

of missing a day of school. Daddy (Creek George) would hitch a horse to a good size log and drag it all the way up there and back to our house to break open the road so we could walk. It was easier than wading in deep snow."

She remembered sitting on peg-legged benches swinging her legs back and forth trying to hold her books in her lap while they kept sliding off. A peg-legged bench was a log split in half with legs pegged in at angles on each side.

Talking about lunch Ethel said, "Oh, we carried it in a basket. We had sausage and biscuits, sometimes ham biscuits and eggs, butter and molasses, sometimes gingerbread, sometimes fruit cake. Not what we call fruit cake today—it was eight or ten layers of cake and a filling made of cooked dried apples, sugar, and spices. This was a nice, moist cake we often had. We would carry a jug of milk and set it in the creek until lunch, and we had cups to pour it in. We would have baked sweet potatoes, and sometimes we took apples to eat too—always plenty of food."

Mrs. McCracken told about her mother making their warm clothes from wool they sheared from the sheep. They had a place to wash and card the wool, and her mother would spin it into yarn and take it to the loom and weave it into cloth. She also sewed on a pedal sewing machine made by Arlington. She knitted stockings for the girls to cover their knees and socks for the boys. Her mother also wove blankets from the wool yarn. They had a seam down the middle because the loom was not wide enough.

On March 21, 1995, we talked about buggies. Mrs. McCracken said, "Oh yes, several people had them. When we left moving out of Cataloochee in 1920, I drove the buggy and took Mother out.... It seems like just about every family had one, Aunt Mag Caldwell, Jarvis Palmer, Aunt Lizzie Caldwell, Aunt Milia Palmer, Steve Woody. We didn't hardly ever see a car in Cataloochee."

In 1920 George Palmer moved his family to Ratcliff Cove, near Waynesville, but Ethel still remembers family life in Cataloochee. Her father, Creek George Palmer was married to Sarah Russell from Fines Creek. They had a son named Jarvis, and Sarah died a short time later. Ethel's grandma Palmer (Mary Jane Caldwell Palmer) kept the baby Jarvis for about three years. George then married Sarah's twin sister, Martha, and they took Jarvis back. Then they had four girls and three boys. George managed to buy up lots of land and was able to give all his children a good bit of property.

The children would go to church for Sunday school and sometimes to practice their singing. It was a social function which they looked forward to. A Mr. Killian came to Cataloochee to teach singing. In the summer, a Mr. Long from Cove Creek came to teach singing school, and he used a tuning fork to get the correct pitch to start the songs.

Mrs. McCracken learned to play violin from her Aunt Jane Rogers who was blind. Mrs. McCracken then played hymns in church. She also learned to play the organ from Myrtle Medford using shaped notes.

On another subject Mrs. McCracken said, "When another baby was about to be born, all the children would be sent to visit some relative until the baby was born." She remembered Aunt Susie Woody Caldwell delivering babies. She said, "She was a big woman. She rode a horse and she would go anytime day or night, no matter what the weather was. Aunt Susie really did a fine service for the community. Of course there was Aunt Annie Caldwell and Aunt Easter Sutton on Caldwell Fork and Aunt Fannie Hannah on Little Cataloochee. They delivered babies wherever they were needed. Sometimes there would be a doctor come in to deliver the baby, but it took so long to ride horseback

Cataloochee Valley

into Waynesville to get the doctor, then maybe the doctor would be off in Crabtree or somewhere out of town. If they did find him, by the time he rode over the mountain he might be too late. Midwives usually delivered the babies. These fine women were very much appreciated and held in high esteem and honored by everyone."

Mrs. McCracken said after they moved to Ratcliff Cove, she and her sister Myrtle went to Waynesville's first hospital to train to be nurses. This hospital was actually a large house on Pigeon Street. She said, "We worked from the basement up to the operating room. We had to keep the fire going, bathe patients, prep for surgery, make beds, sterilize instruments, and for night surgery we had to stand in chairs and hold the light." She said it must have been electric because it was on a drop cord, but it was necessary for the doctor to have enough light. Once when a woman was cut open for surgery, we could see she was just full of worms crawling around in her stomach. That made me sick to see such a thing."

Talking more about working at the hospital, she said, "There were five or six girls working. Three of us roomed in the attic, and it was comfortable. We had our meals in the dining room. The food was good and included. The pay was very little, except when we were on special duty. That was twenty-four hour duty. We were paid $21 per week, and we were right there if they needed us. Most of the time we got off two hours per day. We usually just sat and visited, or sometimes we would walk up town and look around."

We asked her if she ever drove a car, and she said, "No, but I was foolish enough to try once." She smiled as she recalled, "I ran it into the bank. I tell you I quit right then and there—never tried it again!"

We next talked about flying. Mrs. McCracken said, "Well, I tell you, the closest I ever came to riding in a plane, we were at Cataloochee a few years back, and some politicians were there at the reunion and had a helicopter come over there and give free rides. Well, I guess I always thought I could do what everyone else could do. Horace Woody and Uncle Jarvis and several of us got in that "thing," went all the way up to the Uncle Steve Woody place, turned around, and went all the way back down to Uncle Jarvis's place. I want you to know I was glad to get off that "fool thing," and I'll tell you, I was the first one off!

January, 1996, Mrs. Ethel Palmer McCracken is just one month short of 102 years of age. She has been living in a nursing home for a few years. She gets up early every day and bathes and dresses. She checks on others to be sure they take their medicine, get their exercise and anything else they need. She walks with a cane just to be sure she doesn't fall. When the weather is good, she will walk all the way around the big, long building she lives in. She takes some of the other residents with her, if she can find anyone who is able to walk that far.

Recently she had a roommate who needed a bath. They were short of help at the home, and Mrs. McCracken waited and waited and no one came, so she took the lady into the bathroom and gave her a bath. The lady was twenty-five years younger than Ethel. Someone came in and said, "Oh Ethel, you shouldn't have to work like that." She replied, "Honey, I don't mind the work, but the only thing that worried me a little was that I might drop her."

She is truly a remarkable woman. She never forgot her training as a nurse, and she is now 102 years old.

John Cordell Noland

"My name is John Cordell Noland. I was born in Cataloochee, February 14, 1895. My father was William Thomas Noland. My mother was Margaret Smith. My brother, Badger, bid on carrying the mail to the two post offices, Nellie and Cataloochee. Nellie was in a store building, the other one was in Uncle Fayte Palmer's house. Badger carried the Nellie post office mail from 1909 through 1912, and to Little Cataloochee Post Office in 1919. My brother, Frank, walked and carried the mail from Nellie to Cove Creek, about fourteen miles. Sometimes he rode a horse.

"Cove Creek Mountain has them dark caves way back up in there. Snow would stay in there all winter long. We had awful deep snows back then. That Cove Creek Gap looked different in those days. Big sharp mountains and just a little bit of narrow road cut through it. Later it was pushed off and made better. One day

Cataloochee Valley

I was riding a young mare about five years old. It was blowing snow hard. When we came to that cut it had drifted maybe five to ten feet deep. As we came up to the cut, the little mare threw her head back, as if to say 'hold on,' then she jumped and jumped like a big rabbit and got us through it. Yes, we had much worse winters then. Snow would lay all winter long. Then about March comes a warm rain and thaw, so creeks overflowed. I've seen them bottoms in Cataloochee covered in water.

"Uncle Hiram Caldwell, he had five brothers. Doc was one of them. We knew him well—our land joined his. He had, oh, I don't know how many acres. Must have been 200, a big pasture with a big long rail fence. Must have been a mile long, plumb up to Indian Ridge. He owned all that land called Alfred Cove Country. He would bring in great herds of cattle and put them there to pasture.

"I remember when I was just a child, he brought the cattle up there. Doc Caldwell would always stop by and talk to Mother and Daddy, told them if they needed any pasture, just go ahead and put our cows in there. He would appreciate it if they just watched his cattle and notify him if his cattle got out. There would be no charge for the pasture, and we did put a milk cow in there and built a pen on his land. We called it the milk gap, where we went to milk. We lived on Davidson Branch. That's where Doc's land was, but he didn't live up there.

"Doc lived on Shanty Branch in a big white house. (Same house his son Tommy and his family lived in later, painted yellow.) He had lots of hogs, sheep, and cattle. He was a fellow that raised lots of stock. Doc had some men helping him put up a big gang of hogs, some two or three years old. After they brought the hogs in from the woods, off the mast (nuts, etc.) they put them in pens and fed them corn for about sixty days (to harden the fat). Doc would run around this way, the big hog would run the other way around the barn, and they just met up. The hog throwed Doc down. Doc was hurt bad. They sent for the doctor, but he never did get better. Doc died. He wasn't an old man either.

"Doc's children were all small, and his brothers divided them children up and raised them. Uncle William took Herbert. Frank Palmer took Jessie. Thomas Palmer took Tommy. Tommy was about my age. I went to school with him. Uncle Harrison took

Hardy. Uncle Hiram took Minnie. Hardy was the youngest—Minnie and Hardy ate lunch together at school. Big George Caldwell took Eston. I was raised up with them, knew every one of them.

"Eldridge went to school. I would see him every day. He come here to visit me (near Lake Junaluska). He liked my stock of dogs. Eldridge got one of the pups and trained him. He would come by here and tell about his dog. Said he had sowed some grass in his yard, and one day a cow got in the yard. The dog put the cow out, and the cow slid and tore up a chunk of grass. After getting her out, the dog turned the grass back in place with his nose.

"Eldridge farmed, had a big gang of cattle, hogs, sheep, and everything. Eldridge was an awful fine gentleman. I have known him ever since I can recollect; a good friendly fellow, everybody loved him.

"Chauncy Palmer went to school at Rockhill school and met his wife, Lee Parton, when she was going to school there. They lived up here in Mooney Cove. I built their house in 1926. Chauncy drew it out like he wanted it, I scaled it out and ordered the lumber cut for that house pattern.

"My daddy sold out to Charlie Palmer in 1922, and my brother Badger sold to Charlie too. Me and my brother bought out Uncle Jim's place.

"Chauncy and others sold out. Big George Caldwell bought all that land, old mill and all. Chauncy's house material come from head of Campbell Creek. Had a train group there. They run that logging camp about thirty years. Hauled logs to Band Mill bottom where they sawed them.

"My oldest brother lived in Arlington, Washington; my youngest brother, Dave, went there to live. Badger went too, but he came back. Dave and Grady stayed there until they died.

"Verlin Campbell taught school over there (Beech Grove). My daddy named my brother after him. I was afraid of Verlin at first. He had a gruff voice, but he went down to William Palmer's store and bought stick candy. Verlin stuck it in his shirt pocket, some sticking out, and he would break off pieces and give it to us. It wasn't long until the whole class was following him around.

Cataloochee Valley

"Uncle Hiram raised lots of stock. He had that place on High Top for summer pasture. He had Bob Evart stay there looking about the cattle and clearing more land, then planting grass. Hiram raised crops there in Cataloochee to feed the cattle in winter. He would go over to the Indian Reservation and all around, buy up cattle and young mules, keep them until they were three years old, then sell them to people from South Carolina to raise cotton with. This went on and on many years. They didn't have any thing to spend their money for. My daddy went to visit Uncle Hiram shortly after he built that big house. He took my daddy upstairs to show him his house—there he had a big trunk. Hiram opened it up and showed my daddy big stacks of money, $1800 (that was rich in those days.) Hiram would loan it out at ten percent interest if anyone wanted to borrow it.

"Them folks up on Caldwell Fork had no school. Them children tried to go to school at Beech Grove, but that was too far for them to walk. Some of the children boarded up at Uncle Harrison's so they could go to school. I think George Sutton's children, Myrtle Sutton (later Fitzgerald), brother Carl, Jim Sutton, Ted, and several of them boarded there. Their mother, daughter of Harrison, married George Sutton. They stayed there with their granddaddy so they could go to school. They did get a school up on Caldwell Fork, later on when they had enough children

"I told you about Cove Creek Mountain, such a sharp, steep mountain. It had this little bit of narrow road, and when I got to the top I would just stop and look. Bill Boyd had a hundred acres—big blue grass pasture. I could see for miles and miles; it's not like that now. They have cut down the high ridge somewhat."

Raymond Caldwell

Raymond Caldwell remembered being sent to get Aunt Elenor Palmer to come to their house to deliver a baby. She said, "Well, I was going to plant corn today, but I'll go take care of your mother, and you can go to the field to drop (plant) the corn." He worked all day long for her.

He talked about making a wagon to play with. He cut the wheels from a small black gum tree, twelve to fourteen inches in diameter. Just sawed off four slabs about two inches thick, then heated an iron pipe to make holes in the center for the axles. He then nailed some planks on for the bed. He said, "There wasn't much time to play. We were always tending to the livestock, shucking corn, carrying in wood, and all sorts of things." He said he looked forward to spring time when he could go along with the men to take the cattle out to the Ledge, to pasture for the summer. Along the way he fished and caught all they could eat. He said they usually made two trips a year to Waynesville.

Raymond said they had fifty stands of bees. They sold honey for fifty cents a quart. They sold livestock and tobacco. They also had the corn mill. He talked about school in the Beech Grove School. Learned reading, writing, and arithmetic. He said there were eighteen to twenty-five students. When World War II came along, every young man except the ranger and a few maintenance men went to war. All these Cataloochee boys kept in touch, as most of the people do. All the young men in Raymond's class went to war, and all came back. None got serious injuries. He smiled, "We must have been too tough." –interview January 10, 1996

Raymond spoke about Hiram and Lizzie Caldwell. He said, "Hiram Caldwell was a hard worker, work, work, work. Once he had some young fellows working on the place while he was checking on pasture and cattle. He come in about dinner time, and they had stopped to eat and he said, 'You're good fellows, come help me saw a little wood while you rest.'

"I'll always remember Aunt Lizzie coming to Sunday school with her big black shirt and big black bonnet. She'd lead prayer, pray on her knees, with that big skirt all billowed out."

Mrs. Pearl Caldwell

Interview Dr. Carroll had with Mrs. Eldridge (Pearl) Caldwell August 7, 1977 at her home in Maggie Valley.

"Lizzie was a very devout Christian, an active leader in Palmer's Chapel Methodist Church. She was a very intelligent

Cataloochee Valley

Pearl Valentine Caldwell

woman, awfully independent, and could manage to have her way in a lot of things. She taught subscription school when she was a young woman. She was educated in Waynesville by Judge Ferguson and family. Lizzie's mother, Eleanor, was a sister to the Fergusons. Lizzie's daddy was killed when she was a little girl and the Fergusons took care of her, read scripture, and had prayer in home every night and every morning.

"Before going to bed every night she would gather all of us in a room, read Bible and have prayer. In the morning when sausage was cooked, coffee made, everything ready but the biscuits, we had prayer, read Bible, then put the biscuits in the oven. She'd nearly starve me to death.

"She did not joke much, a very serious woman, skilled in taking care of the sick and injured. If anyone got a bone broken, she and Andy (Hiram's brother) Caldwell usually would set the bone.

"Lizzie wanted her casket handmade, didn't want no undertaker. Preacher Roten down at Dellwood made her casket, and we brought it up here (Maggie Valley) about 1936 in a wagon. Preacher Groce came from Asheville to preach her funeral. (He had visited her home many times when he was the circuit riding preacher in Big Cataloochee.)

She was buried beside Hiram in Big Cataloochee."

About Grandpa Hiram Caldwell, Pearl said, "He was a joker, teased a lot. Lizzie liked to argue. Hiram, he would listen a while then finally say, 'Oh, Lizzie you ought to have been a lawyer.'

"Hiram would give each son a place and set him up when he married. Eldridge being the youngest and last to get married, stayed and kept the home place. Hiram really loved his daughter Hattie (married Verlin Campbell) and always had her a good horse to ride. After she married, he gave her cattle and sheep right along. She always rode side saddle. Anytime Hiram got a special gentle riding horse, it was for Hattie.

"Hiram and Eldridge ranged cattle upon mountains. Eldridge had pasture out on High Top Mt. Sterling Ridge. It was Glenn Palmer's, and when he moved away Eldridge bought it. (March 1921 - 105 acres for $2,250. Deed Book 59, p. 37.) Hiram had a pasture down below that at the Orr Place (Hiram bought it in 1902 - 100 acres Deed Book 15 p. 490.) They were noted for making liquor down there, but the law never went down there. If any of our cattle were missing Hiram (and later Eldridge) would ask old Mr. McGaha to bring them back.

"Later Eldridge sold the Orr Place and divided the money among the family. He would drive the cattle to Mt. Sterling for the summer, and drive them back for the winter, using dogs. Hiram and Eldridge were also good dog trainers.

"At the Kerr Place, where you start up the mountain, there was the Asbury Trail, where the dogs would go ahead and turn the cattle up the trail. We sold cattle at Mr. Palmer's scales there in Cataloochee. Buyers were there. Sometimes we would sell them in the pasture at High Top and the buyers would truck them to Tennessee. So far as I know Hiram Caldwell was the first man in Cataloochee to buy a purebred Hereford bull.

"We would winter up to 200 cattle, plus lots of sheep. We had a sheep house, above the big barn. Eldridge built the big barn across the road soon after we married in 1923, also had a calf barn.

"Eldridge took over the farm in 1919. You would think it was lonely, but it was interesting. Most interesting people came there. We boarded a lot of teachers over the years, and once a Mr. Hodges and his wife came to board with us for a while. He was an

Cataloochee Valley

opera singer from New York. He didn't want his voice to go down so he'd go up on the mountain top and practice. We could hear him all over the valley. That sure was a strange sound to most of the folks. They wondered if anything was wrong with him. We had lots of people in the summer, fishers and tourists.

"Three families came often from Marshall in Madison County. If we had room we gave them beds, if not they'd sleep in the hay loft in the barn. We'd cook for them. If weather was good they'd cook out and eat on the porch. The first year we cooked for them, but after that they did their own cooking. (This may have been descendants of Reuben Caldwell, son of Levi, who was the only one of eleven children to live away from Cataloochee.)

"Verlin Campbell (married Eldridge's sister Hattie) would bring lots of his friends, usually drummers (traveling salesmen). Verlin ran a big store and he met many drummers while working.

We raised corn and hay to feed cattle. We ranged hogs and cattle in the mountains in summer, fed them in winter. We raised sheep and did our own shearing. Sometimes we'd go to the store over the mountain (John Harrel's) and mostly paid cash, but sometimes we would take a ham to trade. We had lots of game and fish.

"When the quarterly meetings were held at Palmer's Chapel, we had many guests come stay with us, and of course they had to eat. Aunt Lizzie would send Henry and Mandy Grooms (tenant farmers) to Jackson County to catch a big load of fish because everyone loved them."

11

TODAY

They Kept Their Promise

Descendants of the past generations gather in great numbers at Palmer's Chapel in Big Cataloochee in August and at Little Cataloochee in June at the Baptist Church. Because the churches are packed, many stand in the door and by the open windows to hear the speaker. Each year someone keeps track of those who have passed away that year, and as each name is read, the church bell tolls. The melancholy sound rings out over the valley and in our hearts. The list is longer each year. The last generation born there are now getting to be the old folks. We realize it won't be long until we are gone and the bell will toll for us, too.

We have had some very distinguished speakers. After they finish, prayers are said and we sing familiar old songs, Shall We Gather at the River, Amazing Grace, In the Sweet Bye and Bye and others. Then we go outside, we hug, we laugh, we talk. The picnic tables have been set outside. Everyone is busy setting all kinds of good food on the table. The blessing is said, then everyone starts to eat, but many are so busy talking they barely eat. We meet the newest additions to the families and make pictures.

When we are finished eating, the tables are cleared. Then the crowd scatters out, some going to the family cemeteries, some going to see old family homes. Most homes are gone now, but no matter, they just go to see where the family home once stood.

Cataloochee Valley

A gathering at the Woody's house.

They shed tears because there is not much evidence that a house was ever there. Maybe some stones from the tumbled down chimney or foundation, maybe a lilac bush or some other plant, their grandmother had planted, are still bearing witness that people once lived there. They want to show the younger generation where their ancestors had lived.

Yes, they kept their promises to each other, to always return to the church and have a reunion or homecoming. The first reunion was August 1933. The first years were the hardest to go back and see their beautiful cleared land grown over with briars and brush. Their homes started leaking and rotting, and every year they had deteriorated more and more and the forest had reclaimed the fields, with the exception of the few fields they keep mowed. Even though it broke their heart to go back and see such waste, they would go to embrace their old friends and to keep their promise.

Speakers at the Cataloochee Reunion

Bishop Paul Hardin, Jr.
Bishop Earl Hunt
1972   Lt. Governor James B. Hunt
1977   Congressman Lamar Gudger

Cataloochee people have kept their promise to return to the valley for reunions after more than sixty years. Among the people pictured are Congressman Jamie Clark, Linton Palmer, and Larry Caldwell.

1978	Dr. Larry Wilkinson
	First United Methodist Church, Waynesville
1979	Rev. Mel E. Harbin
	Director, Lake Junaluska Assembly
1980	Dr. Jacob J. Martinson, Jr.
	President, Brevard College
1981	Dr. Joe Hale
	General Secretary, World Methodist Council
1982	William H. Hendon
	US Congressman - 11th District of North Carolina
1983	Rev. David Reeves
	Maggie Methodist Church
1984	Dr. Jacob B. Golden
	Central United Methodist Church, Asheville
1985	Rev. Robert Rawls
	Methodist District Superintendent, Waynesville
1986	Bishop Monk Bryant
	Retired, Lake Junaluska
1987	Dr. Robert T. Young
	Former Chaplain of Duke University and Constituent Services Representative for US Senator Terry Sanford

1988	Rev. John Rooks, Methodist Minister	
1989	Chancellor Myron L. Coulter	
	Western Carolina University	
1990	Congressman James McClure Clarke	
1991	Dr. Roy Carroll	
	Vice President, The University of North Carolina	
1992	Rev. David Melton	
	Central United Methodist Church, Canton	
1993	Rev. Webb Garrison	
	Methodist Minister and Author	
1994	Rev. Charles Maynard	
	Executive Director, Friends of the Great Smoky Mountains National Park	
1995	Dr. James W. Fowler, Jr., Candler Professor of Theology, Emory University	

These are the only names available at this time, but we always had distinguished speakers from the beginning of the reunions in 1933.

This list is from Steve Woody, grandson of Uncle Steve, referred to in this book. His father was named Jonathan and his great-grandfather was named Jonathan.

Education, Schools in Cataloochee Township

An address by Dr. Roy Carroll at the Cataloochee Reunion, August 11, 1991

Dr. Carroll gave all the statistics on these schools and spoke of their closing.

He said the focus for the communities was gone. But those rural schools were far more than cultural centers for their communities. James Rooney captured their significance well in his book with that marvelous title, *Journey From Ignorant Ridge* (1976). He wrote of the little country schoolhouse which he attended:

> It seemed, as I recall it, a lonely little house of scholarship, with its playground worn so bare, that even the months of sun and idleness failed to bring forth any grass. But that humble

little school had a dignity of a fixed and far-off purpose... it was the outpost of civilization. It was the advance guard of the pioneer, driving the wilderness further west. It was life preparing wistfully for the future.

Dr. Carroll finished his speech with this: The tolling of the church bell this morning, as at every annual gathering, reminds us that people born in this valley are disappearing year by year. These reunions were started and sustained by them as a homecoming, as a reminder of who they were, where they came from, and what they had wrought in these beautiful mountains.

I urge you to keep this tradition and that memory alive, and thus in some small measure, to establish the work of their hands.

Our Thanks and Appreciation

We want to express our thanks to everyone who works to make our reunions a success: Steve Woody for finding all the great speakers for the reunions and for being master of ceremonies, as his father, Jonathan was for many years before. Louise Palmer Ross, our treasurer for many years and before her, Jackie Sue Messer. Mark Hannah for keeping a record each year of those Cataloocheeans who have died, and to Raymond Caldwell, Clara Bell Palmer, and Lowell Hannah, all of whom have helped. Hershel Caldwell, who has gone there and cleaned and dusted the church before the reunion, also helping with the tables like his father and mother, Jarvis and Bonnie, did for many years before. We thank the Park employees who mow the grass, haul away the garbage and trash, take care of the cemeteries, and help getting tables cleaned and set up. Steve Woody has a committee: Linton Palmer, Johnny Woody, and Raymond Caldwell. They get together and decide on a speaker, usually taking him over there so he can get familiar with the place and see the historic structures and hear of our ancestors and their accomplishments. We thank the park superintendents and park rangers who have come to our homecomings, some making speeches, all being friendly and nice to talk to, and for their assistance in parking and traffic management.

Cataloochee Valley

Some of the first tables we used were homemade by Jarvis and Eston Caldwell, the tables were nice, strong and sturdy at first, but the weather caused them to become unsteady after a few years. Then fold-up tables were bought, and they are stored and brought out for the reunion.

We extend our thanks and appreciation to all who have helped, for the sixty-three years that we have had the reunion. It is impossible to remember all the names, but know that you are appreciated for your help, keeping everything running so smoothly.

Reunions

It was a bittersweet experience for former residents. Now (1996) almost all of the second generation born there have passed away and several of the third and last generations born there have died. There are only a few of us left. It is up to us to teach the young ones about their heritage and to keep the promise. Remember our link with the past, our pioneering ancestors, those who were born, raised, married, raised large families, died and were buried there.

It is a day of remembering, honoring our ancestors. It is a pilgrimage and a journey of the heart every year.

Many go to the springs to drink the pure cold water and proclaim it to be the best water in the world. They stand on the creek bank and breath the pure sweet fragrance, as they watch their children, or grandchildren play in the cold clear rushing creek, like they did as children.

Please take time and effort to honor our ancestors, choose not to let your heritage die. Choose to preserve the heritage of our families. Celebrate life, and remember our ancestors who gave us this life and grand heritage; always treasure it. Teach your children about their ancestors, the hard work, a labor of love, their courage and strong faith. Yes, it took strong faith and courage to go into that wilderness, such a dangerous place, far out numbered by wild animals and isolated from the rest of the world. Our ancestors formed a partnership in marriage, raising their children, teaching them fine moral standards, respect, and love, striving to leave them a legacy.

Palmer's Chapel

Palmer's Chapel was the only church in Big Cataloochee and was organizationally tied to the Methodist Episcopal Church South. From the earliest days, it had no resident minister and relied on circuit riders provided from a supply pool at either Jonathan's Creek or Fines Creek. Generally, the preacher came to Big Cataloochee (Little Cataloochee was Baptist) on the third Sunday of each month. However Sunday School was conducted each Sunday, with one of the local Palmers or Caldwells serving as superintendent of Sunday School throughout the entire history of the community. Three of the superintendents were Mrs. Hiram Caldwell (Aunt Lizzie), Mrs. Will Palmer (Aunt Eleanor), and Magnolia Caldwell Palmer.

The preacher's salaries were raised from collections and paid from a central fund managed by the conference. They ranged from $300 to $500 per year from 1902 until 1910 or so, then went over $1,000 in the late teens and early 1920s, then dropped to about $150 during the depression. (Minutes of Western North Carolina Conference of the Methodist Church.) Preachers also got paid in kind: hams, beans, dried fruit, etc. They traveled by horseback or buggy and stayed overnight with local families. One of them "always wore a big smile and asked about your family." "Another was a real horse trader, always buying, selling and trading animals" and "some of them didn't do so well." (Palmer, Caldwell, Woody, interview by Ed Trout 1982). Revivals were held each fall for a week, with services morning and night, and socializing in between.

Then there was one substitute preacher, who could really preach but was noted for getting drunk. When he preached he always said, "Brother, do as I say do, but don't do as I do."

Palmer's Chapel Restored

In 1899 a movement was begun to replace the first church/school (at the Schoolhouse Patch) probably because of the age of the structure (40 years) and the general population growth in Cataloochee. Land for the present building was thus sold by Mary

Cataloochee Valley

Palmer's Chapel under repair

Ann (Polly Ann) Palmer to the trustees, in the amount of one and one-fourth acres for the sum of $20 "for and in consideration of the love that I bear to the Christian religion."

The present structure was built by Charlie and Taylor Medford, hired carpenters from the Ironduff section of Haywood County. Members of the congregation donated some of their best trees for lumber, which was sawed on a portable mill about one-half mile up stream at Hiram Caldwell's new house. Information obtained by Gudger Palmer, from Jarvis Caldwell, Eston Caldwell and Floyd Woody, and filed by Dr. Roy Carroll (1977) yields a construction date of 1902. However this conflicts with the statement of Big Charlie Medford, the contractor himself. Former Ranger Mark Hannah interviewed Medford (94) on March 26,

1946. He said that he started the church, April 1899, and finished it in the summer. He said he remembered the date well because his oldest daughter was one year old at the time and took her first steps during the construction project. Then he recently verified this to Hannah.

The design of the building is very simple, being a framed rectangular box with a gabled roof. It originally stood on stone piers, which were later infilled with a continuous stone foundation. The interior is ceiled with handplaned yellow poplar boards and the exterior envelope is beveled lap siding. The stamped metal shingle roof of today most likely replaced an original one made of handrived wooden shingles. The bell tower was added in 1929, and shelters the double doors of the only entrance. The building is ventilated and lighted by three windows four over four sashes, in each side wall. Interior walls and ceiling color was at one time painted sky blue, although the present color is white. There were oil lamps, with reflectors hung between each window and another lamp on a stand that sat on the pulpit when they had night services. Heating once was provided by a freestanding woodburning heater, whose flue is seen piercing the roof in older photographs. By the 1960s or so, the brick flu had disappeared. Fire danger was the reason for removing the unit.

People had already begun leaving for other parts. From 1928 to 1932, church membership at Palmer's Chapel dropped from 110 to twenty-seven; and Sunday School enrollment fell from eighty to fifty-eight. The church building and land (1.47 acres) were purchased in 1929 by the government for the sum of $1,150.00. The congregation was allowed to continue using the church. The money was used to infill the foundation and add the bell tower and bell. The work was done by volunteers from the congregation, and Jim Edwards and his two sons were hired to help the volunteers, Jarvis Caldwell, Jarvis Palmer, among others. It is also probable the metal shingle roof was installed at this time (1929). A flat stone laid into the foundation, with the year 1929 incised into its face, documents this underpinning, the bell tower and bell, and probably the roof, too.

It appears that the people were responsible for the structure, and the park for mowing the ground. Raymond Caldwell told

Cataloochee Valley

Park Historian Ed Trout, that his Uncle Cordell painted the church in the late 1950s or early 60s.

With the formation of the Historic Preservation crew in 1977, church maintenance shifted to the park maintenance division. At this point, Palmer's Chapel was falling into poor structural condition. In 1980 the preservation crew increased the live load capacity of the floor system, which by that time was calculated to be seventy persons, to 280 persons (at 150 pounds each). This was achieved by placing a beam on dry laid stone piers, at mid-span along the long axis of the floor. This was a critical measure, as the Cataloochee reunion at the church attracts 500-700 people (sometimes more).

Additional work at the time included minor repairs to the sills, interior paneling, sanding, and spot painting and replacing of two window panes. A contract in 1980 also resulted in fumigation and soil poisoning and the installation of a vapor barrier under the building.

The next round of work was conducted in 1987-88. Nearly all the window sashes were so badly deteriorated that they were barely holding together. A contract was let to replace all of them with custom made ones of identical design, using most of the old panes.

The structure was then stripped, scraped, and sanded on the outside and repainted by another contractor. The interior was also painted, but did not require as much preparation as the exterior. When all work was finished on the lower portion of the church, the preservation crew removed the metal shingle roof and replaced it in kind. Finally French drains were installed along both long walls to carry groundwater away from the foundation. These measures put the building into its present state of excellent repair. (Source Mr. Ed Trout, Park Historian-Historic Structure Report)

About the Pictures of Homes

It is hard to visualize the many big beautiful homes that once stood in Cataloochee. It seems unbelievable to most people today (1996) because there are few of us remaining who

Homer, Flora and family moved from this house on Shanty Branch. The house was built by George Caldwell. It was first a log house. When the sawmills started operation in the 1880s, the logs were covered over with lap siding and the house was enlarged. Photo Courtesy of GSMNP.

once lived in them and visited in them. The pictures in this book will testify to others that they really were there. It is to be understood that their homes were the people's pride and joy. They were kept up, painted and cared for. It looked like going into an Amish village, everything was kept neat and clean. Farms were never grown up in weeds and briars. I can still see the long straight corn rows, green pastures, fat cattle, and beautiful horses. It is regrettable that more photographs were not taken when people were living there and everything was kept in pristine condition. In 1928 and earlier, the people heard they would be put out, but they could not believe it, but if it was true, they would not spend money to keep it painted or fixed up for the government. But everything looked fairly good up until about 1933-34 when most people finally realized they could not live there anymore, and moved away. Some tried to stay on, by 1937 most had moved away.

If you notice, all the pictures were taken after the paint was about gone, the roofs leaking, fences falling down and in the dead of winter, when everything was bleak, not even a green

Cataloochee Valley

leaf. The yards and fields had grown up in weeds and briars. But at any rate, we are grateful to have these pictures. At least the descendants and others will have something to substantiate that their homes were there. Several of these photos were made by Mr. Wilburn and others and C.S. Grossman about 1937 and can be found in the archives in Sugarland Visitors Center, Smoky Mountains National Park headquarters in Gatlinburg, Tenn. Mr. Grossman was probably hired to photograph the buildings before they ordered them burned down.

Maybe when tourists and others go there and see the few nice buildings, they are surprised because, after all, we had been portrayed as poor whites, living in shacks in the Appalachian Mountains, by outside writers, even in some text books. All the nice homes are not pictured here because all the pictures were not available.

Cataloochee Homes and Families
HOMES ON BIG CATALOOCHEE:

LARGE WEATHERBOARDED HOUSES
John Palmer House
Turkey George Palmer - stayed until he died, 1939
George Caldwell house
Tommy Caldwell house
Hiram Caldwell house still standing
Hub Caldwell house still standing. Now the rangers reside there.
Jarvis Palmer, house still standing, now museum.
Steve Woody, house still standing
Andy Caldwell house
Harrison Caldwell house
William Palmer house
Frank Palmer house
Will Palmer house
Jarvis Caldwell house
George Sutton at the Kerr place
Charlie Palmer house Davidson Gap

LOG HOUSES
Elija Messer house
Levi Caldwell house (grandson of first Levi)
Frank Palmers first house
Jonathan Woody, log, later enlarged and weatherboarded
Rosco Caldwell
Dillard Caldwell
Burl McGaha
Jess Lockman

LOG HOUSES ON LITTLE CATALOOCHEE
Jim Conard
John Connard
Dave Nelson
Jim Hannah

FAMILIES ON CALDWELL FORK

LOG HOUSES	WEATHERBOARDED HOUSES
Jim Sutton	Lige Messer
Jim Evans	John M. Caldwell
Robert Palmer	Ben Sutton
Carson Messer	Ches Long
Bob Parton	Addie Sutton
Neal Franklin	McGee House
Linkie Place	Thad Sutton

FAMILIES ON LITTLE CATALOOCHEE
BIG WEATHERBOARD HOUSES
Bartlett Bennett
Will Messer
Claude Valentine
John Burgess
Rhode Hannah
Mack Hannah
Ervin Messer

Cataloochee Valley

Bennetts Honor Ancestors, 1993

Seventy-one members of the Bennett family from seven states gathered one Saturday at Palmer's Chapel in the Cataloochee Valley of the Great Smoky Mountains National Park to mark with a monument the graves of Allie and Young Bennett, both of whom died in the early 1890s. The Bennetts were among the first few families to settle the wilderness area of Cataloochee in the 1830s. (1836)

When the conflict between the North and South erupted into armed warfare in the 1860s, six of their eight sons (two of whom were killed in battle) served the Confederate cause by enlisting in various companies of North Carolina troops.

The Bennett house was burned by the Yankee regiment known as "Kirk's Marauders" in the spring of 1865 during its march from Waynesville over the mountains into Tennessee. Then in the 1930s the Bennett land was taken over by the government and incorporated into the Great Smoky Mountains National Park. In spite of these losses members of the Bennett family went on to prosper and contribute to the growth and development of Western North Carolina and other communities in which they lived. They became farmers, bankers, investment advisors, doctors, dentists, pharmacists, lawyers, judges, scholars, educators, engineers, religious leaders, members of the armed forces, state legislators, and university trustees. One member, "Doc" Kelly Bennett (1890-1974) a pharmacist, was such a proponent of scenic preservation of the mountain region that he was known, during his years of public service in the House and Senate of the North Carolina legislature, as the "Apostle of the Smokies." Mount Bennett, in the National Park near Bryson City, was named after him. Among those attending the June 29, 1993 memorial service and picnic luncheon were Edward K. Bennett, assistant Vice Chancellor, and James W. Bennett, Vice President of Public Relations, of University of Tennessee in Knoxville, Tennessee; G. Willis Bennett, former provost of the Southern Baptist Theological Seminary, of Louisville; John C. Bennett, Jr., former Asheville assistant superintendent of the U.S. Postal Service; Zelma and Bob Barnes from Candler; Harold Bennett,

Jasper Newton Bennett and his wife Jalie Gillett Bennett. They were among the first permanent settlers on Big Cataloochee. Photo Courtesy of Carolyn B. Mahaffey.

former president of the North Carolina Bar Association; and investment advisors John Bennett Whatley and his wife Molly and their daughter, Katherine Grace, of Asheville; and seventeen members of the Haywood County family of Mary Dell and Robert Ferguson.

After researching the family's history for nine years, Carolyn Bennett Mahaffey of Atlanta decided it was time for the descendents of Allie and Young Bennett to get together (some meeting each other for the first time) and properly mark their graves. After producing proper documentation, she was given permission by the U.S. Department of the Interior's National Park Service to erect a monument to them at the sight of their graves above Palmer's Chapel, the little church which was founded in 1858 where Young Bennett served as a trustee.

In addition to honoring their pioneering ancestors, Mahaffey wanted the present day family to affirm the values of working hard, of being dedicated to the services of one's fellow human beings, of having faith in a higher power, and of never giving up even in tough times, all the values that the pioneer couple bequeathed to their descendants.

Cataloochee Valley

The Bennett Family, which has been in Western North Carolina for over 200 years.[1]

Dancing

In the decades before the Civil War (and long after), social life in this country was quite different from today's. All the county then was rural, and with still much rawness of the frontier. Waynesville, the only town in Haywood County, was just a wooded hamlet of around three hundred population.

Travel was so difficult in the wintertime that the more isolated settlements were left to themselves, with but little ways and means of entertainment. After the crops were harvested and the winter provisions brought in and looked after, there was more time on hand than we today can imagine.

So it was, as the chill of the late autumn nights grew on, that parties or "hoe downs" were in order. These dance parties generally alternating in the homes where they were permitted, constituted the main social events of those days. They were about the same order or pattern wherever they were held, throughout the entire Southern Appalachian region. In Haywood County, they were kept up from our earliest settlements until well into the present century.

A hundred years ago (written 1961) the waltz had not been introduced to any appreciable extent in this county. It came later on with the coming of tourists and the opening of Haywood White Sulphur Springs Hotel, in Waynesville, North Carolina.

It must be remembered that in this period of our history, before the Civil War and on up until about 1875 or 80, the church did not oppose dancing so much. This severe opposition began, probably in the late 70s or at the beginning of the temperance movements in this state. The free-for-all jiggling (now called clogging) and duet contests were often real dance marathons, to see which ones could stay on the floor the longest.

The Old Virginia Reel (with its modified forms and figures) was danced to fast time music, like shindigs and buck dancing.

Fall and winter was dancing time after all the chores were

---

[1]Asheville Citizen-Times, Tuesday, June 19, 1993 - Information from Mrs. Carolyn Bennett Mahaffey, Atlanta, GA

finished, supper over and the gals had dressed. Somewhere in the neighborhood two old masters of the banjo and bow (fiddle) were apt to be tuning up. Come the crisp October air, and long nights, as sure as you're alive these shindig parties were being pulled off, sometimes as often as two or three nights a week. This was kept up until about March, when the demands of the spring work began.

    The fire in the dining room is sending up sparks with a cheerful pop! pop! and the seasoned oak and hickory firewood is piled high in the corner against the chill of the night. The dining table has been moved out to make room, but the long wooden bench has been moved over to the wall to furnish more seats, some stood in the corners and doorway.

    The fiddlers are tuning up, and now comes the call, "Choose your partners!" The gents quickly glide over the floor, each one taking his gal by the hand. Instantly the music starts, there comes a shuffling of feet, and the dance is on! Perhaps they are playing "Sourwood Mountain" or "Cumberland Gap." There were many other favorites like "Cindy," "Shortin' Bread," "Black-eyed Susan," "Cripple Creek," "Turkey In the Straw" and many others. There is a shuffle of feet and whirl of skirts as the pattern of the square dance or Ol' Virginia Reel is carried out with the caller announcing the changes.

    On and on the festivities go until the hour is growing late. The ground outside is hardening with frost, but still the dance goes on, with an occasional rest-spell for all.

    Generally about the time of the "three o'clock rooster crow" the merry making would stop, then all would depart for home on foot or on their horses to catch a little sleep. But doubtless they never dreamed that many of these very mountain tunes and ballads, together with the square dance, would one day become classical folklore music and entertainment.[1]

    In all of Cataloochee, the folks really enjoyed dancing, they gathered and danced every chance they got, with the exception of a few who did not approve. They had some fine musicians, the Hannah family, the Suttons, and Messers and maybe others. Elijah Messer, one of the very early settlers, was called Fiddlin' Lige Messer. But he spoke with an accent (German) and called it

---

[1] Mr. W.C. Medford, Early History of Haywood County p. 91, 92, 191, 192, 193.

Cataloochee Valley

his violin and he could play any tune he heard. Also Cal Messer was an excellent fiddler, they said. But they were all good, could play any stringed instrument, also the harmonica and mouth harp or jews harp.

In talking with Blye Caldwell about dancing, she said, "Dancing was about the most fun we ever had. We had a big dance just about every week, in just about everybody's house, except a few people who didn't want us to. But they would have parties for us. We told jokes and played games." The only game she could recall was Spin the Bottle. "Everyone sat in a circle, the boy spun the bottle, when it stopped it would be pointing at someone, then he got to kiss the girl who was closest to where it pointed."

Blye said, "Another thing that was fun, was the box suppers. They were held in the school house. Women baked cakes and girls packed a box lunch. Some of the folks that made music would always come and play for us. Everyone who wanted to take a chance on winning one of those good homemade cakes, could pay twenty-five cents and line up around the outside of the room. The music played and everyone danced in a single line around and around and around the room. Two or three would be in charge of this event, and they would decide where the winning spot would be, but no one else knew. The music played, the dancers dance around the room until the music stops. Whoever is on the lucky spot won the cake. That went on until all the cakes were gone."

Then lunch boxes would be put up for auction. The auctioneer would tell which girl made it. The boxes had good food in them and wrapped in crepe paper with ribbons or flowers made of crepe paper. The boxes of food were not only good, they were pretty all were decorated.

Sometimes the bidding was fast and boys were outbidding each other, because the highest bidder got to eat with the girl, and the boys always tried to get each other's girl. No one got mad; it was just fun. They would go out and sit on the creek bank or under a shade tree to eat.

"All of the money they made was for the church and everyone had fun, and we had box suppers often," Blye said.

Maggie Mooney Caldwell and her son Roscoe. She was the wife of George Caldwell. This photo was taken about 1900. Photo Courtesy of Maggie Rich Caldwell.

Flora Burgess Caldwell (Laws) said, "Oh yes, we always had lots of dances and when it was over, we ate a big meal. Whoever had it at their house would always have plenty of good food and hot coffee, hot cider, and so forth. While we were eating, we would plan where to have the next dance."

Reuben Caldwell, son of Levi, had a grandson who lived in Spring Creek. He told of Hiram coming from Big Cataloochee to Spring Creek to visit them. He said, "Hiram always rode a fine horse and his shepard dog always came with him. After supper some folks made music for us. We sat around the fire and talked of families, cattle, crops, etc." Then he said, "Uncle Hiram pulled off his boots and said, 'I will show you how to buck dance.' Then he danced for us. It was a real pretty dance; he had rhythm and he did a fancy step called buck and wing. Later, after he had left next morning, we wondered why it was called buck dance. We thought maybe the Indians had taught him that. Back then young Indian men were called Bucks," he said.

The beautiful Virginia Reel has been all but forgotten. It's a shame because it was such a graceful dance and was brought here by our ancestors. Aunt Mag Mooney Caldwell thought it was sinful to dance, but she loved the Virginia Reel and she said it was just a game. That was how she thought of it and danced it.

The square dance has always been popular in the mountains. There are many different patterns: Four Hands over, The

Cataloochee Valley

Sam Love Queen, center, with the Soco Gap dance team. Photo courtesy of Gordon Schenck, Jr.

Garden Gates, The Ocean Wave, The Kings and Queens Highway, The Georgia Rang Tang, the Shu Fly Swing and others.

In the early days square dancing was much smoother than today. It was a shuffle of feet to the exact timing of string music, either fast or slow. The leather soles of their shoes on the wooden floors had a beautiful rhythmic sound, like a light tap to the music. There were no drums needed in the string bands. No metal taps on their shoes either. It was a beautiful dance, quieter, and more dignified than the square dances of today.

Right here in Maggie Valley and all of western North Carolina we have some very fine dancers. In 1939 one group became so well known and famous that they were invited to the White House by Mrs. Eleanor Roosevelt for a command performance for the King and Queen of England. The leader of this dance team was Sam Queen, Sr. On this dance team were Kyle Campbell and his wife Sarah and other relatives, also a daughter of Hub Caldwell's, named Beulah.

After fifty years the same dance team, called the Soco Dancers, were called on to perform again in Washington, D.C. Some of the original team were still dancing and went. The descendants of some of the original dancers, went to dance in place of those who could not go.

The first time they danced in the White House, but fifty years later they danced in the Smithsonian Museum of Natural History, in the Pendulum Room. A man by the name of Alan Lomax had arranged for this dance. After the dance, he showed them a film of the dance fifty years before, and to everyone's surprise, they had danced to the same tunes and done the same figures, it had not been planned, but the tradition had been carried on so well, they had not forgotten.

Maybe some people have a "gene" for dancing. Hiram Caldwell's great-grandson, Kyle Edwards and family own the Stomping Ground in Maggie Valley. When Kyle was twenty years old, he danced in World Champion Clogging Competition, and he won first place and was the "world champion." Again when he was forty-two years old, he was world champion in his age group. His son, Burton, has been World Champion Clogger four times, his daughter Becky Revis, was also World Champion one time. Then Becky and Burton won US Champion duo twice. Now Burton and Becky have two children each, and they are starting to dance.

So here we have Hiram buck dancing, his son Eldridge a good dancer and caller, and Hiram's grandson Kyle Campbell on the famous Soco dance team. Hiram's great-great grandson Burton Edwards and his great-great granddaughter Becky Edwards Revis both world champions.

Square dancing has been a tradition and part of our heritage, which should not be lost. We have a fine young man here who realizes the importance of preserving our tradition of old time dancing and music. He is Joe Sam Queen, grandson of the famous dance leader, Sam Queen, Sr. Each year Joe Sam has a gathering of mountain musicians at Lake Junaluska, and he also has street dances (square) on Main Street in Waynesville, on some summer nights. Mr. Queen is to be commended for keeping the tradition of square dancing alive. Hopefully square dancing and old time mountain music will not be forgotten like the Virginia Reel.

Burton Edwards and his sister Becky Edwards Revis have performed in Las Vegas at the MGM Grand, Hee-Haw, Nashville

Cataloochee Valley

Network, Grand Ol Opry, New York, and at the Stomping Ground with their team called "The Magnum Cloggers." Burton has taught classes at Western Carolina University and in a number of other states.

Becky and Burton have been on many cruises on the Norwegian Cruise Line as part of the entertainment, and they will continue performing in certain seasons on the ship and at the Stomping Ground in summer and fall.

Hiram Caldwell's great-great grandchildren Burton Edwards and Becky Edwards Revis, have dancing in their genes.

12 APPENDIXES

Debt of Gratitude

All the Cataloochee people owe a great debt of gratitude to several people: Mr. Ed Trout, park historian for his interest and dedication to get this church and other buildings restored. Mr. Trout worked faithfully to get funds for these projects. We give him credit for saving our buildings; if not for him, perhaps these buildings would be beyond repair now. Mr. Trout got the old iron bridge replaced.

In a letter from Mr. Trout, dated January 28, 1996, he states, "The Historic Preservation crew actually did the work, and they hardly ever get any recognition. The standbys through the 70s and 80s were Danny Sohn, Paul Qually, Bob Shubert, Herb Willford, and Ray Myers. All but Shubert have transferred or retired. Bob still runs the present crew. I, too, forget who else was involved in the museum, but I do know that Tom Robbins at Lufty, a historian himself, had a lot to contribute in the interpretation. Kitty Mancill, the curator and archivist has long cared for the exhibits. Stan Cantor, chief of interpretation, set up most of what's in the Palmer house."

Mr. Trout is now retired. He says, "I guess I was just the principal cheerleader." But thanks, Mr. Trout, we know how tough it was to get funds. And your sincere interest is more appreciated than you know.

We thank all the others mentioned above. We know it took good teamwork to do it. Tom Robbins did a grand job of making the tape on Cataloochee. It can be heard at the little museum there. We hope he will make more.

Many thanks to Kitty Mancill and others at the Sugarland Visitors Center at Gatlinburg, Tenn. Park Headquarters, who were so kind and helpful when we went looking for information, pictures and such.

Thanks to Mr. Randall Pope, superintendent (now retired) for getting some repairs to the Hiram Caldwell house. After it

Cataloochee Valley

had been repaired, someone had taken something from it. He was very prompt in getting it fixed, and a special thanks to him for getting a picture of Uncle Hiram and Aunt Lizzie Caldwell put in the little museum. Thanks to all who helped. Sorry if I have forgotten some names.

Now we have a new historian, David Chapman, and a new superintendent, Karen Wade, and a new preservation crew. Hopefully they will be able to help maintain the few historic buildings. We also hope that the new organization which calls itself "Friends of Great Smoky Mountains National Park" will be able to help with these buildings as well as the trails and all. This new group is headed by Rev. Charles Maynard of Sevierville, Tennessee. Their interest seems to be to reconstruct trails, rehabilitate wilderness areas, repair backcountry shelters and campsites, study and protect native wildlife, increase access for the physically challenged, and furnish new exhibits and facilities.

Our museum needs to be bigger. The park service collected lots of valuable antiques for that purpose. Wouldn't it be grand if some of the things could be put on display as promised by park officials when they were taking the artifacts from the people?

Gudger Palmer says there was a park ranger stationed in Big Cataloochee about the time the museum was being set up. His name was David Dahlen. He was very much interested in history and had quite a bit to do with the museum. We thank Mr. Dahlen and everyone else who has contributed any help in preserving Cataloochee.

If you want to send a donation, the address is:
Friends of Great Smoky Mountains National Park
107 Park Headquarters Road
Gatlinburg, TN 37738.

You can specify what your gift is to be used for. Even though it seems that trails, etc., are their main interest, they did restore a fire tower on the Tennessee side of the park. They also rebuilt a kitchen in a house in Roaring Fork. This was specified by the donor, also in Tennessee.

We want to express thanks and gratitude to Karen Wade for repairing wind damage to some roofs and other things. We are pleased to have a lady ranger.

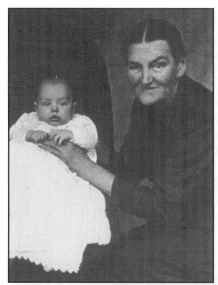

Top left: Lizzie Howell Caldwell with her son Eldridge. Top right: Eldridge Caldwell at the time of his forest service retirement. Left: The interior of Beech Grove School. Below: The interior of Palmer's Chapel.

Sheriff of Haywood County, William Palmer and his horse, Big Mac. William Palmer was born and raised in Big Cataloochee.

Sunday afternoon at Creek Creek George, Laura Palmer Palmer, Harley Palmer, John Palmer and Jarvis Palmer.

Levi Caldwell, grandson of the first Levi.

My, How they grow in the at the Jarvis Palmer House in

lmer's place. Left to right: rrett, Will Palmer, Maria lmer, Polly Palmer, Jim

Emma Valentine with her granddaughter Gladys in her lap. Ivelta is on the right, and Arletha with a Messer child is on the left.

aloochee Valley! A gathering late 1920s.

Jarvis Caldwell in the Palmer Mill.

Cataloochee Valley

Genealogical Information on Caldwells of Cataloochee to 1860 by Roy Carroll, 1984

FIRST GENERATION OF CALDWELLS IN CATALOOCHEE

1. Henry Colwell, born c. 1759 or 1760 in Pennsylvania. Married ? Settled in Buncombe Co., N.C. in 1807. by 1810, he and wife had 3 sons and 3 daughters, all "to 10 yrs of age." Still living in 1850 in Spring Creek district, Buncombe Co., N.C. Died before 1870 Census.

2. James Colwell, son of 1. above, born c. 1801, died late 1866 or early 1867. Married Mary ? in 1814 or 1815 Had at least 4 sons and 4 daughters, including:
a. Levi, born October 14, 1815, died Nov. 4, 1864 (Gravestone, Caldwell Cemetery)
b. Reuben A., born c. 1832, married Nicey Evans on October 11, 1854 (Early Marriage Bonds, Haywood Co., 1808-1870).
c. Alfred, born c. 1834 or 1835, married Elizabeth Hall on September 13, 1857 (Early Marriage Bonds....)
d. Louisa, born c. 1841.

3. Levi B. Colwell, son of 2. above, married Mary Ann Nailand (Neyland?) about 1836. Mary Ann was born May 27, 1817, and died February 18. 1917 (Gravestone, Caldwell Cemetery). She was from Buncombe Co., N.C. In 1830 Census, a neighbor of Henry and James C. was Patrick Nailand. Levi and Mary had 12 children:
a. Harriett Elisabeth, born June 11, 1837, died October 25, 1903 (Gravestone, Little Cataloochee Baptist Church), married Daniel J. Cook. July 25, 1854 (Early Marriage Bonds....)
b. Louisa Matilda, born Aug. 12, 1837 (should be 1838) died March 17, 1896 (Gravestone, Little Cataloochee Baptist Church) Married (1st) Creighton Bennett, June 3, 1856 (Early Marriage Bonds....) and married (2nd) J. Valentine ("Tine") Woody, October 29, 1880.
c. Nancy Jane, born Sept. 9, 1841, died Nov. 22, 1918 (Palmer Family Bible; Haywood Co. Death Certificate Book 5, p. 169). Married George Lafayette (Fate) Palmer in 1860 (Palmer Family Bible).
d. William Jarvis Harrison, born Feb. 9, 1844, died July 20, 1929 (Gravestone, Caldwell Cemetery; Haywood Co. Death Certificate, Book 16. p.102), married Susan Adeline Woody, April 24, 1870, (Index to Marriages, Haywood Co., 1850-1921). She was born March 28, 1848, died Jan. 6, 1929 (Haywood Co. Death Certificate Book 16, p. 98).
e. Andrew C., born May 9, 1845, died Feb. 2, 1916 (Gravestone, Caldwell Cemetery), married Charlotte Matilda Owens, Sept. 27, 1868 (Index to Marriages, Haywood Co., 1850-1921).
f. David Marion, born 1847, died ?, married Eliza Cagle about 1867.

g. Reuben A., born 1849, died ? After 1870 married a Nancy Woody and moved to Spring Creek, Madison Co.

h. Hiram J., Born June 3, 1851, died May 19, 1922, (Haywood Co. Death Certificate Book 10, p. 96; gravestone Caldwell Cemetery) Married Mary Elizabeth Howell, Jan. 22, 1880 (Index to Marriages, Haywood Co., 1850-1921).

i. John W., born 1854, died ?, married Nicey (Nicie) McGee, Feb. 10, 1876 (Index to Marriages, Haywood Co., 1850-1921).

j. Doctor L., born Oct. 1855, died 1901, married Sarah M. Palmer, Feb. 4, 1885 (Index to Marriages, Haywood Co., 1850-1921).

k. George Henry, born Dec. 1857, died 1928, married Margaret (Maggie) Sarah Mauney, April 6, 1881 (Index to Marriages, Haywood Co., 1850-1921).

l. Mary, born 1864, living in 1870, but apparently died young.

3h. Hiram J. Caldwell, fifth son of 3 above, born June 3, 1851, died May 19, 1922. Married (Haywood Co., Index to Marriages, 1850-1921) on Jan. 22, 1880, to Mary Elizabeth Howell, daughter of Albert Howell and Eleanor (Ferguson) Howell. She was born March 17, 1855, died Aug. 25, 1937 (Haywood Co. Death Certificate Book 25, p. 94). Hiram J. and Mary Elizabeth had five Children:

(1) Harriett ("Hattie") born Dec. 1880, died ? . She married Verlin A. Campbell.

(2) William, born March 1885, died ? (The Index to Delayed Birth Certificates, Haywood Co. Book 20, p. 32, lists a James H., son of Hiram and Mary E., born March 10, 1885, is this supposed to be James W. for James William?)

(3) Dillard Wilson, born October 28, 1890, died March 23, 1962. Married Clercy White (Haywood Co. Death Certificate Book 43, p. 35).

(4) John Connie, born 1895, died 1896 (Gravestone, Caldwell Cemetery).

(5) Reuben Eldridge, born Jan. 8, 1898, died June 13, 1973 (Index to Delayed Birth Certificates, Haywood Co., Book 25, p. 29; Interview with his widow, Pearl (Valentine) Caldwell, July 2, 1977). Reuben Eldridge C. married (March 23, 1923) Pearl Valentine, daughter of Robert Valentine and Emma (Killian) Valentine. She was born July 23, 1904, in Cosby, Tenn. (Marriage Certificate, and interview with Pearl Caldwell, July 2, 1977).

3i. John W. Caldwell, sixth son of 3 above, born c. 1854 or 1855, died ? . Married Nicie McGee (Feb. 10, 1876), daughter Jesse McGee and ? She was born Oct. 5, 1857, died Dec. 7. 1923. Her husband was still living at *the time of her death (Haywood Co.Death Certificate* Book 10, p. 140). John H. and Nicie had at least two children:

(1) Charles, born c. 1879, died ?

(2) Robert, born c. 1883, shot and killed Aug. 9, 1922. (The 1910 Census lists a Robert S , age 28, and wife Agnes, age 24, married 6 years, but I am not sure this is John and Nicie's son.)

3j. Doctor L. Caldwell, seventh son of 3 above, born Oct. 1855, died 1901 (Gravestone Caldwell Cemetery);. Married (Feb. 4, 1885) Sarah E. (or

Cataloochee Valley

M?) Palmer, daughter of Jesse Palmer and Mary Ann or "Polly" (Rogers) Palmer. She was born 1867, died 1899 (Gravestone, Caldwell Cemetery). Doctor L. and Sarah had seven (?) children:

(1) Herbert E., born April 1887, died 1903 (Gravestone, Caldwell Cemetery).
(2) George L., born 1888, died 1893 (Gravestone, Caldwell Cemetery).
(3) Jessie, born May 1890, died 1967 (Information from son Frank Davis).
(4) Minnie, born April 1892, died ?. She married Thurman Davis of Iron Duff. (information from son Frank Davis).
(5) Thomas H., born Feb. 21, 1894 (Index to Delayed Birth Certificates, Haywood Co.), died June 12, 1971 (information from daughter Sara).
(6) Eston F., born March 1896 (still living 1978).
(7) Harden ("Hardy") Robinson, born April 1, 1898 (Index to Delayed Birth Certificates, Haywood Co.), died ?.

Levi B. Colwell (or Caldwell) married Mary Ann Nailand (or Neyland) about 1836. He was born Oct. 14, 1815, and died Nov. 4, 1864. Mary Ann or "Granny Pop," as she came to be known, was born May 27, 1817, and died Feb. 18, 1917. Their 12 children are listed above. Levi was captured by Union raiders marauding through Cataloochee in 1864. He managed to escape, but died soon thereafter from the exposure and hardship he had experienced. It is not known whether the youngest daughter, Mary was born before or after his death. At any rate, his widow, Mary Ann, was left with nine children still at home. Levi's son Andrew ("Andy") was made the administrator of his estate. Mary Ann's tragedy was compounded by the death of her father-in-law, James, in late 1866 or early 1867. A few months later (late 1867 or early 1868), Mary Ann Colwell married Jonathan H. Woody, a widower who had moved into the valley with five children about 1866. (Source. Haywood County Commissioners Minute Book, October 5, 1868-Feb. 15, 1881, p. 12; Tax List, Haywood County, 1866-68, C.R. 049.701.1, North Carolina State Archives, Raleigh, N.C.; Estate Records, Haywood Co.; Inventories and Accounts of Sales, 1866-75, pp. 26-27, and 44, N C. State Archives, Raleigh.)

The 1860 Census for Madison County, N.C. (created from parts of Buncombe and Yancey Co. in 1851) lists Jonathan H. Woody, age 41, and his wife Malinda (Plemmons), age 41, and their nine children: William M., born c. 1843; Martha Jane, born c. 1844; James Valentine, born 1846; Susannah A., Born 1848; Nancy M. (or J.), born 1850, Lucinda E., born 1852; Stephen L., born 1853; Robert Jackson, born 1856; and Rebecca E.; born 1860. Jonathan's wife, Malinda, died about 1861. In 1866, he and five children, Susannah or Susan, Nancy, Stephen, Robert Jackson ("Jack"), and Rebecca ("Becky") came from the Spring Creek area to Cataloochee. He and his family had known the Caldwells for many years.

By the time of the 1870 Census, six of the children of Levi and Mary Ann Colwell had married and set up households of their own. Their daughter Harriette Elizabeth and her husband, Dan Cook, had settled on Coggins Branch in the Little Cataloochee area; Louisa Matilda and her husband, Creighton Bennett, had settled next to them; while Nancy Jane and her husband "Fate" Palmer were in Cataloochee, as were the three older sons: William Jarvis Harrison and his wife Susan, the daughter of Jonathan Woody; Andy and his wife Charlotte, and David Marion and his wife Eliza.

The 1870 Census of the Cataloochee area lists Jonathan Woody and his wife, Mary Ann, and indicates that three of his children (Steve, Jack, and Becky) and six of her children (Reuben, Hiram, John, Doctor, George, and Mary) were still living at home. The youngest child, Mary Caldwell, apparently died young. Her name does not appear in any subsequent census.

Seven of the eight sons of Levi B. Colwell married and set up their own households on farms in Cataloochee. The son who left was Reuben A. who married a Nancy Woody (apparently not Jonathan's daughter, but surely related to him) sometime after 1870 and moved to Spring Creek in Madison County where relatives of the Caldwells and Woodys were still living.

3d. William Jarvis Harrison Caldwell, eldest son of 3 above, married, April 24, 1870, Susan (or Susannah) Adeline Woody, daughter of Jonathan and Malinda Woody, born March 28, 1848, died Jan. 6, 1929 (Haywood Co. Death Certificate Book 16, p. 98). The 1900 Census indicates that they had 10 children, 9 of whom were still living at the time:

(1) Sarah Jane, born 1870. She married a William Mitchell Sutton.
(2) Malinda Margaret ("Lindy"), born June, 1872. She married a George Sutton, about 1890
(3) Levi B., born May, 1874. Married (1st) Etta Palmer, Sept. 2, 1900 (Haywood Co., Index to Marriages, 1850-1921), married (2nd) ?.
(4) John L., born Feb. 9, 1875, died March 1, 1942 (Haywood Co. Death Certificate Book 29, p. 73). Married Elizabeth Ann ("Annie") Sutton. daughter of Solomon and Easter (Williams) Sutton, on Sept. 5, 1901 (Haywood Co., Index to Marriages, 1850-1921). Annie Sutton was born March 24, 1884, and died Nov. 7, 1963 (Haywood Co. Death Certificate Book 50, p. 27).
(5) Louisa C., born 1877, died 1878 (Gravestone, Palmer Cemetery).
(6) Louisa A. ("Lou") born Sept. 2, 1879, died Feb. 4, 1968 (Haywood Co., Death Certificate Book 55, p. 268). She married (1st) Jesse Frank Palmer, in January 1900, and married (2nd) Thomas King.
(7) Leona Moselette, born Aug. 1881. She married Lucius Baxter Leatherwood.
(8) Rudolph, born Aug. 1884, died 1928 (Gravestone, Palmer Cemetery). Never married.
(9) James Cleveland, born July 1886, died March 16, 1939 (Haywood Co. Death Certificate Book 26, p. 157). Married Avle McElroy of Fines Creek on Nov. 20, 1910 (Haywood Co., Index to Marriages, 1850-1921)
(10) Fannie, born Jan. 20, 1888 (Index to Delayed Birth Certificates, Haywood Co.). She married Harley Bryson of Iron Duff.

Cataloochee Valley

Andrew (Andy) Caldwell, second son of 3 above, born May 9, 1845, died Feb. 2, 1916. Married Charlotte Matilda Owens, daughter of J. Franklin and Julia Ann (McDonald) Owens on Sept. 27, 1868. Charlotte was born Oct. 1, 1850, and died May 20, 1935 (Haywood Co. Death Certificate Book 22, p. 222). The 1900 Census indicates that Andy and Charlotte had six children, 4 of whom were still living at the time:

(1) Milia ("Milie") Magdala, born May 20, 1871, died Sept. 12, 1962 (Haywood Co. Death Certificate Book 49, p. 232). She married, March 2, 1888 (Haywood Co., Index to Marriages, 1850-1921) William A. Palmer, son of Jesse R. and Mary ("Polly") Ann (Rogers) Palmer. William A. Palmer was born Sept. 9, 1856, and died Oct. 31, 1927 (Haywood Co. Death Certificate Book 14, p. 132).

(2) Alice E. (Cumi), born May 27, 1873, and died Sept. 28, 1947 (Gravestone, Palmer Family Cemetery). She married, Feb. 13, 1890 (Haywood Co., Index to Marriages, 1850-1921) George Newton Palmer, son of Jesse R. and Mary ("Polly") Ann (Rogers) Palmer. George N., or "Turkey" George 26 he was called, was born Jan. 24, 1858, and died Jan. 16, 1939 (Gravestone, Palmer Family Cemetery; Haywood Co. Death Certificate Book 26, p. 107).

(3) Mary E., born c. 1874, died ?.

(4) James W., born 1877, died 1880 (Gravestone, Palmer Cemetery).

(6) Gudger, born c. 1879, died ?.

(6) Gudger, born fete. 1880, died prior to 1910. Married Annie M. ? in 1899.

David Marion Caldwell, third son of 3 above, born 1847, died early 1883. Married, c. 1866 or 1867, Eliza Cagle, who was born c. 1844. She had apparently been married before, because of the 1880 Census Mary C. has a stepdaughter named Elizabeth, aged 17. Other children in the household at the time of the 1880 Census included:

(1) Mary (or Nancy), born c. 1866.

(2) [Laura] Bell, born c. 1868.

(3) Charlotte C., born c 1870.

(4) David A., born c. 1872.

(5) [William] Erastus (or Rastus), born Oct. 25, 1875, died May 18, 1942 (Haywood Co. Death Certificate Book 29, p. 74).

(6) [Silas] Carmine, born April 7, 1877, died July 1, 1959 (Haywood Co. Death Certificate Book 46, p. 31).

(7) Jerry R., born c. Nov. or Dec. 1879.

Marion and Liza had at least two other children born after 1880:

(8) Marion Hubert, born March 4, 1882, died April 25, 1964 (Haywood Co. Death Certificate Book 51, p. 44). Married Maude Lee (Ibid.)

(9) Fred Houston, born Oct. 1883, died Oct. 11, 1964. His death certificate states date of birth as Oct. 1884, but that is too late, because his father died in late January or early February 1883. (Haywood Co. Death Certificate Book 51, p. 41; Superior Court, Haywood Co., Orders and Decrees, p. 272). Married Margaret (Maggie) Moody (Ibid.)

Reuben A. Caldwell, fourth son of 3 above, born 1849, died ?. Married after 1870, Nancy Woody. Moved to Spring Creek, Madison Co.

3k. George Henry Caldwell, eighth son of 3 above, born Dec. 1857, died 1928 (Gravestone, Caldwell Cemetery). Married Margaret ("Maggie") Sarah Mauney (or Mooney) (April 6, 1881), daughter of Hosea ("Hosey") Mooney and Mary (Hill) Mooney. She was born Jan. 11, 1858, died Dec. 23, 1949 (Haywood Co., Index to Marriages, 1850-1921; Death Certificate Book 37, p. 32). George Henry and Margaret had eight children:

(1) James Roscoe, born Feb. 11, 1882, died July 26, 1925 (Gravestone, Caldwell Cemetery; Haywood Co., Death Certificate Book 12, p. 58) Married Eliza Rich, Aug. 2, 1921 (Jarvis Caldwell, Family Bible).

(2) Ida Love, born Nov. 18, 1883, died Oct. 26, 1936 (Jarvis Caldwell Family Bible).

(3) William Claude, born March 16, 1886, died March 9, 1933. Married Gazzie McGee, Sept. 12, 1909 (Jarvis Caldwell Family Bible).

(4) Cordell Millard, born March 15, 1889 (Index to Delayed Creek (?), (2nd) Bessie Owens in March 1917 (she died Aug. 30, 1941), and (3rd) Altha Owens (she died Feb. 28, 1960) (Jarvis Caldwell Family Bible; Haywood Co. Death Certificate Book 46, p. 28).

(5) Doctor Norman, born Nov. 7, 1891, died March 21, 1964. Married Lizzie White of Maggie Valley, Dec. 26, 1915. She died Sept. 16, 1965 (Jarvis Caldwell Family Bible; Haywood Co., Death Certificate Book 51, p. 39). I am not sure of date of birth: Index to Delayed Birth Certificate has Oct. 1, 1891, Death Certificate has Nov. 1, 1891, and the Family Bible has Nov. 7, 1891.

(6) Jarvis Reuben. born Oct. 5, 1895 (Haywood Co., Index to Delayed Birth Certificates). Still living 1978. Married Bonnie Childers, Dec. 24, 1919 (Jarvis Caldwell Family Bible).

(7) Homer Paul, born June 10, 1898, died March 1, 1963 (Haywood Co. Death Certificate Book 50, p. 26). Married Floras Burress, Aug. 8, 1925 (Jarvis Caldwell Family Bible).

(8) Hattie Love, born Oct. 27, 1900, died July 6, 1975. Married Jesse Brooks of Franklin, June 7, 1935 (Jarvis Caldwell Family Bible).

Cataloochee Valley

REQUEST FOR BURIAL WITHIN NATIONAL PARK
United States Department of the Interior
Great Smoky Mountains National Park

PART I - CONTACT
1. Name of Contact _____ Date: _____
2. Relation to Deceased _____
3. Mailing Address _____
   City _____ State ____ Zip ____
4. Home Phone (___) ____ - _____ Work Phone (___) ____ - _____

PART II - DECEASED
1. Name of Deceased _____ Sex: M F
2. Date of birth __ / __ / ____ Place of birth _____
3. Date of death __ / __ / ____ Place of death _____
4. Lived in Park? Y N When? Where? How long? _____
6. Cemetery of choice _____
5. Reason for burial request (OPTIONAL) _____

PART III - FAMILY OF DECEASED
1. Marital status of Deceased: Married Widowed Divorced Single
   If married, will the spouse be requesting a joint burial with the deceased? Y N
   If widowed, where is the spouse buried? _____
   If divorced, single, or the spouse is not requesting a joint burial, will any other members of the family be requesting a joint burial with the deceased? Y N
   If yes, who? _____ Relation to the Deceased _____
2. Names of surviving immediate family and their hometowns:
   Name _____ City, State _____
   Name _____ City, State _____
3. Names of family members buried within the Park:
   Name _____ Relationship _____
   Cemetery _____ Documented? Y N Initials ____
   Name _____ Relationship _____
   Cemetery _____ Documented? Y N Initials ____

PART IV - DECISION ON BURIAL REQUEST
1. Request for burial within Park was GRANTED / DENIED
   Reason: _____
   Signed: _____ Date: __ / __ / ____
2. Date of Ceremony: __ / __ / ____
3. Mortuary/Chapel: _____ Phone: (___) ____ - _____
   Name of Contact at Chapel: _____

Copies to ☐ Staff Park Ranger ☐ Archives ☐ Historian ☐ Dist. Ranger notified

[Use reverse side for additional remarks.]

Descendents of the displaced families can still be buried in the Cataloochee cemeteries. The form has to be obtained from the park service.

BIBLIOGRAPHY

The history of Cataloochee has been condensed from the list of research material of:
Dr. Roy Carroll's *Historic Structures Report*
Edward Trout's *Historic Structures Report On Big Cataloochee*
Mr. Hiram Wilburn's Notes
Mr. Clark Medford's *Early History of Haywood County*
Judge Felix Alley's *Random Thought and Musings of a Mountaineer*
Employees of The Great Smoky Mountains National Park
Mr. Fred Grose and Mr. Frank Davis for the map (*a copy of this map can ordered from Hattie C. Davis, P.O. Box 274, Maggie Valley, N.C. 28751. Please enclose two dollars for each copy.*)
And all former Cataloocheeans who so graciously gave us information and stories.

Acknowledgments

The author acknowledges gratefully the contributions of Dr. Roy Carroll and his staff, who wrote Historic Structures Report, Little Cataloochee, N.C. Great Smoky Mountain National Park, Department of History, Appalachian State University for Great Smoky Mountains Natural History Association, Gatlinburg, Tennessee, June 1976. Dr. Carroll and his staff also did the genealogy of The First Generation of Coldwells on Cataloochee and The Second Generation of Coldwells on

Cataloochee Valley

Cataloochee, by which we have been able to document the dates in this book.

The author acknowledges gratefully the contributions of Mr. Edward L. Trout, park historian, who had a true sense of history and was so dedicated to restoring the few historic structures we have left in Cataloochee. He wrote *The Historic Structures Report On Big Cataloochee*. He and his preservation crew worked faithfully to restore the buildings, as near the original as possible. We realize it was a difficult task for Mr. Trout to get funds for these projects. We appreciate the support of Boyd Euison, park superintendent, Stanley Canter executive secretary, Tom Kloos, Cataloochee sub-district ranger.

I am grateful for all the notes and information that Mr. Hiram Wilburn made, as he interviewed the Cataloochee people, during the time he was there surveying for the park, just before the people moved out. By Mr. Wilburn's work I have been able to document many of the stories I had heard. Mr. Wilburn's notebooks were found at Haywood Co. Library, Western Carolina University Archives, and Great Smoky Mountains and National Archives at Gatlinburg, Tenn.

I am indebted to Mrs. Kitty Mancelli and Annetta Evans, Great Smoky Mountians National Park archivist and library staff, who so graciously aided in locating pictures taken in Big Cataloochee, Little Cataloochee, and Caldwell Forks, in the 1930s. Also to all others who have furnished pictures to be reproduced for me to use in this book. Most of the photos found at the park headquarters were made by Mr. Hiram Wilburn and Mr. Charles S. Grossman.

Mr. Frizzell, archivist, Western Carolina for his assistance in finding some copies of Mr. Wilburn's work and Mr. Curwin, librarian. Lowell Hannah for furnishing pictures of his family, and some information.

I would like to express our many thanks to Mr. Wilson Medford, for permission to use some of his father, Mr. W. Clark Medford's books. *The Early History Of Haywood County*, copyright 1961 by W. Clark Medford. Asheville, N.C. Also *The Middle History Of Haywood County*, copyright 1968 by W. Clark Medford. Asheville, N.C. Mr. Medford spent many long hours searching through the old records at the Haywood County courthouse to collect and record many of the old documents.

Mrs. Ethel Palmer McCracken—born on Big Cataloochee 1894—has a vivid memory and many wonderful stories and furnished photos.

Mrs. Flora Burress Caldwell Laws—born on Big Cataloochee 1911—has a clear mind and wonderful stories. She could shoot well enough to have been Annie Oakley. She gave me some pictures.

Thad Sutton and his son Floyd—my only source of information from the Caldwell Forks area—both have told interesting stories of how life was. I could not have documented the information with out them. They furnished some photos.

Many thanks to T. Frank Davis, who made the map of Big Cataloochee, Little Cataloochee and Caldwell Fork. He is a registered surveyor who walked all the trails and roads and climbed steep mountains in order to get the correct location of the home sites recorded on this map. Larry and Loyd Caldwell helped identify the sites. Both were born and raised on Cataloochee. Loyd stayed on and worked with the Park Service until he retired. Frank make this map in honor of his mother, Minnie Colwell Davis, who was of the second generation born there. (All three of these men were great grandsons of Levi and Granny Pop.)

I wish to thank Betty Gene Alley for permission to use some of the writing of Judge Felix Alley, *Random Thoughts and Musings Of A Mountaineer*, 1937.

I want to thank Gudger Palmer, who has been a big help in gathering information for this book, for his support and encouragement all the way. He so graciously gave me pictures and stories. (He is also great-grandson of Levi and Granny Pop.)

A special thanks to Mr. Fred Groce, son of the circuit riding preacher, Mr. T.A. Groce. He responded to my request at the reunion for information and pictures. He so kindly supplied all the information and pictures of his father found in this book.

I want to express our appreciation to Mr. Kyle Campbell (grandson of Hiram and Lizzie Caldwell and great-grandson of Levi and Granny Pop), who made special trips from South Carolina to contribute to this book.

Cataloochee Valley

I am grateful for the taped interview (1979) with Mr. John Noland, born in Cataloochee in 1895. He revealed much about Cataloochee in the early 1900s.

My many thanks to Paul Woody—born in Little Cataloochee. Paul furnished many pictures and stories of the homes and people on Little Cataloochee. He so carefully preserved and treasured all the history he could.

Steve Woody—son of Jonathan, grandson of Steve and Great grandson of Jonathan—has been the master of ceremonies at the reunion and furnished a list of the distinguished speakers for the last several years. I wish to express my thanks to Steve and all the fine speakers listed and others which are not listed.

Clay McGaha for stories of both Big and Little Cataloochee; his help is much appreciated.

I also thank Raymond Coldwell, Blye Caldwell, Helen Hannah and all others who have contributed stories and pictures for this book.

I appreciate the guidance and instructions so graciously and willingly given to me by Mrs. Ernistine Upchurch (great-great-granddaughter of Levi and Granny Pop.)

My thanks to Linton Palmer, who gave us much information on the Palmer house and family.

Many thanks to Bob Palmer and his brother Judson for pictures and stories. They are the grandsons of the late Turkey George Palmer.

I want to express our appreciation to Louise Palmer Ross, who has been our reunion treasurer for many years. Before her was Jackie Sue Messer. Thanks to all who have helped.

I am grateful to all who have helped with stories and supplied pictures. Hopefully I have not left out any names, if so, please know your help was appreciated. After a hundred and sixty years of oral history, there may be several versions of the stories. The former Cataloocheeans shared a wealth of information with me, and in every conversation they displayed that deep heartfelt love of home and heritage which only exiles can have.

INDEX

Alexander, Judy 184
Alexander, Tom 184
Alexanders, Tom 195
Allen, Maggie 54
Allen, Ronnie 131
Alley, Betty Gene 299
Alley, Judge Felix 13, 53, 198, 299
Allie, Bennett 276
Allison, Jarvis 54
Allison, Joshua 25, 47
Andrew, Jackson 19
Arrington, Eli 213
Arrington, T. Frank 97
Asheville 22
Barnes, Bob 276
Barns, Zelma 276
Bennet, George 218
Bennet, Young 24, 27, 34
Bennett, A.C. 202
Bennett, Allie 27, 28
Bennett, Amanual 77
Bennett, Andy 129
Bennett, Archibald 77
Bennett, Bartlett 78, 218, 275
Bennett, Callie 211
Bennett, Crate 88
Bennett, Creighton 77, 78
Bennett, Edward K. 276
Bennett, Eldridge 78, 218
Bennett, G. Willis 276
Bennett, George 78, 97, 129, 201, 208
Bennett, Harold 276
Bennett, Jalie Gillett 77, 277
Bennett, James W. 276
Bennett, Jasper Newton 277
Bennett, John C. 276
Bennett, Kelly 276
Bennett, Matilda 78
Bennett, Newton 52, 77
Bennett, Sophronia 70
Bennett, Sylvanus 77
Bennett, Tyne 78, 218
Bennett, W.B. 201
Bennett, Wash 77
Bennett, Weaver 218
Bennett, Young 52, 70, 76, 125, 173, 276, 277
Big Cataloochee 17, 18, 24, 54
Big Cataloochee Valley 25
Big Creek 21
Black, Margaret 204
Blount, John Gray 16
Boone, Keder 20
Boyd, Bill 258
Boyd, D.J. 202
Boyd, Dave 100
Boyd, J.R. 202
Boyd, Little Dave 100
Boyd, R.T. 202
Bradley, Bill 243
Brown, Bob 218
Brown, Jane 54
Brown, Jonah 97, 132
Bryant, Monk 265
Bryson, Lillian 54
Burgess, J.W. 97, 201
Burgess, John 218, 275

Burns, Ned 210
Burress, Callie 128
Burress, D.H. 232
Burress, Julia 128
Burress, Mattie Lockman 232
Burris, D.H. 201
Burris, Dock 208, 219
Byrd, Thomas R. 202
Cagle, Eliza 55
Cagle, Gordon 132
Caldwell, Addie 126
Caldwell, Alice Cumi 91
Caldwell, Andy 89, 274
Caldwell, Auie 85
Caldwell, Arvil 128
Caldwell, Blye 128, 280
Caldwell, Bonnie 85, 243
Caldwell, Boone 128
Caldwell, Brown 126, 250
Caldwell, Burl 152
Caldwell, Charlie Ray 19, 126,162, 217, 200, 231
Caldwell, Charlotte 91
Caldwell, Connie 52, 85
Caldwell, D.W. 200
Caldwell, Dave 126
Caldwell, David 56
Caldwell, David Marion 54
Caldwell, Dillard 47, 52, 104, 109, 176, 217, 275
Caldwell, Doc 256
Caldwell, Dock 215
Caldwell, Doctor 54
Caldwell, Doctor L 55, 56
Caldwell, Dr. Bob 56
Caldwell, E.R. 55
Caldwell, Eldridge 7, 23, 27, 30, 46, 51, 52, 56, 94, 96, 104, 109, 114, 116, 117, 119, 126, 145, 147, 157, 178, 183, 188, 197, 200, 205, 207, 217, 239, 261, 287
Caldwell, Elizabeth 55
Caldwell, Elizabeth Howell 85
Caldwell, Ella 225
Caldwell, Eston 55, 268, 270
Caldwell, Eulala 231
Caldwell, Flora Burgess (Laws) 85, 86, 281, 232, 299
Caldwell Fork 28
Caldwell, George 91, 126, 134, 208, 212, 217, 274
Caldwell, George H. 57, 200, 210
Caldwell, Gilmer 176
Caldwell, Glenn 126
Caldwell, Guy 126, 128
Caldwell, Hardy 55
Caldwell, Harrison 80, 274
Caldwell, Hattie 104, 109, 126, 159, 247
Caldwell, Helen 109, 222
Caldwell, Herbert 55
Caldwell, Hershel 267
Caldwell, Hiram 50, 51, 52, 55, 61, 66, 81, 83, 84, 85, 101, 104, 106, 109, 111, 116, 121, 126, 127, 145, 161, 167, 217, 226, 247, 256, 259, 261, 274, 281, 283, 285

Caldwell, Homer 146
Caldwell, Hub 90, 135, 175, 176, 217, 249, 274
Caldwell, J.L. 200
Caldwell, J.M. 202
Caldwell, James 200
Caldwell, Jarvis 50, 85, 146, 179, 219, 243, 268, 270, 271, 274, 289
Caldwell, Jessie 55
Caldwell, Jim 51, 85, 119, 151, 163, 215, 217, 236
Caldwell, Jimmy 76
Caldwell, John 156, 196, 219
Caldwell, John Mull 149
Caldwell, Ken 109
Caldwell, Larry 165, 299
Caldwell, Lenn 126
Caldwell, Levi Belese 7, 8, 45, 88, 104, 119, 275, 288
Caldwell, Lizzie 55, 63, 103, 109, 179, 180, 182, 193, 221, 229, 253, 259, 286
Caldwell, Lizzie Howell 30, 241, 145, 287
Caldwell, Loyd 299
Caldwell, Lush 110, 126, 217
Caldwell, M.H. 200
Caldwell, Maggie Cope 55
Caldwell, Maggie Mooney 110, 128, 212, 234, 253, 281
Caldwell, Magola 54
Caldwell, Magolia 126
Caldwell, Marshall 146
Caldwell, Mary Elizabeth 104
Caldwell, Mary Elizabeth Howell 81
Caldwell, Mattie 128
Caldwell, Minnie 55
Caldwell, Nell 109, 160
Caldwell, Nettie 128
Caldwell, Norman 217
Caldwell, Pearl Valentine 109, 118, 158, 161, 175, 180, 221, 222, 259
Caldwell, Phillip 8
Caldwell, Ray 176
Caldwell, Raymond 50, 114, 214, 234, 258, 267, 271
Caldwell, Reuben 281
Caldwell, Rosco 275
Caldwell, Sarah P. Palmer 56
Caldwell, Susie Woody 80, 253
Caldwell, Thomas 55, 200
Caldwell, Todd 79
Caldwell, Tommy 162, 217, 274
Caldwell, Turkey George 195
Caldwell, Wayne 192
Caldwell, William 52, 104, 109
Caldwell, Wilma 128
Campbell, Bill 93
Campbell, C.A. 202
Campbell, Carlos 208
Campbell, Kyle 228, 282, 299
Campbell, V.A. 200, 201
Campbell, Verlin 54, 247, 251, 257, 262
Canup, Leona 126
Carpenter, Charlie 54
Carroll, Dr. Roy 30, 123, 266, 297
Carver, Alden 208

301

Cataloochee Valley

Carver, Alps 74
Carver, John 74
Cataloochee 21, 32
Cataloochee Creek 17, 52
Cataloochee Toll Road 24
Cataloochee Turnpike 47
Chambers, Cromer 54
Chambers, Maggie 54
Chapman, David 286
Charleston, S.C. 22
Charlotte Lane 19
Cherokee Indians 17, 31
Clark, Dee 202
Clark, G.C. 202
Clarke, James McClure 266
Coldwell, Blye 300
Coldwell, Harriet (Hattie) 52
Coldwell, Henry 17
Coldwell Palmer, Nancy Jane 33
Coldwell, Raymond 300
Caldwell, Sally Teague 227
Coldwell, Thomas 17
Coldwell, Tommy 250
Colwell, Andy 76, 80
Colwell, Betsy 20
Colwell, Daniel 19
Colwell, Doctor L. 80
Colwell, Harrison 75, 80
Colwell, Henry 18, 19, 20, 24, 30
Colwell, Hiram 45, 74, 80
Colwell, James 19, 24, 30
Colwell, Jimmy 27, 34
Colwell, John W. 80, 275
Colwell, Levi 27, 30, 41, 50, 52, 57, 71, 74, 77
Colwell, Marion 80
Colwell, Mary 76
Colwell, Mary Ann 28, 30, 52, 58, 70
Colwell, Nancy Jane 32
Colwell, Reuben A 80
Colwell, Thomas 19
Colwell, William 19
Colwell, William Sr. 19
Conard, Jim 275
Conley, James 20
Connard, John 218, 275
Conner, Dock 208
Conrad, J.A. 201
Cook, D.J. 96
Cook, Dan 41, 199
Cook Lane 47
Cope, William 97
Coulter, Myron L. 266
Cove Creek 25, 47
Cove Creek Mountain 17
Dahlen, David 286
Davidson Branch 33
Davidson, Edwin 20
Davis, Falsom 54
Davis, Felder 20
Davis, Hattie Caldwell 221
Davis, Mary 54
Davis, Minnie Coldwell 299
Davis, Pat 187
Davis, Rev. D.C. 97
Davis, T Frank 299
Deadmen 28
Dell, Mary 277
Doughty, Mary Ann 30
Early, W.A. 202
East Fork 24, 25
Edwards, Burton 283

Edwards, Jim 271
Edwards, Kyle 283
Eggleston, Laura 201
Evans, Annetta 298
Evans, Ethan 251
Evans, Jim 149, 219, 275
Evans, Thurman 251
Evart, Bob 258
Ewart, Rachel 128
Ferguson, Burder 63, 64
Ferguson, Garland 63, 65
Ferguson, Judge 260
Ferguson, Lillie 54, 126
Ferguson, Ora 54
Ferguson, Robert P. 66, 277
Ferguson, Roger 54, 130
Ford, Arthur 201
Fowler, James W. Jr., Dr. 266
Franklin, Hobert 204
Franklin, Neal 275
Frazier, Tom 131
Gardner, Kenneth 98
Garrison, Webb 266
George, Bennett 78
George, Turkey Palmer 167
Golden, Jacob B. 265
Grace, Katherine 277
Granny Pop 60
Green, Eula 54, 248
Green, Mary 138
Greenville 22
Groce, Fred 299
Groce, T.A. 99, 100, 103, 299
Grooms, Addie 126
Grooms, Anderson 67
Grooms, Eliza 68
Grooms, George 67
Grooms, Henry 262
Grooms, Mandy 262
Grooms, Walter 202
Grossman, C.S. 274
Gudger, Lamar 265
Hale, Joe 265
Hall, Americus 132
Hall, Andy 54
Hall, "Doc" 96
Hall, Ella 175
Hall, J.R. 200
Hall, L.N. 201
Hall, M.N. 201
Hall, Mercus 159, 175
Hall, W.M. 201
Hall, Will 34, 218
Hannah, Alexander 34
Hannah, Blaine 203
Hannah, Evan 20, 34
Hannah, Fannie 203, 253
Hannah, Fannie Hoyle 146
Hannah, Fred 130, 131
Hannah, H.T. 96
Hannah, Helen 131, 300
Hannah, I.V. 201
Hannah, J.B. 201
Hannah, James H. 201
Hannah, Jethro 201
Hannah, Jim 26, 275
Hannah, John 129
Hannah, John J. 90
Hannah, Levi 19
Hannah, Lewell 298
Hannah, Lois 98
Hannah, Lowell 34, 267

Hannah, Mack 97, 275
Hannah, Mack W. 201
Hannah, Mark 48, 50, 130, 132, 207, 215, 217, 227, 267, 270
Hannah, Mont 131
Hannah, Rebecca Wilkins 34
Hannah, Rhode 275
Hannah, Robert M. 97
Hannah, Verda Messer 130, 216
Hannah, W.R. 201
Hannah, William 129
Hannah, William J. 97
Harbin, Mel E. 265
Hardin, Paul 264
Harrel, John 262
Hayes, Mattie 54
Hayes, President 79
Hemphill 28
Hendon, William H. 265
Henry, Mary 54
Hopkins, I.H. 202
Hopkins, J.C. 89, 202
Hopkins, L.A. 202
Hopkins, Parker 125
Howell, Albert 52, 63
Howell, David 20
Howell, Eleanor Ferguson 52, 63
Howell, James L. 20
Howell, John 137
Howell, Mary Elizabeth 52
Howell, Mr. 32
Howell, Nelson 20
Howell, Robert 69
Howell, Rufus 101
Howell, Will 54
Hunt, Earl 264
Hunt, James B. 209, 264
Indian Bottom 58
Indian Creek 33, 50, 58
Jackson, Andrew 78
Jarvis, Maggie 202
Jonathan Creek 17, 25, 28, 32
King, Lou 200
Kirk, George 69
Kirk's Marauders 68, 276
Lackman, J.B. 201
Laws, Flora Burress Caldwell 233
Leatherwood, Clara 54, 137
Leatherwood, Mamie 54
Leatherwood, Samuel 20
Liner, Dr. 73, 236
Liner, Louise 73
Linton, Fate 32
Linton, Harley 33
Linton, Jarvis 33
Linton, Maria 33
Little Cataloochee 17, 59
Little Davidson Branch 33
Lockman, Boone 128
Lockman, Fannie 128
Lockman, Jess 275
Lockman, Jessie 128
Lockman, Odell 128
Lockman, Paul 128
Lockman, Wayne 128
Lomax, Alan 283
Long, C.M. 200
Long, Ches 275
Long, Chris 149
Long, Mr. 179
Love, Col. Robert 16
Madison, Susan Caldwell 56

Maggie Valley 17
Mahaffey, Carolyn Bennett 78, 277
Mancelli, Kitty 285, 298
Marley, Miss 198
Martin, Gussie 54, 131
Martinson, Jacob J. 265
Maynard, Charles 266, 286
McCracken, Ethel Palmer 8, 53, 69, 124, 251, 252, 298
McElhaney, Mr. 54
McElluth, Lee 54
McFalls, Edward 20
McGaha, Burl 218, 247, 275
McGaha, Clay 164, 241, 245, 300
McGaha, Gene 246
McGaha, I.B. 201
McGaha, Zeoma 183
McGee, Ira 68, 149, 212
McGee, Jessie 156
McGee, Nicie 156
McMahan, Burnice 54
Medford, Bob 116, 240
Medford, Charlie 270
Medford, Clark 139
Medford, Juanita 54
Medford, Myrtle 253
Medford, Robert 78
Medford, Taylor 270
Medford, W.C. 22
Medford, Will 139
Medford, Wilson 298
Mehaffey, P.W. 202
Melton, David 266
Messer, Anderson 150
Messer, Cal 218, 280
Messer, Carson 120, 149, 214, 315
Messer, E.M. 202
Messer, Elijah 275, 279
Messer, Ervin 132, 275
Messer, G.M.D. 202
Messer, J.L.C. 202
Messer, Jackie Sue 267, 300
Messer, John 20
Messer, Lige 149, 219, 275
Messer, Mack 219
Messer, Rachel 145, 173
Messer, Vanalie 145
Messer, W.G.B. 97, 129, 201
Messer, Will 40, 97, 119, 145, 173, 175, 191, 215, 218
Messer, Willie 204, 205
Methodist Episcopal Church South 52
Miller, Clarence 213
Miller, Ernest 162, 193, 231
Miller, Joe 213
Miller, Mae 161, 180, 192, 221
Miller, Pauline 193
Miller, Polly 161
Moody, C.M. 202
Moody, Ruben 20
Mt. Sterling 17
Mull, John 212
Mull mill 58
Murrow, Edward R. 231
Museum of North Carolina Handicraft 46
Myers, Ray 285
Nailand, Mary Ann 30
Nailand, Patrick 30
Nalan, John 299
Nalan, Mary Ann 30
Needham, John 215

Nelson, D.B. 201
Nelson, Dave 218, 275
Nelson, Sidney H. 201
Noland, A William 20
Noland, Badger 255
Noland, Bill 214
Noland, Elizabeth 34
Noland, Eula 54
Noland, Frank 255
Noland, John Cordell 255
Noland, Laura 128
Noland, Letha 54, 137
Noland Mountain 20
Noland, William Thomas 20, 34, 255
Owens, Josie 54
Owens, Rass 54
Palmer, Arlo 128, 218
Palmer, Bill 126
Palmer, Bob 300
Palmer, C.L. 201
Palmer, Carl 128
Palmer, Charlie 126, 167, 218, 257, 274
Palmer, Chauncy 126, 257
Palmer, Clara Bell 267
Palmer Creek 50
Palmer, "Creek" George 91
Palmer, Dave 126
Palmer, Della 54, 126
Palmer, Eleanor 54, 109, 179, 217, 218, 245, 258
Palmer, Elizabeth 136
Palmer, Elmer 126
Palmer, Elthel 118, 126
Palmer, Eulala 128
Palmer, Fayte 33, 255
Palmer, Flora 54, 126, 128
Palmer, Frank 55, 173, 274
Palmer, George 32, 34, 52, 77, 180, 253
Palmer, George LaFayette 82, 92
Palmer, George N. 201
Palmer, Glenn 54, 127, 140, 197, 217
Palmer, Gudger 48, 71, 85, 89, 102, 128, 135, 140, 163, 173, 179, 209, 217, 244, 270, 286
Palmer, H.R. 200
Palmer, Harley 54
Palmer, Flora, Medford 219
Palmer, Hazel 126
Palmer, Hilda 49
Palmer, Hilda Dotson 95
Palmer, Hiram 126
Palmer, Jarvis 53, 114, 119, 173, 181, 192, 200, 217, 253, 271, 274
Palmer, Jessie 49, 50, 55, 74, 91
Palmer, Jessie R. 39
Palmer, Jim 126
Palmer, John 274
Palmer, John M. 201
Palmer, Jud 167
Palmer, Judson 94
Palmer, Julia 33
Palmer, Julian Ann 52
Palmer, Kimsey 128, 131, 218, 219
Palmer, Lavade 54
Palmer, Lavada 128
Palmer, Linton 32, 126, 191, 200, 267, 300
Palmer, Lonnie 126

Palmer, Lou 55
Palmer, Lura 126
Palmer, Maggie 128
Palmer, Magnolia Caldwell 179, 269
Palmer, Maria 173, 181,191, 192, 193, 200
Palmer, Mary Ann Rogers 39, 55, 270
Palmer, Mary Davis 242
Palmer, Milia 174, 175, 209, 217, 248, 253, 294
Palmer, Myrtle 126
Palmer, Nancy Jane Caldwell 82
Palmer, Nellie 126
Palmer, Ola Messer 173
Palmer, Pauline 128
Palmer, Reuben 128
Palmer, Robert 128, 202, 219, 275
Palmer, Roy 126
Palmer, Sarah 55
Palmer, Thomas 50, 55, 214
Palmer, Turkey George 88, 94, 217, 274
Palmer, Vaughn 217
Palmer, Velma Childers 33
Palmer, Verlin 126
Palmer, Vernon 128
Palmer, Vincent 191
Palmer, Vinson 218
Palmer, W.H. 200
Palmer, Will 109, 218, 245, 274
Palmer, William 35, 39, 55, 179, 180, 217, 274, 288
Palmers, Frank 275
Palmers, Jessie 212
Parham, Kimberly 209
Park, James 133
Partin, Robert 202
Parton, Bob 219, 275
Parton, Lee 257
Pease, Guy 200
Phelps, Yvonne 56
Phillips, George 93, 202
Phillips, Jonah 89
Phillips, Tobe 89, 93, 94
Pigeon River 24
Plemmons, James 19
Plemmons, Malinda 79
Pop, Granny 59, 66, 241
Pope, Randall 285
Price, Mrs. 213
Prince, R. 202
Purchase 28
Qually, Paul 285
Queen, John 54
Queen, Sam 282
Rawls, Robert 265
Ray, Charlie 130
Reeves, David 265
Reno, L.C. 133
Revis, Becky 283
Robb, Tom 285
Robbins, Tom 285
Rockefeller, Laura Spelman 209
Rockhill School 28
Rogers, Frank 54
Rogers, Fred 128
Rogers, Goldy 128
Rogers, Herman 150
Rogers, Hugh 54
Rogers, Jane 253
Rogers, Nellie 128
Rooks, John 266

Cataloochee Valley

Roosevelt, Eleanor 282
Roosevelt, Franklin D. 177, 209
Ross, Louise Palmer 267, 300
Running Wolfe, Molly 183
Sandy Mush 25
Sanford, Terry 266
Schoolhouse Patch 52
Settlemire, Hazel 54
Shanty Branch 33
Shelton House 46
Shubert, Bob 285
Simmons, Miss 54
Sloan, B.J. 200
Smathers, Ruth 54
Smith, J. Oss 201
Smith, Jacob 20
Smith, John L. 20
Smith, Margaret 255
Smith, Vic 203
Smith, Vick 213
Soco Mountain 17
Sohn, Danny 285
Stiles, Mrs. 159
Stokes, Dick 216
Strikeleather, J.G. 201
Sugarland Visitors Center 285
Surrett, Polly 32
Sutton, Addie 137, 202, 219, 275
Sutton, Annie 150, 154
Sutton, Arthur 126
Sutton, B.H. 202
Sutton, Ben 275
Sutton, Bob 126, 149
Sutton, Carl 201
Sutton, Easter 253
Sutton, Fannie 126
Sutton, Floyd 154
Sutton, Gene 126

Sutton, George 258, 274
Sutton, Grace 126
Sutton, Harrison 219
Sutton, Huston 138
Sutton, Jim 148, 219, 258, 275
Sutton, Mitch 90
Sutton, Myrtle 176, 258
Sutton, Pearl Rogers 148
Sutton, Sol 120, 153
Sutton, Thad 120, 137, 155, 219, 275, 299
Sutton, Thelma 54
Sutton, W.M. 200
Sutton, Willie 126
Teague, Albert 67, 69
The Good Samaritan 28
Thomas, Will 32
Trantham, Helen Hannah 130, 145
Trout, Ed 20, 111, 272, 285
Turkey George 58
Upchurch, Ernistine 300
Valentine, Claude 275
Valentine, Emma 193, 289
Valentine, Press 158
Valentine, Ressie 158
Vance, Zeb 79
Vessell, Lynn Caldwell 56
Wade, Karen 286
Whatley, John Bennett 277
White Oak 21
White, T.H. (Bud) 202
Wilburn, Hiram 57, 90, 207, 210
Wilkinson, Larry 265
Willford, Herb 285
Woody, Carl 132, 172, 203, 218
Woody, Charles 126
Woody, Clay 206
Woody, Ethel 126

Woody, F.W. 200
Woody, Floyd 59, 135, 136, 200
Woody, Horace 254
Woody, J. Valentine "Tyne" 78
Woody, J.R. 201
Woody, J.S. 201
Woody, J.V. 96
Woody, Jack 48
Woody, James Valentine 79
Woody, Johnny 267
Woody, Jonathan 19, 34, 52, 60, 81, 126, 200, 275
Woody, Jonathan H. 79
Woody, Lou White 98, 203
Woody, Lucinda E. 80
Woody, Major 119, 249, 251
Woody, Nancy 80
Woody, Paul 26, 78, 132, 172, 206, 218
Woody, Rebecca E. 80
Woody, Robert 227
Woody, Robert Jackson 80
Woody, S.L. 200
Woody, Sherman 219
Woody, Silas 19
Woody, Stephen L. 80
Woody, Steve 57, 59, 83, 115, 126, 127, 128, 134, 135, 195, 208, 217, 247, 253, 266, 267, 274, 300
Woody, Steven L. 135
Woody, Susannah A. 80
Woody, Tint 204
Woody, Tyne 203
Woody, W.C. 202
Woody, William 19
Young, Dr. Robert T. 265

We would like to make a book of Cataloochee photographs. If you have pictures you can identify and would like them in our next book, please send a *photographic copy* of the original to: Hattie Caldwell Davis, P.O. Box 274, Maggie Valley, N.C. 28751 or call 704-926-1291. Pictures can keep memories alive. Also, we and future generations can see what our ancestors looked like.

If you send a photo of a person or several people, building, or an object, please identify completely on the back. Write a short history including dates or events or anything of interest and importance to the photo. Tell when buildings were erected, by whom, and who lived in them in order of occupancy.

Several photos were offered too late for inclusion in this book. If we receive enough we will put together another book consisting of photos, accompanying material, and credits.

It would be great if entire families were organized together complete with identification and background material. Let us hear from you by July 31, 1998.